Praise for *No Ordinary Assignment*

"For all the upheaval and conflict she's seen, Jane Ferguson has never lost sight of the ordinary men and women caught in the middle of it all. This is the story of her journey, and it's told with breadth and verve and humanity."
  —Dexter Filkins, Pulitzer Prize–winning author of *The Forever War*

"So much has been packed into this young foreign correspondent's remarkable life, you'd think she's far older than she is. From Ireland to Yemen, Afghanistan, Somalia, Syria, and Ukraine, there's hardly a war zone she hasn't covered. But what most draws you into this finely written memoir are the raw accounts of a childhood short on love and long on criticism that no doubt pushed her in the direction of a high-wire career, and, along the way, a soulful search to understand who, really, is Jane Ferguson."
  —Judy Woodruff, former anchor of *PBS NewsHour*

"Growing up in Northern Ireland during The Troubles, Jane Ferguson gained a visceral, instinctive understanding of conflict. She brought an inquisitive eye and innate empathy to the greatest stories that have defined our age, from the wars in Syria, Yemen, and Afghanistan to the Russian invasion of Ukraine. Her courageous book is an honest, searing examination of these events—and of the toll they inflict on journalists who give up so much to keep telling the stories of those who often can't speak for themselves."
  —Yaroslav Trofimov, author of *The Siege of Mecca*, and chief foreign affairs correspondent at the *Wall Street Journal*

"In a haunting memoir of disarming honesty, Jane Ferguson evokes not only the far-flung wars she has covered with a lucid passion, but also the internal battles of a woman raised amid The Troubles of Northern Ireland where 'a separate, quiet strength began to grow inside me.' Driven to pursue an unordinary life, determined to bear witness to the humanity of the desperate, torn at times between the temptations of a settled existence and her longing for the road, Ferguson delivers a remarkable testament to the anguish and the beauty of foreign correspondence."

—Roger Cohen, *New York Times* Paris bureau chief and author of *An Affirming Flame*

"*No Ordinary Assignment* is an intimate portrait of a journalist coming into her own. For some of us that happens in boardrooms; for Jane Ferguson, it happened in war zones. Her memoir is a thrill to read and an inspiring example of what can happen when we confront fear and great risk with purpose."

—Pat Mitchell, author of *Becoming a Dangerous Woman* and cofounder of TEDWomen

"Jane Ferguson's breathtaking memoir takes us inside the savage wars of the last two decades with greater immediacy and compassion than any news report. Her inspiring and sometimes nerve-jangling account shows what it takes to bring us the news: tremendous courage and determination, qualities she has in spades. Whether dreaming up an adventuresome life beyond Belfast or facing down murderous Yemeni warlords or Syrian torturers—or indeed network resistance—she is unflinching. Her book will forever alter the way you look at the news."

—Kati Marton, *New York Times* bestselling author of *The Chancellor*

"With vivid details and pointed reflection, [*No Ordinary Assignment*] draws readers into the world of war that exists beyond the "bang-bang" of most news coverage. . . . Ferguson clearly demonstrates the devastating, oft-overlooked impact of war on civilians from every side. . . . She is an expert storyteller. . . . A captivating, honest, and powerful attempt to do justice to the hardest stories to tell."

—*Kirkus Reviews* (starred review)

No Ordinary Assignment

A MEMOIR

Jane Ferguson

Mariner Books
New York   Boston

HarperCollins books may be purchased for educational, business, or sales promotional use. For information, please email the Special Markets Department at SPsales@harpercollins.com.

FIRST EDITION

Designed by Chloe Foster

Library of Congress Cataloging-in-Publication Data has been applied for.

ISBN 978-0-06-327224-8

23 24 25 26 27 LBC 5 4 3 2 1

For Fanny Marr

Contents

Author's Note

I WROTE *NO ORDINARY ASSIGNMENT* with one main purpose in mind: to answer with total honesty the question, Why do you do this work? Really, why? I am asked this question often—most war reporters are—at public events, on panels, when speaking to people anywhere in the world, and always, always at dinner parties. There are neat answers, popular ones, about speaking truth to power and bearing witness. I am, as you will learn in these pages, wholeheartedly dedicated to human rights, truth, and helping the world understand itself in all its beauty and ugliness. But that's not the whole story of *why* I made the choices I did in my life and *why* this particular work became so important to me.

Investigative reporters, financial journalists, aid workers, human rights lawyers, they all do worthwhile, impactful, and sometimes dangerous work. But it takes a certain type of person to be a war reporter. We are complex, curious creatures with wandering souls, and we are shaped and driven as humans and professionals beyond our grand ideals and neat, noble phrases. We are shaped by where we came from and, as we progress, by the things we have seen.

As I wandered through the hallways and rooms of my memories, connecting my life's events, however triumphant or painful, I found it impossible to answer the question *why* without digging deep into my own personal journey. Who I became as a reporter grew out of the life I led. In this book, I have included many personal details of my life, not for entertainment—although some are funny—but to help you understand the choices I made, the roads I traveled. I have laid out the facts and events of my life and career as honestly and clearly as possible. It was my intention not to glamorize or gloss over parts of my life, but to tell the true story of a real person. Most of the people mentioned are named, but in the interest of privacy, pseudonyms have been used for a few key people in my life. As with most memories, mine is not infallible, and any errors are unintentional. However, sweary language, bad jokes, and excessive mentions of chicken excrement are all entirely intentional.

Prologue

SEVERAL DOZEN REPORTERS FILLED THE Serena's lobby, some trying to leave, others trying to figure out how to stay. Few had any way of going anywhere. The Afghan drivers who had worked for news organizations wouldn't pick any reporters up, including ours. Who would want to be stopped at a Taliban checkpoint with Westerners in the back of your car?

The hotel security chief walked by and I grabbed him by the arm. A blond British former soldier, he looked awkward in a suit. It was too tight around his wide, burly body. I'll call him Mike. "Is it safe to stay here?" I asked, eyeing him for an honest assessment.

"I can't get the security staff to come for the next shift of work at the gate," he replied, whispering in my ear to avoid frightening the others. "I'm leaving to go to the Baron hotel by the airport," he said. "The British paratroopers are based there managing the evacuations."

Mike agreed to give us a ride to the Baron in his armored car. My cameraman Eric and I would relocate just for the night, to be safe.

When Mike came marching across the carpark to his armored SUV, he had changed. He had taken off his suit and wore camouflaged body armor and an ammunition belt around his chest. A 9mm pistol hung from his hip, and he carried a military-grade automatic rifle in his hands. As we climbed into the back of the vehicle, I was painfully aware that we looked like soldiers. The decision to leave the Serena and careen out into Kabul's streets as the Taliban arrived was impossibly tough. Was it safer to stay and take our chances with potential looters at the hotel, totally unprotected, or to make a run for it with this former British soldier? It was too late to change our minds now, I realized as we pulled out of the hotel gates and Mike cocked his gun with a loud clack-clack. My heart beat fast as the city's streets, once so familiar and benign to me, rushed by, now so unknown and dangerous.

At first there was no one around, the roads and sidewalks completely abandoned. After we made it past the outer walls of the U.S. embassy and swung around the Ahmad Massoud roundabout, we headed down the airport road. Traffic was backed up in the direction of the airport. Everyone was trying to make it there. The commercial flights had stopped shortly after Eric and I had landed. Crowds of people were gathered outside the gates, desperate to get in. The road was jammed with cars filled with fleeing families and whatever belongings they had been able to gather.

Mike started to panic. Total chaos had gripped the area outside the airport walls. Government officials and Afghan special forces in Humvees and flatbed trucks had driven there, trying to get to the airport, too, further clogging up the roads. Groups of people were abandoning cars and carrying luggage above their heads the last few hundred yards. Others, standing on the sidewalk, approached our car and stared through the windows in disbelief at what was happening.

A wooden fruit cart had been left on the side of the road, blocking our way forward. Mike was irate. It was starting to get dark. Eric and I asked each other quietly if we should get out and make a run for it. The crowds were too thick, perhaps angry. It was too risky. Mike began yelling at the people standing around the car. "Get the fuck out of the way!!" he roared, now pointing his pistol through the car's bulletproof glass at a group of men at the hood of the car.

Now I was losing my own cool, panicked this irate British gunman was going to get us all killed. "Please calm down," I begged. "Don't point your gun."

On the sidewalk, Afghans stood and stared at the traffic, watching the city fall. Suddenly I saw two Talibs walking nonchalantly down the sidewalk, their long curly hair, leisurely gait, and automatic rifles unmistakable. They were walking in the direction of the city center. I slid down lower in my seat.

"Did you see that, guys?" Mike asked from the front. "Two Taliban on the right." Yes, I had, but I'd hoped I was somehow mistaken. Mike placed his pistol on his thigh. His finger was still on the trigger.

Vehicles started passing us on the left, heading into the city. I sat frozen in the back of the SUV as cars and pickup trucks full of Taliban fighters drove by. I felt certain that we had only seconds before a Taliban commander spotted us, stopped our car, and ordered us killed or detained. The fact that we were still alive seemed so improbable the scene felt dreamlike, yet the dread racing through me was far from ureal. They didn't stop us, seemingly content that we were headed in the other direction. As one truck passed us at a painfully slow crawl, the driver and passengers, all Taliban, with long wavy hair and wide eyes, guns on the dashboard, stared at us as we stared back, unable to look away, at the same time completely entranced and gripped with intense fear. No one honked their horns, fired their guns, or even shouted. We watched the Taliban drive back into the city they were driven out of almost twenty years prior.

For the first time in two decades, the Taliban were taking back Kabul. When they were last here, in November 2001, I was a teenage girl in high school in Northern Ireland living under a different sort of conflict. But it would be this war, this city, that would define me.

Part I

Uncle Desmond Got Kicked by a Cow

WHEN I WAS A CHILD, war was a secret. And you certainly couldn't call it war. It was known as "The Troubles." Even its name was a kind of disguise.

The Troubles were what my parents whispered about in the kitchen at night after my siblings and I had gone to bed. I would sometimes slip out from under the covers and onto the staircase, crouched in my pink nightie, knees tucked under my chin, looking down at the light coming from our farmhouse kitchen, listening to the hushed voices, so soft I had to hold my breath to hear. When they talked about The Troubles, my parents called each other by their names, not Mom and Dad. We children were not permitted to discuss the topic, and doubly so for me, as the youngest. *No one ever tells me anything,* I would grumble to myself. *Like why Uncle Desmond walks with a limp.*

Uncle Desmond had a limp so pronounced he almost dragged one leg behind him, moving in a slow, labored gait as he herded black and white cows from the field down the road to his milking parlor each morning. He was a quiet man, always with a cigarette between his pursed lips and a flat cap on his head.

My mother answered my questions about Uncle Desmond's leg with irritation, finally and reluctantly telling me a story that didn't seem to warrant her level of resistance to telling it. "Because he got kicked by a cow. So you should never get too close to the cows, see!" she snapped.

As a little girl, I was always asking questions. The world seemed full of secrets to me. I wanted to understand, to be let in on the things other people seemed to know.

I asked incessant questions and rarely got answers. The more the answers were fudged, the more I wanted to know. Particularly about The Troubles, the adults were always having conversations above my head, and no matter how hard I tugged on trouser legs or how eagerly I swung on their hands, the answers just didn't come. How is bread the body of Christ? How does fertilizer make a bomb? What is a Fenian?

My mother would field my inquiries about the events I saw on TV—car bombings, murders, and angry, hateful politicians—with growing unease. By the time I reached my third question, she would end the conversation, shouting, "Whisht!" This meant *shush* in Northern Irish. *This is all so unfair,* I thought. *Nobody ever gives me a real answer.*

I grew up on a small pig and sheep farm within rolling green hills in Northern Ireland. When you stopped and looked around, you would see a spectacular collage of different shades of green spread out into the horizon. Neat hills known as drumlins rolled into one another. Most of the time they were slick with a soft, mist-like rain. The air smelled like fresh wet earth. Motorists slowed for tractors and herds of sheep and cattle on the move. I was sixth in a family of six: Mom and Dad, and us four kids. Our farm was about seven miles north of the border with the Republic of Ireland, and very close to the restive, lawless rural areas of South Armagh, where the rugged, heathered farmland sheltered units of the Irish Republican Army—the IRA—as well as fortified hilltop outposts of young, often terrified British soldiers.

The IRA was the latest iteration of armed Irish uprising against British rule. For over four hundred years Irish nationalists had been taking up weapons at various moments in a violent history of repression and rebellion. In the 1980s and 90s, we kids in Northern Ireland grew up hearing the word *terrorist* as regularly as most Americans did in the wake of 9/11. That's what we British Protestants, descended from poor Scottish farmers sent over four centuries earlier to secure Catholic lands stolen from the locals, called the IRA men.

The IRA had launched a deadly campaign against the British in the 1970s, hoping to unite the full island of Ireland, free from British rule in the north. County Armagh was where many of the most senior leadership of the organization lived, and where some of the deadliest attacks took place. Few Protestant families where I grew up were not impacted by the violence. Mine was no exception, unable to escape the inevitable, hushed grief that weaves itself into the legacies of Northern Irish families. This made the idyllic green hillsides of South Armagh the most dangerous place in the world for a British soldier when I was growing up. Long before it agreed to negotiate with the IRA, the British government responded by sending in more troops.

By the time I was born in the public hospital of the town of Craigavon in 1984, South Armagh had already become a heavily militarized zone. Improvised explosive devices (IEDs) that could be detonated from afar using a radio were invented and refined there. Village police stations were surrounded by blast walls and huge metal frames to protect against regular mortar and car bomb attacks. Ambushes of British soldiers on the move became so common in certain areas the British army began transporting troops only via helicopter. I remember the slow thumping sound of massive Chinook helicopters flying low over our farm, watching them land in fields and take off in seconds, the grass underneath trembling flat as soldiers with camouflage paint on their faces scattered into the hedges. The Army Men.

Trotting around country lanes on my pony, I sometimes came across them walking in formation. If they saw me, they hid in ditches until I passed. I'm sure I was hardly a threatening vision—a little girl in corduroy and gum boots on top of a muddy pony, stopping to reach across hedgerows to pick wild berries. I desperately wanted to stare, but instinct stopped me. My parents' *whisht*s taught me that. I would push my pony, Lady, onward, keeping my eyes firmly on the horizon.

In those moments, I obeyed the unspoken rule: acknowledging The Troubles only invited them in. I would pretend to ignore the troops, quietly desperate to ask what in the world they were doing.

What had really happened to Uncle Desmond was much more violent than a kick from an angry cow. On New Year's Day in 1987, a gunman from an IRA splinter group, the Irish National Liberation Army, waited near Desmond's small, pebble-dashed bungalow. As Uncle Desmond was leaving the house by the back door, he opened fire, hitting both him and his seventy-year-old mother, Iris, who had been waving goodbye to him. My cousin Stephen, eight years old at the time, was standing next to his father. The bullet grazed his ear. Iris died of her wounds five weeks later. Stephen suffered from chronic irritable bowel syndrome, which turned to Crohn's disease, which turned into a cancer that killed him thirty years after the shooting

I learned the truth in my twenties, when I was deemed old enough to be told, piecing together foggy and mysterious childhood memories like snippets of bad dreams coming into focus when my sisters finally answered my questions over a beer in the pub. I understand now how the crack of bullets echoes long through the years, triggering a cascade of tragic events in individual lives.

Part of the secrecy was to protect us, but it was also a reflection of our stern Ulster Scots Protestant community. There was an unofficial insistence on discretion, a culture of cautious circumspection when talking about the violence around us. Hysteria was frowned upon. When the IRA blew up the police station in our nearest village, as they tended to do every few years, the enormous car bomb took with it the local cattle market and a number of small homes from a nearby working-class street. I watched the evening news with my family, as we all did every night, but especially when an attack had been close to home. A woman who had lost her house was talking to the TV reporter, yelling and denouncing the IRA, swearing bloody revenge. My mother tut-tutted and shook her head at the TV. "What a scene she is making," she said, rolling her eyes.

In reality, the silence was likely due to how complex the conflict was. Uncle Desmond was a member of the Ulster Defence Regiment, a locally recruited regiment of the British Army in Northern Ireland, Protestant dominated and known to be infiltrated by loyalist paramilitaries that carried out extrajudicial murders of Catholic civilians. I have known since long before covering wars as a reporter how there are often no good and bad sides, and that reality is a complex and harsh collection of truths. Morality bends.

Another time when the police station was attacked, I was in the local village school. Just around fifty feet of grassy soccer pitch sat between the corrugated steel barriers of the police facility and my classroom. Six years old, I was sitting with several other children when we heard bangs outside. Rushing to the windows, we saw smoke and flames leaping over the fortified walls. Our noses pressed against the window glass, elbowing and shoving one another as we strained to see, we watched open-mouthed as crackling flashes of what looked like fireworks in the daylight exploded in the air. The IRA had hit the station with mortars. None of it seemed frightening initially, just enormously exciting—much more interesting than our times tables. When our teacher realized what was happening, she screamed at us to get away from the window, pulling us over to the other side of the room. That's when everything felt different, suddenly scary. I took my cues from the adults. If they weren't scared, then I wasn't. When they showed fear, I was petrified. It was like watching air hostesses panic on a bumpy flight—suddenly those in charge seem not to be so in control after all.

Six years later, sometime during the summer break, a huge bomb exploded outside the police station, damaging the school and injuring a teacher who was there preparing for classes. It never occurred to me to ask why they didn't move the school away from the police station. Children accept everything around them as perfectly normal, even the trappings of war.

Years later I would wander through makeshift refugee camps on the Lebanon-Syria border, settlements filled with Syrian children smiling and laughing, playing in the trash, covered in mud. As much as they had experienced appalling trauma, there was a duality to their normalization of everything. A pure acceptance: *No one knows where Dad is, and we all left home to come here and live in this tent.* Children will say such things with a smile. My childhood experiences in Northern Ireland were far from the trauma millions of children in Syria have been forced to endure, but I would come to recognize that sense of normality, an unquestioning tolerance of ways of life that seem disastrous to the outside world.

As a kid, I presumed everyone went to parades celebrating military victories over the Catholics hundreds of years ago, parades filled with marching bands from local sectarian armed militia. Everyone except Catholics, of course. Surely everyone had to travel through military checkpoints when they drove down the road. That's what soldiers did. They disembarked from helicopters, walked around in fields, and randomly stopped cars.

When soldiers stopped my dad's car at the checkpoints, they would glance in the back seat, see four smiling muddy children squashed on top of one another, and ask him his name, where he was going, and if it was his car.

"Why would they ask you if this is your car, Dad?" I would whisper as we drove away. "I mean, whose car would it *be?*"

"Whisht!" my father would reply, stony-faced, checking the rear-view mirror.

I didn't understand until I was older the sectarian nuances of my father telling them our Scottish Protestant name Ferguson and being smiled at and waved on. Our community viewed themselves as fiercely British, and so the British army were, as far as we were concerned, there to fight the IRA, the terrorists, the Bad Man. The British Army was on our side. That still didn't seem to cut the tension at checkpoints, however, where my parents' body language and *whisht*s showed this was a serious business. "They have special machines that mean they can hear you when you talk in the car, so don't say anything!" my mother would say. My two sisters and brother caught one another's eyes and sniggered, aware that only I, the youngest, would still believe that yarn from Mom. "Whisht!" came again from Dad, turning to look at us with a death stare while gripping the steering wheel.

"I don't see why we should care if they hear us," I would declare out the window with a growing insolence. The older I got, the more I bridled at the constant shushing and secrets. Sometimes when I was feeling particularly brazen, I would lean forward between the front and back seats just as a soldier was talking to my dad through the window and snap, "Hello!" before shrinking down behind the front seat, grinning at my little show of bravery in front of my bigger siblings. I would have to wriggle away to avoid a thump from Mom.

Northern Ireland was a completely yet informally segregated society back then. Neighborhoods, streets, grocery stores, pubs, and schools were all either Protestant or Catholic. I attended a Protestant school on the Protestant side of Armagh town. Save for a few exceptions, Catholic kids went to schools run by the Catholic church. They lived in Catholic areas, where their moms shopped in Catholic grocery stores and their dads drank in Catholic pubs, with other Catholic dads. Northern Ireland was full of families who would have loved to see their kids playing with and studying alongside those from other communities. But as the conflict and social strife between the two communities intensified, sectarian divisions dragged everyone along with them.

Our people came to Ireland from the peasant lowlands of Scotland in the 1600s. Land was handed down, farmed, coveted, bought, and left to sons, and the cycle continued. In a deeply patriarchal society, the rural Ulsterwomen I was raised by and around held a gender identity wrapped tightly around motherhood, farming, God, and Britishness. My mother's mother, my grandmother Isabella Anderson, was the clearest blue-blooded example of a Protestant Ulsterwoman I have ever known. A stout, plump farmer's wife with huge glasses and her hair in a tight white perm on her head, my granny Anderson raised seven children in a tiny single-story farmhouse attached to a farmyard and barns. She insisted that we read the Bible to her when we visited. Her house had images of the Queen hung on the walls. The only time I ever saw her not wearing an apron was when she was dressed for church. Granny spoke with a kind of good-humored shout, as though constantly talking over the racket of small children and the roar of tractor engines, even when she wasn't.

Granny and the other women in my family cooked from scratch every meal we ate. This was as much a tradition of women where I grew up as it was the most economical way to feed and raise children. There was a stern, frowning disapproval of the preprepared. These women insisted on doing things themselves.

My sisters and I were expected to do the same. Still, we looked out for each other. Until the age of twelve I don't have a single significant memory that doesn't involve my sister Laura. One of the earliest memories in my life is being crouched under the stairs with her. Laura had her hands cupped over my ears and was telling me not to listen, her face twisted in fear. She kept standing up to steal glimpses though the glass door into the kitchen before crouching down again, afraid she would be seen. She kept saying, "Everything is okay," over and over again. I was terrified and mute.

My parents were having a fight that was much worse than usual. I never knew what they were fighting about, just heard my mother's screaming and my father's shouts, things falling and the sound of chairs being scraped over tiles. Laura was my protector. She was only eighteen months older than me and barely more capable of handling the fear. Yet she seemed so much more grown up.

My mother's mood swings were as unpredictable as they were frightening. She was rarely violent, just verbally abusive. She would lean down and place her face close to mine and yell, "You are an ungrateful bitch!" If I was slow to answer a question or, as was often the case, because I had escaped by getting lost in daydreaming, she would call me "thick," meaning stupid. Her anger terrified me so much I was finely attuned to just a subtle change in the tone of her voice. And her mood could change at any time, from laughter to a violent, spiteful rage that I was too small to escape beyond running out the back door and up to the farm. I never understood where my mother's anger came from, but it seemed to me to center around a deep hatred of her children. To this day, the sound of kitchen cabinet doors being slammed prompts a fear response inside me—like a bullet a little too close.

The morning of my confirmation at church, we posed for a photo taken by my eldest sister, Lesley, in the garden. I stood between Mom and Dad. Mom had been in one of her worst moods all morning. She had bought me new shoes for the big day and seemed now to resent me for it. I was fifteen years old and deeply depressed. I was wearing a blue skirt just above the knee and a sleeveless blue blouse. My hair was cropped short, my face pale and thin. I look blank and faintly shocked. There were days in my life I just had to get through, and this was one of them. I stared into the camera and managed a half smile while Mom muttered under her breath, "You look like a slut." My father pretended not to hear. I pretended not to cry.

There were times when my mother seemed happy, and when she was happy, she was different. She baked birthday cakes from scratch, hosted children's Halloween parties, laughing as we bobbed for apples, and took pictures of us on the first day of the school year. Yet times like this were the exception. I learned not to rely on this woman, this version of my mother, as she came so infrequently, and as the years passed by, disappeared entirely.

My parents were not physically affectionate. I most craved a loving touch from my mother. Missing something I had never really known made me ache. I was so rarely touched as a child that I felt the absence of being held before I really understood what it was. I desired physical human connection so much I noticed the intensity and comfort in moments when it happened in mundane ways. At the hairdresser's, when the smiling lady would touch my shoulder, my head, my ear. Or at the optometrist, getting fitted for glasses, when the doctor would lean over my face and stare into my eyes, illuminating them with a tiny light. No one knew my little heart beat faster at the rare intimacy I so desired from life.

My father was an intense, much more brooding presence at home. His silent rumination, often quietly fuming at us children, was in stark contrast to my mother's angry fits. My father seemed to resent any softness in me. He was affronted by my sentimentality if I wept when lambs on the farm died or worried that the injections he gave to the piglets hurt them.

One day he brought home a puppy—Samy—which we raised on the farm. Samy was white, with brown patches and shaggy hair around his neck. My father intended that Samy be a sheepdog, but he was a runt without a shepherding pedigree. He didn't have any talent or natural ability, and no one on our farm took the time to train him. So, inevitably, he began to chase traffic, bark, and make a general nuisance of himself. I adored him. My father, on the other hand, couldn't stand him. He saw Samy's uselessness as shameless freeloading, an existence that only someone with indulgent sentimentality would tolerate.

One day I came home from school and Samy wasn't there. I crouched under the kitchen table to look for him, asking aloud where he was. My siblings exchanged glances and fell silent. My father had taken Samy in his truck to a rural spot far from our home, opened the door, and pushed Samy out. When I heard this, my little heart closed over. My sense of right and wrong in the world around me began to recognize a deep cruelty in my father.

In keeping with our traditional patriarchal family structure, Dad concentrated on ensuring that we were maintaining his standards. Those standards boiled down to a fear of coming in second, an anxiety to excel. To my father, all the world was a competition, and failure was catastrophic. Lectures on our shortcomings of character would be dispensed if we got anything but As. He constantly compared us to one another ("Lesley never got a C in chemistry"; "Laura made the hockey team by your age"). As we got older and more competitive, it tended to pit us against one another, on an endless treadmill for approval. The crumbs of approval that seemed too little to go around.

I studied constantly, so my grades were usually top of the class. I would come home after a field hockey match on Saturday afternoons and Dad would march down to the house from the farm to find out if we won. "Did you score any goals?" he would ask. If the answer was no, it required an explanation. Who did score the goals? Which father's daughter was scoring goals? Why was I not scoring the goals? What was it I needed to do better to score the goals? In the seven years I attended middle and high school, he never came to a single game. The sport was simply used in the abstract to underscore my weaknesses and point out how to squash them.

Neither of my parents ever said, "I love you." Ever. Very occasionally, my father said it in the third person. "Your father loves you very much, you know." I wonder sometimes if it was said as an apology.

I felt safe in our house only when I knew my oldest sister, Lesley, was there. I was fortunate that she lived at home for the earlier part of my childhood. Yet she always seemed elusive, hard to reach, absent in some way. Whereas Laura was constantly by my side, Lesley was the one person I was always trying to get closer to. I would watch her drive Dad's old car down the driveway and long for her to come back, not quite settled under that roof without her there, too.

Lesley listened to music from Pearl Jam and R.E.M., wore Doc Martens boots, cropped her hair, and studied to go to college in Dublin. That all seemed endlessly glamorous and grown-up to me. Like Laura, Lesley was a bodyguard, protecting me from my brother Andrew's bullying. She taught me to ride a pony. I was ten years old the day Lesley went to college; I silently cried myself to sleep each night for weeks. My sisters were my refuge.

It wasn't unusual for us to be away a lot, heading off to relatives' houses when my mom "needed a break" from us children. Fanny Marr's house was my favorite place to go. Fanny was in her seventies and adored children but didn't have any of her own. I was about seven years old when Laura and I started spending summers at her cottage on the rugged County Down coast. The area was still subjected to the sectarian social divisions across Northern Ireland, but by that stage was spared much of the violence. Our tiny, rugged seaside world there felt sheltered from it all. Eventually as Laura grew older, I visited Fanny on my own. It felt like heaven. Simply driving down the grassy laneway to her cottage, a summer home she bought as a ruined fisherman's cottage and renovated in her younger years, I could feel a weight lift from me. Still today the smell of the ocean, salty and ripe with seaweed and cold air, makes me think instantly of searching for seals in the bay near the townland of Tara, where her cottage sat, and attaching cockles to pieces of string to lure crabs out from under rocks with my friend.

Fanny had grown up in Belfast and had gone on to work as an executive for various companies there. She never married and had traveled the world. To me, this made Fanny a unicorn: a woman in the 1950s and 60s with a good job and a house of her own who threw parties and had no husband and children. In the evening she would make me cups of cocoa, and in between moves in the Scrabble game we played by the fire, she would tell me about Hong Kong. I listened, enraptured. Chain-smoking long cigarettes, Fanny would cradle a whiskey in one hand as she introduced me to new words and talked about books and movies and faraway countries. Biographies of famous British broadcasters and politicians lined her shelves. She loved Humphrey Bogart movies, introducing me to the classic film *Casablanca* when it was shown on her tiny TV in the corner of the living room.

After these visits to Fanny's cottage, I always went "home" to the farm with a heavy heart. I would steel myself on the drive back for another long stint on high alert.

I was deeply afraid that my mother would go insane. This fear left me with a sense of always being on the edge of some sort of disaster, one completely beyond my control, a kind of chaos dangling in the winds of my mother's moods. Anxiety became simply a state of being. The very air I breathed felt heavy, like a weight on my body.

One summer, when we were traveling the south coast of Ireland in a small RV my dad had rented for a holiday, we had to pull over by the side of the road for my mother to get out and rant and rave on the sidewalk while my father tried to persuade her to get back inside. I sat on the pavement and stared at my sneakers, watching my mother in a very public, uncontrolled rage nearby. *This is it,* I thought, *the moment when my mother loses it.* My fear felt so all-consuming, so existential, that I was shaking.

The emotional turmoil had physical manifestations. When I was around twelve, the night before a piano exam, I was suddenly petrified as I gasped for breath, weeping. I could not breathe. It was my first panic attack. My mother walked in from the kitchen, looked at me, and walked out again in disgust.

Long before then I had developed a heavy sense of anxiety, a deep shadowy fear that followed me around. Sometimes as a toddler, when my parents were fighting, I would run into walls. This must have resulted from some sort of need to feel something to escape the fear in my mind. I grew hardened to this anxiety, and a separate, quiet strength began to grow inside me. I was never comforted, so I learned to live with fear as a kind of presence, under the weight of which I grew impenetrably strong. My ability to make peace with fear, to let it hitch a ride along with my life, began under that staircase in my childhood house. My siblings developed their own physical signs of trauma. Mine were primarily emotional.

Lacking Lesley's charisma, I was much too socially awkward for hard partying, and unlike Laura, boys were certainly not interested in me. My acne, thick government-subsidized glasses, and thin, boyish frame were perfectly aligned with my choice of escape: books.

Stories were my survival. Books didn't just allow me to flee the farm, they let me slip out the back door and into a wider world. A bigger, better one where I had freedom. I read every Enid Blyton Famous Five and Secret Seven book, many of them several times. I could think of few things as thrilling as pushing through fur coats in the back of a closet and into the snowy forests of Narnia.

In my bedroom at night, by lamplight, I leaned low over world atlases and *National Geographic* magazines. I traced a finger over the maps, mouthing the names of places like Lalibela, Ethiopia, Antarctica, and the Cape of Good Hope. My heart would beat faster at the symbols of mountains, beaches, and roads I ached to travel, places even Fanny hadn't been.

As I grew older, the weekend papers brought news from the conflict in the Balkans. The outside world in *The Sunday Times* magazine seemed like a much less fair place than I had pictured it. Photographs showed elderly women in headscarves, weeping. I thought of my grandmother and wondered how anyone could take a picture of an old woman crying and not stop to help her fix whatever problem she had. Who was that old lady? Where were her children? What did she say to the person who took her picture?

I inhaled Martha Gellhorn's biography. I was thrilled to learn the life I desperately wanted had been lived already, by remarkable and pioneering women. A life lived deliberately, according to my own design and not some arbitrary set of four-hundred-year-old rules. This life was about travel and adventure, actually charting your own course in the world, seeing and feeling all there was out there. And the ability to make some sort of difference, however vague that felt in those early, excited glimpses. Martha Gellhorn had lived in Cuba and on the Kenyan coast. She had reported on the Spanish Civil War, the invasion of Normandy, and the liberation of the Nazi concentration camps.

Lesley bought me a book by the BBC's lead foreign correspondent Kate Adie, which I read near breathlessly. Her descriptions of defying Chinese security forces to report from the street on the night of the Tiananmen Square massacre in 1989 and of interviewing young American soldiers during the first Gulf War thrilled me.

I read, enraptured, about how Dervla Murphy, the Irish explorer and travel writer, went to Ethiopia in the 1960s and bought a mule, upon which she trekked across the country, solo. I learned how Gertrude Bell, a British diplomat, explorer, archaeologist, mountaineer, writer, and linguist, had campaigned for Iraqi independence in the 1920s and established its national museum.

The more I read, the more I questioned authority. In the increasing insolence of my teen years, I argued with the male preacher teaching us Sunday school lessons about the Protestant Reformation and the errors of Catholicism. The preachers were always men, and they were often deeply bigoted against Catholic communities. I had grown old enough to read history books about The Troubles and the civil rights marches and the abuses by British rule. Calvinist Ulster Scots culture seemed inextricably intertwined with the men who were always in leadership positions.

"He's not even an educated man," I scoffed to my startled mother when I came home from Sunday school one day. "He shouldn't be teaching us history he knows nothing about. He's an idiot, a bigot." Authority figures, in my world, rarely lived up to their titles.

My teenage defiance was not about boys or drugs—I was much too nerdy and shy, a growing cigarette habit my only rebellion—but about politics. I professed myself an ardent republican feminist. A defiant collection of political beliefs neatly and completely the opposite of my father's.

When I pulled my nose from Gellhorn's and Murphy's books, TV news was the one place I saw living, breathing women being heard. It was as though the TV screen was a special portal into another world, one where people listened to and respected women. One where women were asking questions of powerful people and—my eyes widened—they were answering them! Where women traveled all over the world to explain things to us and help us understand. And all the men watched and listened in a way I knew they never would have listened to me over dinner. I saw the power these women journalists held: Kate Adie and Orla Guerin of the BBC reported from wars, revolutions, and environmental disasters. Women like Moira Stuart anchored the shows and shared breaking news with us all. I looked around the room when the news was on and saw my family watching. When these women spoke, everyone listened. Everyone was whisht.

Soon I was going to leave home and go to college, I told myself. I was going to travel all over the world and keep going. I felt like the only way to crawl out of South Armagh was to make peace with my sense of not belonging. *I don't need to belong anywhere,* I thought. *I can belong on the road.*

I focused with a mighty intensity on my studies, entirely as a means to an end—a way out. My high school politics teacher Mr. Millar could see my appetite for international and current affairs books and encouraged me to read about varying political systems, in the UK and United States; landmark legal rulings like *Roe v. Wade*; and foreign affairs scandals like the Iran-Contra Affair. Under his guidance, the world seemed like a place where good and bad could be deciphered, decoded, and understood. A place where injustice and abuse of power—issues I felt deeply attuned and reactive to— were to be uncovered and shared in stories.

I read books on Irish politics, The Troubles, and the IRA, searching for and often finding the answers to my many questions as a child. I got lost in British classical fiction, the sisterly stories of Jane Austen novels and the class politics of D. H. Lawrence. There were stories everywhere, in the poems of Seamus Heaney and the music of Van Morrison, in newspapers and magazines. In his novels, Thomas Hardy seemed to speak right through the page directly to me. He created wonderful headstrong and brave female characters like Bathsheba Everdene in *Far from the Madding Crowd,* who without family or money charts her own course through a patriarchal world. "I don't see why a maid should take a husband when she's bold enough to fight her own battles," she declares.

In the midst of one of my daydreams of driving 4×4s across the African Sahel, camping in the Panjshir Valley, meeting revolutionaries in Tiananmen Square, riding a horse across Cuba, my mom yelled up the stairs to my bedroom that there was a phone call for me. It was my teacher, Mr. Millar.

I stampeded down the stairs and grabbed the phone in both hands. "There's a woman here from the United States who is looking for potential scholarship students to go study there," he said. "I think this is important. Can you come and meet with her?"

"I'm coming now, I'll be there!" I told him.

2

Chicken Shit

I WHEEZED AND PANTED SO hard I thought I might well faint. A fitness instructor, unmoved, whistle pursed between his lips, sent me and around two dozen teenage girls sprinting up and down the neat cut grass of a field hockey pitch again and again. I bent over and rested my hands on my knees for a gasp of air while sweat rolled down my forehead and into my eyes. The thick New Jersey humidity was stifling. I looked up at the majestic trees surrounding the field and the pale blue sky beyond, listened to the laughter and cheers of my teammates caught in the warm air around me, and despite my exhaustion, I was thrilled. This was America.

Beyond the clearing in the trees where we were training, the rest of the Lawrenceville School grounds spread out in all their green splendor. I had never seen a place this grand, save for old mansions and country houses back home that were open to the paying public. The sprawling lawns here were neatly trimmed, with towering mature sycamore and oak trees casting shadows over the greenery between buildings spaced so gracefully the campus looked like a giant Zen garden. There was no concrete anywhere. The classrooms inside smelled of smooth wood paneling and new carpets. People smiled at one another as they walked between buildings along walkways through the grass or lounged under trees in circles of friends.

That spring, someone had contacted my school in Northern Ireland looking for students who could qualify for a one-year scholarship at a boarding school in the United States. An Irish American alum of Law-renceville named Katie McMahon had created a scholarship endow-ment and was overseeing the recruitment herself. She met me in my teacher's office, standing up and holding out her hand with a smile. She had perfectly blow-dried blond hair and wore a suit and high heels. She was American. I had never seen anyone smile so much. I stared at her in wonder, this representative from the wider world. To me, she was the embodiment of a more sophisticated world. I stood awkwardly, shoving my glasses up my nose and not knowing where to place my hands.

My heart pounded, but I was already adept at appearing calm. I gripped the sides of my seat, forcing my trembling hands still. Katie was looking for students who were well-rounded, those who got top grades, played sports, and would speak up in class, not intimidated by culture shock. I tried to figure out what she wanted to hear from me so I could follow her out of there.

"Tell me about your family," Katie asked. "What are you guys like as a group?" I looked at her as she smiled, waiting for me to tell her all about my nice family and our lovely, quaint farm life.

"We are all really close," I replied, smiling back at her. "My par-ents are very supportive." I felt certain she wanted to find a nice, stable, well-put-together teenage girl from a lovely family. So I put on my best face, and lied. I described a close-knit family who loved one another very much. I said what I would find myself repeating throughout the next decade when asked about my family: I told her what she wanted to hear. I couldn't escape the secret fear that there must be a reason why parents would refuse to love their child and that I must have provoked them. Maybe there really was something wrong with me.

Katie seemed very happy with my answers and wrapped her arms around me in a bear hug, something highly unusual in Northern Ire-land back then. As I walked away and headed for the bus stop across town, a rare kind of calm rested on my shoulders. I had a feeling my life was about to change.

When I landed at Newark Airport several months later, I could see in the far distance the outline of Manhattan's skyscrapers, gray against the haze. A world I had seen a thousand times in movies was now right in front of me, real. Like so many before me, I was captivated immediately. Here no one knew anything about me other than what and who I chose to be. That feeling of reinvention, however much a half-truth, is a seductive promise.

No tired limbs could overshadow the joy I felt as I prepared for field hockey preseason tryouts. I was so excited to be where there was a place for me. Katie and others had detected potential in me. For the first time in my life, I felt that people really believed in me, and I was determined to prove them right.

The other girls had known each other for years and screamed and laughed and chatted among themselves with the thrilled intimacy unique to teenage girls. I sat in the grass nearby as they caught up after long summers away at something called hockey camp. They looked like professional athletes and played like them, too. Back home we practiced once a week and played a game once a week, sucked on orange slices at halftime, and stopped the game if someone's mouth guard came off or if someone got a cramp. We stopped scoring goals if we were winning by four or more because it was considered unsporting. Few parents bothered to come to watch our games.

These girls were serious. They wore Under Armour gear, cleated shoes, knee supports, and sunblock. They iced bits of themselves after practice. I had no idea why and was too afraid to ask what putting ice on yourself was for. They drank bright-colored energy drinks their parents brought to their games and practices. Yes, their parents didn't just come to the games—they came to practice. The two main coaches were middle-aged women, each sporting a visor and a fanny pack, with faces more serious than General Douglas MacArthur. My white Celtic skin looked almost transparent, save for my purply red face, as I strained up and down the field. By some miracle, I made the team.

Katie was beyond excited that I was a varsity field hockey player, calling me on the phone in my bedroom to tell me how proud she was of me. No one had ever said that to me before. The other girls on the team were sure of themselves, the most popular and pretty girls in school. I spent much of my time in those early days smearing makeup on my inflamed acne and adjusting my glasses in the sweaty heat of New Jersey's summer. I wanted to fit in more than anything.

My roommate, Katy-Jane, was from Texas. She was only four-ten and always wore blue jeans with a big cowboy belt, sneakers, and a T-shirt. She had wild, curly auburn hair. We became instant friends. As we unpacked our things into our respective wardrobes, Katy-Jane looked over and asked, "Is that all your clothes?" I looked at her and then back inside my closet. There were about three shirts and one sort of smart Sunday-best pair of pants. It seemed perfectly normal to me. I felt a sudden flush of embarrassment and mumbled something about wanting to pack light for my flight over.

My scholarship fund had placed enough there for me to buy things like the books and sports equipment I needed, as well as some decent clothes for the seemingly endless school events, formal lunches, and get-togethers. It also meant I could afford to keep up in small ways socially. At weekends I would catch the bus to Princeton with my housemates, too shy to suggest we just buy bikes, which seemed like the smarter option. When someone asked if I would like to get a pedicure, I would respond with confidence and say, "Of course!" aloud, and *What is a pedicure?* inwardly. When the others wore pastel-colored cardigans, I would purchase one from J.Crew as soon as possible. When ordering Thai food I would do so with utmost authority. I wandered among the beautiful, neo-Tudor buildings of Princeton as the leafy streets turned red and orange in the fall and watched myself ease into a new version of myself.

There were other scholarship students at Lawrenceville who came from deeply underprivileged backgrounds. Many more came from enormous wealth and privilege, often from some of the richest families in the country and wider world. Buildings, gyms, and libraries even bore the surnames of some of my classmates. Classes were no larger than fourteen students, and we all sat around oval boardroom-like tables with our teachers. There was no way to hide at the back. I adored it.

I had no shortage of support from adults on campus. My house mistress, Ms. Stewart, was equal parts teacher and mom to several dozen of us senior girls. In her mid-forties, she was tall and thin, with long limbs and cropped brown hair and a wide smile. Ms. Stewart always seemed to know when to stop us in the corridor and ask what was on our mind and when to let us be. The morning I was due to fly back to the UK for my university entrance interview, Ms. Stewart came bounding out the front door and down the building steps to where I was waiting for my ride to the airport. She grabbed me by the shoulders, looked me straight in the eye, and said, "Remember, Jane, they would be *lucky* to have you," before giving me a bear hug. I was silent. At times like this, when people were so kind to me, I didn't know how to respond. This was the first place besides Fanny's cottage I had felt truly valued and loved in my life.

Despite the confidence I presented in class, I was terrified my hill-billy roots were obvious, no matter how hard I tried to disguise them. My laugh was louder. I cursed more. I pulled awkwardly at the smart shirts and khaki pants I had bought for events on the campus lawn, filled with small herds of boys in blue blazers and khaki pants and girls in sweater sets, shuffling between tables spread with foods I didn't know the names of. No matter how welcoming and friendly people were to me, it felt like there was dirt under my nails I could never quite get out and everyone could see it—especially the parents who drove up in Mercedes and BMWs, confident the investment here meant their son or daughter was making important connections with the right sort of people. Not a kid like me with tobacco stains on my teeth and government-subsidized glasses.

The moment I opened my mouth to speak, I was exposed as an outsider. My classmates were friendly about my accent, treating it like a great source of novelty and reveling in the different phrases and words for things and pronunciation. "What is it you say for *elevator?*"

a housemate asked. "Ah, *lift,* yes!" At other times they did imperson-
ations of Mel Gibson in *Braveheart,* even though the movie was set in
Scotland. Close enough, I suppose. I set about quickly shaving off the
edges of my Northern Irish brogue.

There was one way in which I could not conform to this new
environment. I arrived at Lawrenceville in August 2003, five months
after the invasion of Iraq. By the next year, the weapons of mass destruction President George W. Bush had warned about were still not
found, and reports of abuses by American soldiers in Abu Ghraib
prison burst onto the front pages and through the near-impenetrable
bubble of campus consciousness. A modern history teacher assigned
our class an article in the *Atlantic* magazine—the first time I'd ever
heard of it—about how the war was descending into chaos. After we'd
read it, the students slouched into their chairs until one boy finally
declared, "I don't care about the weapons of mass destruction, if they
are there or not." He shrugged his shoulders and the teacher waited
for another student to respond. "I don't really think it's fair to criticize
the soldiers over the prison photos," said another boy. "It's a war, they
are soldiers." I was appalled.

Two years before, I had come out of Mr. Millar's politics class and
walked out on the playground, where my classmates were standing
together in serious conversation. One of them looked up at me and
asked, "Jane, what's the World Trade Center?"

"I don't know." I shrugged in response.

In Northern Ireland, we had watched the United States grapple
with being hit on its home turf with an uncanny understanding. The
rubble, thick dust in the air, shocked and bloodied civilians being
helped to safety, however much on a greater scale—this was all too familiar to us. But those were the streets of New York. To my American
classmates, acts of war had happened so far away for so long that it was
an appalling shock to experience mass casualties in the heart of New
York City. We watched the news each night as they openly discussed
their horror at being targeted "at home." It was a strange feeling for us
in Northern Ireland, watching the United States seem so vulnerable.

America had always been another word for success in Ireland, on both sides of the border. "Now living in America" was always followed with the phrase "Och, sure, she's doing awful well for herself." To live in America, even to visit America, was synonymous with some sort of personal life advancement. The place seemed immune to bad things. The tragedies of that day seemed to narrow the gap between us.

The war in Afghanistan was soon on our screens nightly in South Armagh, images of helicopters and soldiers and weapons, and then, in my final year of high school in Armagh, the buildup to the war in Iraq. It seemed so fast, so rushed and frightening. Suddenly American politicians were asking us to "trust them" about the evidence of weapons of mass destruction in Saddam Hussein's Iraq. In Northern Ireland, politicians were just angry men driven by prejudice and personal agendas. Trusting them seemed like an act of willful stupidity to me.

My American classmates' agnosticism toward the war in Iraq shocked me. I had come from a place so ravaged by sectarianism that the lexicon of ending conflict was second nature: building bridges, healing the wounds of war. The Troubles had been bound up in cross-community efforts, appeals for peace, peace processes, cease-fires. War was something everyone around me was always trying to stop, and here I was surrounded by people cheering on a new one. Although I had grown up amid entrenched political disagreement, I had never been so out of sync with my peers' perspectives. This was the first time that I had ever felt like I was speaking another language. A culture shock that my naive young heart felt was morally wounding.

While I was at Lawrenceville, I read British papers and followed BBC reports. Much of the U.S. reporting was taking the statements by White House and Pentagon officials about weapons of mass destruction at face value. I read about the enormous million-man marches going on across Europe as the Bush White House tried to form a coalition, turning to France, the UK, and Germany. It felt like everyone except the Americans knew the "intelligence" was phony.

So I kept asking questions. Why would you believe a politician over hard and fast evidence? "I just can't believe that our president would lie to us," a friend's dad replied, shrugging, during dinner on a visit. He didn't like the idea of the war, but he couldn't accept that a president would send young men to die in an ambitious experiment.

I understood by now that there was no such thing as peace and justice. You had to pick one. To have lasting peace, there would be no justice. The man who shot my uncle Desmond and his mother was a mass murderer, and he was released from jail early on the terms agreed to with the British in the Good Friday Agreement that brought our war to an end in 1998. He walked free and returned to his home not far from my uncle's. That's what war is. It is killing and sacrifice until a monstrous bitter pill—the ultimate wound—must be swallowed to make it stop.

Following the U.S. invasion of Iraq, Lawrenceville organized a debate on the issue for the senior class in the main lecture hall. Those who wanted to speak prepared their own arguments and speeches. The class gathered, around a hundred of us in the tiered rows of benches. One young man got up, blond hair neatly combed to the side above his small round glasses. I sat and listened as he presented a well-spoken and passionate statement in favor of mandatory conscription. "We all must stop questioning the war and go and volunteer to fight in it!" he argued. In times of war, it was not for us to question orders, he continued. Those who refused to fight were shirking their responsibility.

I slipped out quietly before it ended and sat on the building's steps. It was a beautiful night, warm at last after a long winter, with stars crested over the outline of the campus. My despair over the war seemed to touch a sadness in me, and a deep sense of loneliness washed over me.

The American TV reports from the initial invasion of Iraq, the "Shock and Awe" operation in Baghdad, had breathlessly recounted the bombardment as though it was a fireworks display, with no real attempts to convey how the Iraqis were experiencing those terrifying moments. Other than the occasional painfully brief sentence from a man-on-the-street sound bite, Iraqi voices were literally absent from the reports. I thought perhaps that if the nightly newscasts presented the Iraqi point of view in a meaningful way, Americans might feel more connected to the human rights of Iraqis.

Despite my fiery teenage indignation over this senseless war, my adolescent self-consciousness sometimes threw cold water on my ardor. At times, when I argued most passionately in class, I would catch the smirks of my classmates, often the cooler boys by whom I only ever longed to be noticed. In those moments, I would flush with embarrassment. Back then, to be seen as "political," overly fired up about the war, was uncool. It's better to be ignored than to be actively uncool, a smaller, frightened part of me would concede, and I would stop talking.

My school friends were more likely to discuss their summer plans than the war in Iraq. I spent spring break with several other girls from Lawrenceville on an eighty-foot yacht in the Caribbean owned by a classmate's parents. Slicing through aquamarine waters as we sailed from island to island, an onboard staff that included a chef catered to our every need. I felt the warm teak wood under my toes and sunshine on my face. When the girls began discussing summer travel in Italy together, I lied and said I'd join them, knowing there was zero chance I could get the money to travel around Europe. Despite our close bond—in fact perhaps because of it—the other girls still didn't realize that I was a visitor in their world, and not of it.

I was focused on getting into a university in England, where I would study literature and international politics at York. One more stretch at home in Northern Ireland before I truly left home for good. I would need a job.

I lowered my paper time card into the metal box on the wall, and as it thumped an angry stamp, my first day at Moy Park Chicken Factory began. I hoisted my pale blue uniform trousers up around my waist and walked down the hallway and through the door to the factory. The heat and smell hit me first: chickens and feathers and eggshells.

The main hatchery floor was paneled with white plastic sheeting along the walls. Workers stood at tall steel tables, various stations where baby chicks went through layers of processing. The whir of ventilation machinery mixed with the high-pitched chirping of thousands of chicks sounded like a muffled endless scream.

Each day started in the huge incubators, where hundreds of overnight hatchlings stood blinking and shaking in plastic trays among the wreckage of eggshells. The trays were layered in metal wheeled carts, like those you see in bakeries. Every morning we would carry the newborns out into the main factory floor and place the trays on the shiny metal tables in the center for processing. We would sort the chicks into cardboard boxes, stack them onto wooden pallets, and load them onto trucks to be delivered to farms across Northern Ireland, to grow into eligible adult chickens.

There were deformed chicks waiting for us in the morning regularly, some with one leg, some with three. I once found one with four legs and two heads, two tiny beings trying to pull themselves apart. The deformed ones that had survived till morning were tossed onto the conveyor belt and a worker would sit and ring their tiny necks, usually squeezing the chick on the side of the bucket until its beak opened in a silent gape.

Each morning in the factory changing rooms, I took off my jeans and T-shirt and pulled on a blue and white factory uniform from my allocated locker. I would look in the mirror, straighten the floppy blue hat, and wonder who the person was looking back at me. I had slipped from one planet to another, a different person in each. In this factory world, in an industrial park just outside a small Northern Irish town, I was not sure how to be. I didn't fit in here.

The adjustment from the excitement and care and warmth of Lawrenceville back to my parents' house and into this factory was difficult. I had spent all those months surrounded by friends and teachers. They were everywhere: in the dining hall, the gym, the classrooms, the common rooms, I had even shared a room with someone I adored, staying up late and talking and listening to music. Now, back in my parents' house, I felt more alone than I had as a child. Because back then I had not known these other friends. The companionship I had enjoyed felt like a dream, my loneliness now a painful longing. My siblings had moved away, and I sat alone in rooms that sounded and smelled of the past.

My school friends wrote me a big group letter from Italy, folded over until it was thick and stuffed into an envelope. I cried hard when it came, sitting alone in my parents' living room. I had not told anyone from Lawrenceville that I was working in a factory that summer. I was too ashamed. The smell of chicken shit on me, the seeming downward tumble I had taken. When girlfriends had asked, I told them I had wanted to spend time with my family before college.

At work I felt a different shame. When I walked into the canteen where we sat at long tables to eat our packed lunches, the room would fall quiet. I had gone to grammar school, studied for exams, was planning on going to college on "the mainland" (in the UK). I was different; they probably considered me snobbish. I quietly ate my ham sandwiches and smoked my cigarettes near the others but at a socially acceptable distance until the break was over. The last thing I could admit was that I had just graduated from one of the world's most exclusive boarding schools. I dropped my new American accent and readopted the rural Northern Irish brogue. Here I was again, working hard to fit in, feeling lost and in the wrong place.

As the new girl, I was often assigned the worst job: taking the eggs that had not hatched overnight out to the large open bins on the other side of the carpark to be thrown out. To avoid breaking any eggs, which would engulf me in a smell beyond description, I struggled to steady the cart across the uneven tarmac of the carpark. But it was enormous, taller than me, and rattled along violently, making it impossible to keep the odd egg from exploding, spurting out black chunks of rotten baby chick and appalling fart gas into the air. The smell took all day to erase, no matter how much bathroom hand soap I rubbed into my pink cheeks.

Things weren't much better at my parents' house. My mother was resentful that I was home, and my father was upset at me for disturbing her with my presence. Mom would storm around in a rage, slamming kitchen cupboard doors and yelling at me before storming out of the house. My siblings were not there to defend me or redirect Mom's rages toward themselves, or to simply dilute her anger among the four of us. My father could think of little to say to me.

I would wake up in the morning and leave the house before they got up. Lesley had gifted me her car before leaving for England, an old white Toyota Corolla with over 150,000 miles on the clock. Her unruly dog had ripped out sizable chunks of the driver and passenger seats and door lining, and she had "fixed" these holes with vast amounts of black duct tape. It was of no monetary value but was worth everything to me. I climbed in with my packed lunch at dawn and enjoyed twenty minutes of bliss driving rural roads in the clear summer air, the window down, radio blasting, smoking.

On the way home from work one day, I stopped in the village near my parents' house and bought a bottle of crisp, cold white wine from the local store, wrapped tight in a brown paper bag. It was worth about four hours of chicken shit hosing. It was a warm summer's evening and the back door of the house into the kitchen was open to the driveway when I pulled up. My mother was home, angrily banging around and mumbling to herself in disgust. I silently pulled off my shoes, opened the bottle of wine, poured myself a tall glass, and walked outside. I crossed the garden and stepped over the rotten brown fence, moving across the laneway and over the steel gate into a large field. The grass was as tall as my thighs and cool under my bare feet. At a safe distance from the house, I sat down, and the world was gone. I drank wine in my private world. Lying on my back I stared up at the sky framed by swaying grass. Tears rolled down my temples into my ears and hair. *I'm going to get out of here and never come back,* I told myself. This, I decided, was the last time I would ever cry here.

My refusal to wallow in self-pity worked. The other women at the factory softened, eventually turning to chat with me at lunch. Diane, the oldest, was the natural leader of the group. She was in her fifties, thin as a rail and with graying blond hair tied back in a bun under her factory blue hat. Diane smoked as much as I did—more than a pack a day—but had been at it longer, so it showed in wrinkles across her top lip and her raspy voice.

Young, loud, and fun to be around, Niamh was the number two. Niamh was pretty, with long auburn hair and olive skin. She always had one hand on a hip and the other either waving in the air as she talked or balancing a cigarette, her elbow clasped to her side. She tilted her head when she talked. And Niamh talked loudly. She roared with laughter. When Niamh was telling a story, everyone on the factory floor could hear it, and no one minded because her stories were always hilarious.

Naimh and Diane were from different sides of the religious divide in Northern Ireland. The reality was that those from varying "sides of the community," as we referred to it, didn't socialize at all outside work. This was an unacknowledged fact—these friendships were strictly work ones. Outside the wire fencing of the factory parking lot, the sectarian system still ruled their communities. Inside the fence, everyone was relying on the same $6 an hour. Tribalism doesn't work on an individual level, when people are broken down into small groups of nominal enemies just trying to make a living. It works on a collective level, when larger-scale communities are separated. Across Northern Ireland all the workplaces were full of people making money to put food on the table.

The women chatted with me about my college plans and the men asked about my dad's farm. Numbers of pigs and sheep, acreage, easy small talk.

Sometimes they asked about university, what I wanted to do once I got my degree. I told them I wanted to be a journalist. Their responses surprised me: they understood entirely. As I sat with those ladies at a long table in the factory canteen, all of us wearing the exact same blue and white uniform, smoking the same cigarettes, and earning the same hourly wage, I realized something that should have been obvious from the start, when I was wiping rotten egg off my cheek and feeling sorry for myself: what separated us was not where I came from but where I was headed. My privilege lay in my future and its endless possibilities. These women lived dignified lives filled with family and laughter and a sense of belonging, but they didn't have the advantages I had. To get out of here and build the life I had pictured for myself would be near-impossible for every single one of them.

A lottery of birth had placed me in a tumultuous family, but a family where education was everything. When I was a kid, chance, fate, God, or whatever had placed issues of *National Geographic* and newspapers under my nose, David Attenborough documentaries on gorillas in Uganda and BBC reports from the Gulf War and Bosnia before my eyes. In that moment of looking around at the other workers in that factory, I recognized acutely that I had far greater options than these women did, and continuing to ignore that was unworthy of me. I might not be in Italy for the summer with my Lawrenceville friends, but in the grand scheme of things, life's lottery had been good to me.

I volunteered to stay later for extra hours power-hosing shit from the factory walls. I also found out from some of the younger lads that there was additional weekend work on Saturdays, offering $2 more per hour to the guys for heading out to farms to weigh chickens. *Perfect work for a girl like me,* I thought. Our family weighed the fat lambs on the farm every year to see if they were ready for butchering. I did that work for free. This would be for $8 an hour, big bucks. I wasn't going to miss out on a windfall like this just because I was a girl.

From then on, every Saturday began bundled into a small car with several men driving to a different chicken farm. I pulled on blue overalls, a hairnet, a face mask, and gum boots in the single changing room while the guys waited outside. They had never had a woman do this work before.

We were told to weigh the chickens and place them into one of three pens—too fat, too thin, and just right. There were thousands and thousands of them, all being fattened up for slaughter and supermarket shelves. Perspiration ran down my forehead and into my eyes, stinging them and blurring my vision. My glasses would sometimes fall off my sweaty face when I leaned down close to the chicken shit floor and I would grab them out of the dirt, wipe them on my overalls, and shove them back on, keen not to hold up the group.

The too-fats and too-thins were to be killed. By us. By hand. Right now. Again, eager not to look like this fazed me at all—and Jesus Christ alive, it did—I nodded, stern-faced, ready to go. This was entirely normal, I pretended, using the same face I had applied to pedicures and pad Thai in Princeton.

If nature versus the corporate food system is a war, for $8 an hour, I was special forces. What followed was a barbarous massacre. No time to waste feeding up the thin ones a little longer. And the fatties? Goners, too.

One of the other guys kindly showed me how to wring a chicken's neck. Holding the chicken upside down by the feet with my left hand and clutching its neck, just before the head, between my right hand's index and middle finger, I tugged down hard and twisted it back until I felt a click and the chicken went limp. The first few times I did it, my face crumpled in disgust behind my mask. My heart beat faster as I panicked that if I didn't do it right I would just hurt the chicken. And I wasn't some sort of chicken-torturing monster, so I closed my eyes tight and pulled down so hard the chicken's head came off in my hand. My coworkers howled with laughter as I stood in shock. We killed chickens until our backs and hands hurt. In the end we were left with dead white feathered bundles all over the ground around us, twitching and smelling like feathers and shit and a criminally senseless waste of food.

After all the chicken carnage and long days in the factory, by September I had several thousand dollars ready for college. In a much more valuable sense, however, those hours clocked in had readied me for college in a way Lawrenceville alone couldn't. I had the greatest skill any human can possibly have: adaptability. I had drawn a deeper line in the sand between myself and the place that raised me. I could trust myself to step beyond it.

3

The Highest Point

I HAD NEVER MET A real journalist before. In the BBC's Belfast newsroom, they were everywhere, but I was too shy to talk to them. I beamed with triumph when I was accepted into their internship program. This was surely a way into the BBC, I thought. All those years watching and admiring the capable, authoritative women anchors on the evening news, and now I would be on the inside. The one catch: I was being assigned to Northern Ireland. I'd wanted to go to London. Still, not even the word *Belfast* on the screen in front of me could make me feel as though this was anything other than the next chapter of my life starting. My whole career, my BBC career.

When I called Aunt Fanny with the news about my internship, she insisted I spend the month staying with her. She was so excited to see me that she had stocked the fridge with beers and piled the fire high with logs until it could melt your face from the doorway. On my first night in Belfast, she found some old office clothes of hers from the fifties and sixties, pulling them out of the closet upstairs and onto the bed. She was delighted to have someone to wear her beautiful vintage cashmere sweaters and wool jackets.

Fanny's small redbrick cottage in Belfast's Georgian suburbs was filled with books, paintings, and cigarette smoke. This was Fanny's old family home, and her relatives, now all gone, smiled out from photos on the walls like friendly ghosts. Her sister, clad in a thick brown fur coat, clutched her Member of the British Empire award from the Queen outside Buckingham Palace. Her workmates on a trip to Hong Kong in the sixties. Accomplished people. I was ready to become one of them.

I had graduated a few months before from college in York, England. University was a hurdle I had to clear to get here, but I loved it. I adored my studies, reading English literature and attending classes on the Islamic world and the Middle East, developmental aid in Africa and political philosophy. My new best friend, Ruth, and I eventually worked at the student newspaper together, she as editor in chief and me as deputy news editor. Ruth had grown up in various countries in east Africa with parents working in international development. We would sit up at night in the newspaper office, a mess of piles of newspapers and old donated computers, drinking cans of beer and smoking rolled cigarettes, talking about our future careers as journalists. As much as I loved the books and studies, I longed much more to embark on my life as a journalist, traveling and living abroad, meeting people and telling stories every day for a living.

On the first morning of my internship, I walked purposefully into Belfast city center. As I rushed toward my new life at the BBC, images of my old one surrounded me: red brick and cement under the constant mist of fine rain, too faint to see; you just feel it on your face. The soft rolling green hills surrounding the city appeared when a cloud shifted, dark racing green and smoothed over. The old Harland & Wolff shipyard cranes, two angular yellow iron squares, squat over the brown and green of the city, next to the slow-moving River Lagan. Woodsmoke rose from the chimneys, adding to the acid earthiness of the misty air. This was a place that I had pushed so far back in my mind—so firmly labeled "the past"—that it seemed both new and familiar at the same time, like walking through a memory that felt less painful than before.

I was given a guest pass at the reception desk and was shown to the newsroom upstairs. Patricia and Paddy were the bosses, desks piled high with paperwork and coffee cups, set next to each other at the top of the room. I walked up to them and extended my hand, smiling, excited and nervous. It quickly became clear that I had been sent to those in charge of BBC Northern Ireland by their bosses in London, and they were frustrated by the additional work of having to find me something to do. They shook my hand and then returned to their computer screens, telling me to find a seat anywhere. They began talking intensely to each other about plans for that night's show. I sat at a desk in the middle of the newsroom, quiet as a mouse, watching the newsroom around me.

The inside of the building had been given a 1980s makeover and was varying shades of beige and white. No one seemed to have an office. If they did, they never used it. There were piles of newspapers on desks, masses of paper merging one person's space into another's. Seats soon emptied as reporters hung up phones, grabbed their coats and briefcases, and headed for the door, off to do their jobs.

Finally I overcame my shyness and approached a reporter staring into a computer screen, fingers typing violently. I asked if there was anything I could help the person with. "If you are going anywhere today and there's room, I would love to come," I appealed, pulling awkwardly at my inherited sweater. I tried to mask my English accent now, to once again be as Northern Irish as I could.

The journalist gave me a mildly irritated look. This person had little time or patience for a youngster with zero professional-level skills. I was getting nowhere with him. For much of my time I felt like an impostor, consigned to being removed from whatever seat I was "taking up" and thus being moved around the newsroom on rotation to the tutting and headshaking of busy reporters and editors.

In the evenings as I marched back across the city, under patches of orange streetlights, Fanny would be lighting a fire in the dining room and finishing preparations for a three-course dinner cooked from scratch. She used things like ivory-handled cutlery, fine china, and linen napkins. She would tidy her hair for dinner and decant the wine, niceties that were foreign to us in Armagh. I relaxed into that feeling of being securely loved by an adult, just simply for being myself—the way I told a story, my jokes, my constant refusal to wear shoes, whatever it was about me she seemed to enjoy.

For all the energetic love she showed me, I couldn't shake how she seemed a little weaker than before—a little less steady in her vibrancy and chatter and stories and laughter. She appeared to stop and start sentences abruptly sometimes, forgetting what she was saying. But I never allowed myself to believe this meant Fanny wouldn't be around for decades more. When a stab of fear that she was fading hit me suddenly—watching her sleep in her armchair or standing in the kitchen confused by what she was doing there—I would brush it aside, snapping it shut like a heavy book.

I wanted to freeze her in time—quilted vest over corduroy pants and bow tying up the last strands of her hair over an almost bald head. Scarlet lipstick carefully applied in the hallway mirror before we left for a walk around the neighborhood. "I really hate these walking sticks," she would complain, waving her cane above her head. "They make me feel so old." I feared for my life without Fanny—her love, her advice, her careful mixture of bohemian rebelliousness and Victorian sensibilities. I needed her.

"Maybe I should marry Mark now I'm finished at college," I broached one night toward the end of our month together. My college boyfriend was in a North England town working on his first job, calling every day. I had promised to move back in with him once I was done with my internship. After a careful silence, staring hard at her Scrabble letters, Fanny looked up at me and said, "I wonder if he's fun enough for you, Janie." We both knew the answer.

On the last day at BBC Northern Ireland, the day I was imagining weeks prior as being the fateful moment I might (would, must!) raise the subject of a job with the management, I asked Paddy and Patricia for a meeting. Perched close to the edge of the red sofa, ready to leave at any moment, they looked impatient to get back to work. I commenced my "job, please" speech—I would be willing to do anything if they didn't have a job as a reporter. I could start as a junior member of the staff and work the news desk, answer phones, report to the editors, research story ideas. I was not fussy at all. Eventually I dreamed of being an on-camera reporter, but to get there I would do any job at all and learn the ropes.

Patricia stared at the ceiling while I spoke. She was a lost cause. So I spoke directly to Paddy. Once my speech was over, Patricia was silent for a few moments as we eyeballed each other. I held on for the verdict, trying to look calm, my legs folded twice over.

"We can't offer you anything other than perhaps, we might just be able to, in a little time, quite possibly, offer you a position as a regional weather girl. Um, I mean meteorologist," said Paddy. This, I realized, was not my ticket.

The next week, I sat cross-legged on the floor of Mark's tiny apartment in the North of England, bent over my laptop. I scrolled through media job websites for anything that was entry level. It was cold outside, and frost rimed the edges of the room's one window. I pulled the sleeves on my wool sweater down to my hands and rocked back and forth against the chill. My days revolved around the search for jobs that seemed like unicorns and shopping for groceries to cook in time for Mark's return home.

We had talked the night before in the local pub about my hopes and dreams for my career. All the cities we could live in. The travel, the teams, the bureaus around the world for newspapers and broadcasters. In truth, I had talked while he cradled a pint of beer in his hand and stared at me, occasionally glancing over my shoulder and around us. "Maybe if I get a job on the south coast of England you can commute into London on the train," he had said. Boredom threatened to give way to sadness.

I don't want to buy a house, I thought. *I don't want a mortgage. I don't want to get married, and I don't want to commute to a job I hate. I cannot live that life.* I knew in my soul it would be a sort of death for me.

I flicked over to the other open tab on my laptop, filled with Arabic school websites across the Middle East. One in Yemen made me smile when I hit enter, instantly playing the haunting singular melody of an oud, the traditional Arabic stringed instrument similar to a guitar. Images of Sana'a, the capital, surrounded information about the school. Tall ancient structures made of brick, with ornate white window frames, sat between mountains that were ocher.

In another tab, I studied a map of Yemen, its roughly rectangular shape, the Red Sea and Indian Ocean against its shores, the mountains and deserts. Looking at the map of a country you have not visited holds so much promise and excitement. "There is a certain madness that comes over one at the mere sight of a good map," wrote Dame Freya Stark, the much-loved twentieth-century British Italian explorer and travel writer. Stark had struck out, lived in Baghdad, traveled across Yemen with archaeologists, and eventually drew maps of much of the Middle East. She had found her way.

On my map Yemen was a tidy oblong chunk at the bottom of the Arabian Peninsula. It had mountains and deserts and a long coastline. A historic wonder of a capital city. I knew little else. Jagged mountain symbols were placed around Sana'a. With my finger, I traced the names and places and felt my heart swell with an excitement of adventures still to come. I had no idea how I could afford to get there.

Later that day, there was a white envelope in the mail that I instantly knew was from Fanny. Her small envelopes, the letter folded over twice inside, and the old-fashioned ornate handwriting on the front. I tore it open and pulled out a check in my name for $4,500, enveloped in a letter. "Please use this for something fun."

I had never been given a gift like this before. Fanny had given me—at that vital moment in my young life—something more valuable than money. She gave me options. The door to a world I wanted to be a part of opened just enough for me to slip through it. I returned to my laptop, wrote to the school in Yemen with the catchy website music, and asked for a spot. I would stay for as long as I could afford.

Weeks later, I was sitting in the passenger seat of Mark's car, staring at the distant WELCOME TO HEATHROW sign up ahead. It moved painfully slowly toward us in the heavy traffic. The atmosphere in the car was stifling. We both struggled to say anything.

"I'll be back before you know it!" I chirped. No, I wouldn't. Somewhere inside me I knew I was never coming back.

It seemed that all the men around me were puzzled and amused when I talked about my dreams of being a foreign correspondent. But this one was quiet now.

His hand jerked the gear stick into place between us. *He thinks he's in love with me,* I thought, *but he doesn't even know me.*

I didn't yet know how to end things, how to look someone in the eye and say goodbye. I was so scared I strained to keep my voice steady. I burned to get out of the car and as far away from this scene in my life as I could. If only I could climb out and walk the last mile with my rucksack on my back, through the pouring rain. Free.

The rain never stops in this country, I thought as drops of water fell down the windscreen in front of me. When we pulled up outside Heathrow's departures terminal, I leapt out of the car, trying to look calm. He opened the trunk and handed me my huge rucksack, helping to heave it onto my back. "Call me when you arrive!" he said, smiling, pulling me into his chest for a hug. "Thank you," I said, my face against his sweater. And I meant it. Breaking free, I waved as I walked through the sliding doors. I had half my body weight in that rucksack but for the first time in months felt lighter than air.

The plane landed at Sana'a like it was touching down on top of the world, flying over the city of earthen brick buildings, gray concrete suburbs, all held within a basin between high peaks, dark red and jagged. We gently bumped down just beyond the outskirts of town as the sun was rising. *No turning back now,* I thought as I stepped onto the tarmac, the morning air cool and crisp and light. Bored taxi drivers leaned on one hip, arms folded, their traditional Yemeni skirts, called *mawazes,* draped around their legs.

Assam was waiting for me. He grinned as he shook my hand with a viselike grip. I was awash with relief at the sight of him. The strength of his handshake helped me believe that he was real, and that I had made it from one world into another, one part of my life into the next, with Assam here to help me. "Welcome in Yemen, Jane." He beamed. Assam was so friendly even his thick dark mustache appeared to smile. I was grateful for it. He was now the closest thing I had to a friend for thousands of miles. That stark, perfect vulnerability lone travelers feel when they are in a country for the first time was even more potent at that tender age. It's a thrilling mixture of fear and hope.

He wore a collared shirt, slacks, and a suit jacket. He was polite and welcoming, but not obsequious. He had high cheekbones and a noble arched nose, and his eyes smiled constantly. On the plane I had ruminated about the danger of kidnapping. Could I be grabbed at the airport? The building was calm, friendly even. Everyone stared at me, but there was no hostility, and a few even shouted "Welcome!" over their shoulder as they walked by. Alongside my relief was a touch of shame at my mistrust.

Assam was a college student and spoke perfect English. He picked up extra work at the Arabic school I was about to attend, helping make students feel at home, ferrying them to and from the airport and arranging weekend trips around the country for them. At twenty-one, he was two years younger than me but seemed much older. As we walked out of the airport building, I could feel the cold night air give way to the rising sun. The dawn appeared in light blue and orange around the tips of the burnt red mountaintops in the distance. We climbed into his small 4×4 and careened down the highway, the wind in my hair as I hung out the window watching the streets as we sped by. Assam chatted about trips that could be taken and things to see and how much I would love Yemen. I closed my eyes and smiled into the warm wind.

The next morning, a loud wail yanked me from my sleep. Resounding, declarative Arabic I didn't understand. The voice sounded sharp, almost electronic. Was the speaker in my room? No, the sound came from outside, in the street. As I sat upright, dread spiraling in my chest, I stared into the darkness, and remembered I was in Yemen. I was alone.

It sounded like a man bawling into a loudspeaker. I crept below the windowsill. The room was dark save for a faint light from outside seeping in under the curtain. The man's cries were stopping and starting now, the moments between his outbursts profound silences. Could it be cops? Were they raiding our building? Was this crime or terror related? My heart beat fast against the inside of my ribs. I pulled my knees to my chest as I crouched on the floor. With trembling fingers, I raised the curtain a few inches and peered down through the thin glass window. There was no one in the street. I followed the noise to the spires on the top of a nearby mosque. I felt my body relax as I realized this was the call to prayer, the start to each day for most Yemenis. Resting my chin on the windowsill, I exhaled and laughed at my idiocy. Soon the mountains around the city showed themselves, their rocky peaks sharpening in the dawn light.

As I studied for my end-of-school exams several years before, I had written *Fortune Favors the Brave* on a piece of paper and taped it above my desk. I hoped it was true, because if bravery really is the act of moving forward amid fear, it was a way of life for me already. At twenty-three, I was mostly filled with fear, defiance, and a faint hope that what I was doing would work out. I had to find somewhere to belong.

Every call to prayer from that first morning on served as a reminder to me that many things in life can be trusted. That few people are out to hurt you. They may even care about your soul enough to call you closer to God, each morning. Maybe belonging had something to do with trust.

The Arabic school was not in the ancient part of the city, like the few others in town. Those charged more for their lessons and accommodations. The Yemen Institute for the Arabic Language was a new cinder-block structure in a more modern, working-class neighborhood just off the city's main ring road. From a table in the entrance hallway the scent of cardamom-spiced tea would drift through the living room and up the stairs to the bedrooms. Sweet and full of spice and hot. Quickly, that smell became the smell of home.

As I labored slowly up the stairs, the altitude of the city knocked the wind out of me in a way few twenty-somethings, even smokers, are accustomed to. I would get used to it, I heard someone say. Every part of my life now was something I would get busy getting used to. It felt good.

My room was clean, new, and basic. It was perfect. In the distance, next to the highway, were large billboard signs selling products in Arabic—giant, mysterious curved letters held up individually by supports. One of them was bright green, advertising something in Arabic I couldn't yet decipher.

Sana'a terrified and thrilled me. It is believed to be the oldest continuously inhabited city in the world. Yemenis say that when Noah's ark hit land, that land was Yemen. Noah's son Sam founded the city and reinhabited the world. It is one of the most spectacular Old Cities in the world, a precious UNESCO World Heritage Site with towering buildings, some eight hundred years old, resting on the foundations of those built a millennia before that. If you stand on the city's walls by the massive wooden main gate and look down at the complex of buildings and laneways, tiny doorframes and old red and brown bricks and stone, it appears as though time does not exist. There is a point at which something is so old it becomes a part of the geography, where we can never imagine a time before it. My ancestors were living in caves when people here were crafting intricate gold jewelry and using complex mathematics to design the world's first seven- and eight-story buildings.

Although Yemen is technically in the Middle East, it straddles several worlds. Just across the Gulf of Aden are Djibouti, Somalia, and nearby Ethiopia, and it shares much in culture and history with those people and places. It has traded with neighboring Oman and India for many centuries. The cosmopolitan nature of the food, architecture, dress, and language of the coastal areas of Yemen is a result of millennia of history.

The city's myriad multistory ancient structures, placed so close to one another, created a surreal image that seemed to deceive scale, like miniature playhouses stacked next to one another. I looked up and beyond, at the mountains flanking the city. It was the most beautiful place I had ever seen. I couldn't have known then what a huge part of my life this city and nation would become, how many times I would return here, any more than I could forecast the coming storm that would tear Yemen apart, its forces sweeping me up and along with it.

The streets were filled with a constant flow of people. Men and women were shopping, on the move between neighborhoods. Older men and traders sat in doorways. Younger women were covered in black cloaks, flowing full-body covers called abayas that fell from their shoulders to the ground, as well as black headscarves and face coverings called niqabs. The black abaya and niqab are largely Saudi imports that arrived with the oil-dollar-fueled exportation of Wahhabism from the 1970s onward. The older women wore the more traditional costumes of the rural areas: loose baggy pants and long shirts with bright-patterned red and green shawls resting on their heads and flowing all the way over their bodies to the ground. Many of these women had face tattoos, and they sometimes smiled and embraced me when our paths crossed, offering words I couldn't understand. They seemed so tiny, often shorter than me by a whole foot, their rough, hardworking hands holding mine as their smiling eyes looked at me with amazement. They made me think of my granny Anderson. She would hold my hand tight like that when she talked to me.

The men were dressed mostly in the traditional *thobe*—a long white shirt with a collar at the top—with an embroidered cotton scarf across their shoulders and a thick belt around their waist. At the front of the belt, just below the navel, rested their *jambiya,* an ornamental curved dagger in a sheath. The jambiya is unique to Yemen, a precursor to the AK-47 resting over one shoulder. It's an important part of any Yemeni man's dress, with designs and ornamentation indicating regions and tribes and wealth. Many are very old, handed down through the generations as boys become men. The most expensive and traditional ones have handles carved from rhino horn and are adorned with silver.

Camels and donkeys pulled carts, but the narrow streets were mostly filled with small motorcycles, their male drivers in mawazes or thobes hoisted up above their knees as they straddled sheepskin-covered seats, weaving through the crowds of people on foot. I would learn to take a quick step to the left or right when I heard one coming. The open-air spice market in Sana'a's Old City was spellbinding. Ground ginger, cardamom, and cumin reached soft peaks like cones. Wide strips of fabric were draped between the buildings and over the small courtyard, softening the sunlight and protecting against the breeze that could carry the precious powders away. The sun's rays reached through the spaces between the flowing sheets and cast straight lines of golden light across the scene. My Arabic was too spotty to ask questions, so I mostly wandered, mesmerized. Sometimes people would shout "Welcome!" at me, as they had at the airport when I first arrived, and I would respond by smiling, placing my hand on my heart, and saying thank you back.

Taking a small bus into the Old City would become my favorite pastime. My first trip there, I saw a man selling different types of nuts and plucked up the courage to smile at him and point to a huge pile of pistachios. He jumped off his stool and scooped up a few of them, depositing them in my hand. "Hello, how are you?" he asked in perfect English. Relieved, I ate the nuts and chatted with him for a while, talking about where I was from and what I was doing in Sana'a. I asked for a small bag of nuts. Handing the brown paper bag to me with one hand he held up the other and shook his head, smiling and refusing my handful of local cash. "You are welcome in my country," he said. The traders on each side of him nodded, seeing him insist on the gift.

Fourteen hundred years ago, the Prophet Muhammad made the long journey from Mecca to Medina with his followers to escape persecution. His journey was called the Hijrah, but he isn't the only Prophet in Islam to have been forced to travel great distances for safety or to preach their beliefs, which were considered radical and heretical for their societies at the time. As such, a respect for travelers and strangers on the road was ingrained in many cultures in the Islamic world. In the post-9/11 climate of wars and insurgencies and animosity toward the West, these traditions had eroded across much of the region. But here, in this ancient fort, seemingly hidden away from those problems, customs held true. I was treated like a welcome guest, and I felt like one.

Adnan sat across the table from me, leaning in close and watching with intensity as I gripped the pencil, slowly forming clumsy letter shapes on the page. His face showed every emotion, and he cared that I learned correctly. I twisted the letters on or through or below the lines on the page with precision, trying to keep him from frowning. Adnan came to the school every day of the working week to teach me for several hours. Tall for a Yemeni, he was thin and had sunken cheeks and kind, tired eyes. He looked like he was in his forties, but I suspected he was much younger, just a man under enormous pressure and grateful to have another paying student. Yemen was not a major destination for foreign students, like Damascus or Beirut, and the few jobs paying U.S. dollars here were precious.

On my first day at the school, he offered a thin, strong hand emerging from the sleeve of a blue suit. He would throw his head back and laugh hard at a joke, open his eyes serious and wide when telling a scary story, and stare with concentration as he listened to me talk about life in Europe and the United States. He asked me why I was learning Arabic. Because I am going to be a journalist, I told him. I want to be a TV foreign correspondent, and I will need to understand Arabic to work in this region if I want to be any good, I explained. He nodded in agreement. Stern face. This was the first time I had ever elicited a response from a man that seemed entirely serious. His acceptance of my inevitable success, his casual certainty about it, surprised me. Of course, to Adnan, my Western privilege meant all the things I wished for came true. If you should compare the difficulties in my life to those in his, he was absolutely right.

Adnan was an exacting teacher; he took pronunciation very seriously, and we practiced the correct throaty guttural sounds of Arabic again and again until his furrowed brows eased into a smile. Every evening after memorizing my flash cards, I went to the window and smoked a cigarette, looking out over the rooftops. That green sign was still impossibly alien to me. I knew it started with a K. That's all. It ended with a long tail of a letter, trailing off in a massive decorative font.

The best way for me to use my small handful of words beyond my bedroom warbling in those first weeks was my daily grocery shopping. I would head to the local corner store, called a *baqalla,* and refill my gallon drum of drinking water, buy local eggs and vegetables, milk, and Gauloises cigarettes. Every interaction was an opportunity to use the few words in my vocabulary, which was growing by the day.

"*BaSala,* onion."

"*Gir gir,* lettuce."

"*Mawz,* banana."

"*Law Semaht,* if you please."

"Gauloises *Ahmer,* red, please."

"*Shukran,* thank you."

The shop owner would smile and nod in approval with each little attempt, my diet getting more varied by way of my expanding vocabulary. As my Arabic improved, I relished my fleeting moments of communication with anyone—a cabdriver, a shop owner, or a child in the street racing up to me to ask my name. Each was an opportunity to hold someone's gaze as they smiled at a foreigner offering them crumbs of their own language.

The new vocabulary, writing from right to left, the ancient, complex grammar system, made the effort of learning Arabic feel like swimming across an ocean and finding the far shore appearing ever more distant the more I swam. But the harder the task, the more deeply rewarding and joyful the small victories. Understanding snippets of what the TV newsreaders on Al Jazeera were saying, overhearing Adnan bragging about my test scores to the other teachers, turning a page in the book to a new one.

One day a few weeks into my stay, I looked out the window and mumbled automatically, "Canada Dry." The green sign by the highway read Canada Dry, the soda, in Arabic.

"Canada Dry!" I yelled out the window, grinning like a lunatic. "It says Canada Dry!"

Assam came by the school one day to see if anyone wanted to go away for the weekend to the mountains. I practically dove headfirst into the back of his car. We were headed to Kawkaban and Thula, areas northwest of Sana'a high in the green peaks. We swung from side to side up the mountain road out of the city, the traditional oud music twanging from the car's cassette player.

I felt the warm, dusty air on my face from the rear window of Assam's car, an old white Toyota Corolla identical to the one I raced to and from the chicken factory the summer before college, less than four years earlier.

We climbed to the crest of the mountains overlooking the city. Sana'a is one of the highest capitals in the world, situated for two thousand years at well over 2,000 meters above the Red Sea and Indian Ocean. Assam stopped the car by the side of road, turned to us in the back seat, and declared, "This is the highest point in the Middle East." Smiling, he told us that this was also very close to his ancestral village, where he belonged. That meant everything to Yemenis, the pride of where one's family's past and future legacy would always rest. Beyond culture, religion, and race, this was our greatest difference, I thought, as I watched him beam with that sense of belonging.

We stood on the edge of the world, with valleys so far below us the earth seemed to disappear. The mountainsides were indented with terraces held up with ancient stone structures so crops could be farmed in even this forbidding landscape. Perched on top of each ridge was a small village, built from stone quarried from the mountain itself. Each hamlet looked like it had sprouted naturally from the soil, outlined against the blue sky.

We dropped our bags at the little village hotel in Kawkaban and spent the afternoon hiking from one village to another, along the pathways well worn by farmers. The clouds lifted, and we could see we were surrounded by the highlands of north Yemen. Some peaks were simply too steep and tall for cultivation and remained untouched, majestic. Orange butterflies trembled and bounced around in the air. Villagers occasionally walked by, driving their goats or sheep back home for a safe night in the stone forts. They raised a hand and smiled, welcoming us.

We climbed to the highest hamlet around. Assam had arranged for us to visit the village leader's house for lunch. On the top floor of the highest home in the highest village, we collapsed onto the cushions surrounding the traditional living room, my lungs heaving in the cool, thin air. Light poured in from the windows, and I leaned back against the wall. Assam and the elder sat cross-legged on the floor, chin resting on a fist, the other hand on a hip. The two men shared news and gossip in animated chatter. Their headscarves were neatly arranged around their foreheads and fell down their backs. I watched them as the light streamed in, casting a glow over the room, the afternoon sun beaming into the same spot it had every day for hundreds of years, through these windows at this exact time of the afternoon. Several women appeared, smiling and shy and carrying trays of fried eggs, goat stew, rice, and flatbread. They spread the feast out on the floor, and we leaned over it, hungry, scooping it up with our hands.

In the hotel the next morning, I woke at dawn, climbed onto the windowsill, and dangled my legs over the edge. Laid out before me, the mountain peaks spread out and disappeared into the horizon's dawn light. For not one day in my life had I ever felt so at peace, my heart so untroubled, as here in the middle of nowhere, yet to me the center of the world.

Life in Sana'a over the next couple of months took on a welcome routine of studying, exploring the city, and spending weekends away. I visited the same little square in the center of the rabbit warren of ancient streets and ordered lunch. The meat was charred and oily, tucked into chewy bread rolls to be dipped in a local salsa. I quickly came to embrace the moments of familiarity: the same old man with a blue hat, turning the kebabs over the coals, my seat at a table, alone but mine, watching the people moving through the market around me.

As I adventured around Yemen, learning to let myself fear life a little less, the danger inside the country was growing. While I was in class with Adnan repeating verb conjugations, in rural Shabwa province, a few hours' drive to the southeast of that classroom, extremist religious cleric and U.S. citizen Anwar al-Awlaki was in touch with Western Muslims online, gently, skillfully goading them toward violent epiphanies of glory. Awlaki had been on the FBI's and CIA's radar since it became apparent that from his own mosque in Virginia, he had preached to three of the 9/11 hijackers. Eventually Awlaki fled to his ancestral province of Shabwa, as the Yemeni government called for his arrest. From the safety of tribal protection in Shabwa, he ran a propaganda campaign online for Al Qaeda. Through skillful sermons that mixed clear radicalization with a light informality in English, he appealed to disenfranchised young men from Muslim backgrounds in the West.

Al Qaeda's franchise in Yemen was on the rise, and Awlaki's young recruits were to be an essential part of that. According to U.S. intelligence reports, Al Qaeda in the Arabian Peninsula (AQAP) was considered the most dangerous wing of Al Qaeda globally and was determined to attack America at home.

Of course, I didn't know anything of Awlaki's movements as I carried on with my studies and travel and dreams for the future. The country seemed safe for us foreigners because the local people had embraced us and treated us with such kindness. Yemini hospitality was legendary, and each of us at the school would share stories of Yemenis inviting us into their homes.

I had been happily wandering in the Old City one day when a woman dressed entirely in the traditional black robes, with her head and face covered, came up to me and in broken English invited me into her house, which was nearby. She waved her hand, covered in a black glove, firmly in the direction she wanted me to come. She even pointed over to an ancient stone house just about fifty yards away. Sure enough, another woman, clad in black, was leaning out the door waving emphatically. A small part of me wondered if this was a kidnapping. I turned out, partly, to be right. As soon as I arrived, I was taken hostage by a bevy of women, smiling and laughing and pulling off their headscarves and face coverings, forcing me to sit in their living room on cushions on the floor as they plied me with strong Yemeni coffee and made me look at every family wedding photo album in their possession. This was an upper-middle-class home, as many of the most beautiful Old City houses are, that had been passed down from one generation of a trading family to the next. The women were bored, and I was a remarkable novelty for their afternoon. They had trapped me like a spider in a glass jar. I was delighted.

We laughed and attempted conversations, with them employing their broken English and me my broken Arabic. I was desperate to talk to them about life here, much more interesting to me than wedding photos, but every time I skipped a page or two, they would pull me back to the pictures of complete strangers I had missed. Over the years, this type of sisterly kidnapping would become a common and welcome occurrence in my life, from Taliban-controlled villages to Syrian Kurdish fighting units, a form of female bonding made sudden, insistent, and deeply intimate in its lack of formality.

By March I felt confident in my Arabic abilities and needed to face the fact that my time in Yemen would end soon. The stash of local bank notes in my wardrobe was shrinking each day. I knew I needed to go to Soqotra before I left this place.

Soqotra is an island paradise resting in the Indian Ocean, officially in Yemeni territory but far from the mainland, closer to Somalia. Just about eighty miles long and twenty miles wide, it is a protected ecological treasure. Despite its remoteness, it is not volcanic and is a jewel of biodiversity, with nearly seven hundred endemic species found nowhere else on earth. A few school friends and I traveled there on a tiny Yemenia Airways flight, and the island's otherworldliness enveloped us. There were few roads, unspoiled beaches, and mountains covered in wildflowers. On hikes we marveled at the local dragon's blood trees. Around ten feet tall, they have a thick, neat trunk and a layer of spiky branches at the top that spread outward like a parasol and provide shade from the sun. Their name comes from the bright red sap that oozes from their trunks, as though they are bleeding. These sturdy evergreen testimonies to time exist nowhere else on earth.

This was the longest I had gone without studying since I had arrived in Yemen, and the visit—the sea air in my lungs, the long walks—was heaven. I had yet to really sit still and consider where I was going after all this. The future was too frighteningly unclear.

I sat on a hilltop on the first night on the road in Soqotra, watching the sun drop below the horizon as hummingbirds hovered close by, and allowed myself to begin to accept that this part of my life was ending. The future was a blank page. I had no job, no relationship, no money, and no home. But I had at last found a sense of myself and my place in the world. In less than four months, Yemen had given me everything. This adventure had been about vastly more than learning a language; this place felt like it had saved my life. I was booked on a flight back to London as soon as I returned to Sana'a. I would have to build my life from the ground up. I was going to stay with Ruth, my best friend from college, while I looked for a job. A job in the Middle East, I told myself. I'll come back.

On our last night we camped on a spectacular wide golden beach. A powdery-white sandy peninsula reached out into clear water that turned turquoise and then a brilliant blue in the distance. As we set up our tents for the evening, fishermen were tidying away their nets and heading home. The nearby rocky hills swept down dramatically to the beach's soft sand, creating a natural backdrop. We sat around the campfire that night, passing around a bottle of whiskey, talking and laughing. The only other sounds were the fire crackling and the waves breaking against the beach.

Someone suggested we go skinny-dipping. Running toward the water's edge, I pulled my clothes off and laughed as I fell over in the sand. I caught a glimpse of the paleness of my legs in the moonlight. Pulling my clothes over my head and tossing them high in the air, the warm night breeze soft on my naked body, I let joy sweep over me. I dashed into the water like a crab and it started to glow. Phosphorescence sparkled all around us as we swam and twirled and treaded water with our hands and feet. I lingered by the shoreline as everyone else ran back to the fire. As I looked out at the sparkling moonlit Indian Ocean, the horizon disappeared into a black unknown.

4

Dubai Girl

THE LADY BEHIND THE TICKET counter at Heathrow Airport's bus terminal was unimpressed. I was trying to buy a ticket to Oxford, a two-hour drive away. Every time the automatic doors slid open, a wet cold wind blew in around me. I had stepped off my Yemenia Airways flight less than an hour ago. My rucksack beside me, I stood at the counter, pulled the sleeves of my shirt down, and shivered.

"Fourteen pounds," the lady said, looking at me in contempt. I wasn't sure if I had that much in my bank account. I handed her my credit card.

Ruth had said I could come and stay with her when I got back. Mark still had everything I owned that was not in the rucksack next to me, in cardboard boxes in his home. I thought of my collection of books, the only real things I owned in the world, those travel books and explorers' memoirs.

"Declined," the ticket counter woman declared, loudly. "Do you have another card?"

I felt my eyes water and fought the tears. I called Ruth on my cell. "Hand the phone over to the lady," she said. Ruth was the big sister of three siblings, and it showed. The ticket lady started punching in Ruth's card details, and within minutes I was in a (heated) bus, watching the English countryside rush past. Ruth had a habit of being there whenever my path ahead seemed frighteningly unclear. Her curly blond hair framing her face, she was waiting at Oxford's bus station, beaming and waving. I threw my arms around her and knew I had reached a safe harbor. All the way to her house we roared with laughter as I told her stories about Yemen.

Ruth had prepared dinner and invited several other college girl-friends over. I bounced around the house, luxuriating in things like sofas and a wood fire, a garden with grass—small marvels I appreciated after months without them in Sana'a. We all crowded around the kitchen, wineglasses full, toasting one another as Ruth pulled a huge meat pie from the oven, made from scratch, with JANIE spelled out on top in pastry. A crispy golden gesture of love and friendship and sisterhood. I had gone from one of the worst days in a very long time to one of the best. Leaving Yemen felt like falling out of a plane. My friends had caught me.

Their love came with something like an ache. Being unloved as a child makes love like this, as though you are nostalgic for something you cannot remember because you never had it. I so longed for love that receiving it made my heart hurt.

I quickly got a job bartending in the local village pub. Between shifts Ruth and I cooked meals and took country walks, and I relentlessly clicked through job websites. Within a few weeks I spotted something promising. The Middle East's largest English-language newspaper, based in Dubai, wanted an assistant editor for their sports section. Yes! A paid job in a real-life newsroom in the Middle East!

On a phone interview that felt more like an informal chat with a very polite and very English middle-aged editor, I was asked about my specific interest in the sport they tend to cover at the paper. "I love cricket!" I declared. "Huge fan!" Ruth almost choked on her corn-flakes, laughing as she eavesdropped on our conversation. It was an okay lie, I argued afterward. I could love cricket and not even know it. Within days I was on an Emirates flight, 35,000 feet in the air again, headed back to the Middle East. This time, one way.

I landed in hot and dusty Dubai with $100 in my bank account and a rucksack of clothes and books. This glistening new world of promise was at first filled with the wailing of car horns and the sight of throngs of people. This was the first time in my life any company had ever rented me a hotel room. It was a cheap place in a scruffy neighborhood, but to me, it was a palace. I dropped my things and headed outside immediately to explore, passing through the hotel's sliding doors into the thick, humid heat of Dubai's streets. I moved through crowds of people from South Asia, Africa, and the Arab world, wandering between malls and shops and restaurants, down wide avenues packed with bumper-to-bumper traffic, streets lined with palm trees and small storefronts. Signs bleached out by the strong sun spelled out words in English and Arabic. Some streets were strung with lightbulbs, creating a carnival atmosphere. There were shops filled with nothing but gold bangles, their entire front windows displaying thousands of the shiny gold hoops, glistening in the streetlights. It was 2008, and economic recession was devastating economies all over the world, but the Persian Gulf still glittered.

I bought cigarettes and snacks in a small shop and wandered back to my hotel. High above the streets, I sat in the window of my room and ate potato chips for dinner. I stared out at the city's night lights, in absolute wonder at my good fortune.

This was my chance to be a real journalist, working for a real newspaper. The hunger I felt for that life—in a place filled with journalists and writers, overseas—had been with me for as long as I could remember. From my early days reading about Martha Gellhorn and all those BBC journalists reporting from abroad, I had never really wanted anything else at all.

The next morning, I bounced around the room, the news on the TV blaring over my hair dryer. I slipped a dress over my head and high heels onto my feet, one of the two outfits I'd bought with my bartending tips. I buzzed with excitement as I looked in the mirror and smiled. The shoulder pads in my jacket felt like they had magic powers. I was becoming new again.

The headquarters for Gulf News was modern, covered in shiny gray cladding and glass, with four floors of offices and the main newsroom. I followed Tom, the Englishman who had interviewed me on the phone, as he marched me through the newsroom's various sections, pointing out sports, business, news, the *Tabloid* magazine. A few people looked up and smiled briefly at Tom, but most were too busy typing, brow furrowed. Obsequious in my impostor syndrome, I smiled and waved a crumpled sort of an apology for a hello. I knew I was the only person in that whole huge room of people who had zero experience as a reporter. Back then, I feared making eye contact with colleagues in case my face would reveal my total lack of knowledge.

My desk in the sports section in the newsroom was next to those of several other associate editors, mostly English reporters in their thirties fleeing the collapsing newspaper industry in the UK. Although the whole building was sleek and modern, the one anarchic detail was a smoking room, which was where I could meet and chat with other reporters and editors and photographers, a cadre of Indian and British journalists firmly old school enough to still smoke heavily. We were to check for grammatical mistakes, spelling, and phrasing, and usually find ways to keep the articles within the page. Our readership reflected Dubai's many middle-class expatriates from India, Pakistan, the Philippines, the UK, South Africa, and Australia. As such, our coverage tended to swing toward news from their home countries or local national issues of interest and the sports adored by many of these nations. Having stretched the truth in my job interview about my love of the sport, I spent many evenings during my first days in Dubai googling the rules and lexicon of cricket. After having spent most of my life living through conflict within the UK, I was now covering its national sport from the Persian Gulf.

I found a room for rent in a shared house advertised as "girls only." One of the roommates, Sarah, came to pick me up at my hotel in her small car. She was blond and wore enormous sunglasses covered her smiling face. She was a classic Dubai expatriate woman, as much as the stereotype holds. Her fingernails were polished to a turn, her golden tan was perfect, and her green caftan floated around us as she drove fast down Dubai's highways, the car's windows down and pop music blaring on the radio.

Sarah was a cabin crew member for Emirates. In her mid-thirties, she had moved here from England five years ago and had encountered plenty of newcomers in that time. In the house with her were a number of former flight attendants, all of whom had recently left their jobs to pursue lucrative careers selling property in a booming market. Standing in the middle of their villa in my ripped jeans and T-shirt, I dropped my backpack on the immaculate white-tiled floor and looked around at the perfect white furniture and faux fur accoutrements while the girls chatted about the evening's plans for clubbing. Smiley and friendly, they were all impeccably well groomed. I was suddenly self-conscious about my sweaty red face and flip-flops. Compared to these young women, I looked like I had wandered off the street after several nights sleeping rough.

Hours later I was surrounded by sequins and red velvet, clutching a vodka and Red Bull that had been handed to me by a man much like a child might be handed a sandwich. I would be lying if I said I didn't also have fun. The club was new, and in Dubai, the newer the better.

I nodded along to dance music and chuckled at the sexism of it all, as my new friends danced around tables lorded over by several men pouring drinks from liquor bottles. Once in a while, barmaids in tiny costumes would parade past with a massive bottle of vodka or a magnum of champagne with a huge roman candle sparkling out of the top of it, the beaming young bartenders walking in line behind like an entourage for the alcohol. I choked on my drink when I glanced at the bill: $3,500. The few young men at the table settled it without much more than some mumbles and card swipes. I fumbled for my wallet and asked if I could "chip in," causing widespread smirking and an ostentatious display of side-eye. It was a bizarre exhibit of sexist chivalry, normalized by the luxurious surroundings and friendliness of everyone around me.

Still, I enjoyed the novelty of cocktail dresses and high heels. Despite my backpacker wardrobe of sandals and T-shirts, deep down I craved the ability to be seen as more feminine. Ever since my first brushes with fashion at Lawrenceville, I had wanted to feel more elegantly female. I just didn't know how. What I viewed as my coarseness had made me think I must be predestined to be a tomboy. Now I had an opportunity to reinvent myself. But I would never shake the uncomfortable feeling of waiting around for a man to pay a bill. It felt humiliating to me. Perhaps defensive about my working-class roots and certainly about my gender, I bristled at the assumption I would never be able to pay. Was it possible, I wondered, in those clubs to be both feminine and powerful?

To the outside world, Dubai is a place of crass materialism, but I understood the draw. It was the modern New World, where young people who didn't go to the most elite colleges and have family connections in the right industries could still thrive. Those circumstances didn't dictate ambition here. When I got to Dubai, no one asked me if I went to an Ivy League school or to Oxford or Cambridge. No one wanted to know about my family and where they were from. In fact most of the people I met, including the most financially successful ones, were from working-class backgrounds. And no one seemed to think it was odd to start a job having never done it before. I felt I could find my way in Dubai regardless of my upbringing. All that seemed to matter was that I had a vision for my future and a willingness to work hard.

The system was not fair to everyone, though. Exploitation of expatriates brought in as foreign laborers on construction sites was and continues to abound in the United Arab Emirates (UAE) and across the Persian Gulf. Desperately poor workers from countries like India, Pakistan, and Afghanistan often come based on empty promises of good, reliable salaries but end up working for very little, providing property developers with enormous profit margins. Every morning when I drove to work, I would pass buses filled with construction workers headed to and from construction sites, places where yet another glass building would rise from the desert. They wore hard hats and were jostled about as their bus slipped into the flow of the traffic—another part of the life of the city, another collection of human experiences sweeping past. I wondered how I would ever be able to talk to any of them. These men were always either on the job or in their "labor camps," cordoned off from the city.

Those working in the newsroom were a fantastic mix of cultures and backgrounds. Many of the reporters and editors were Indian, Pakistani, Filipino, Lebanese, Egyptian, and South African. My accent didn't matter. Blending into this mélange of voices and twangs felt simple. Each day I would arrive early and leave late. I often volunteered to do the final edit on the front page, which would involve staying until eleven p.m. for the final version of the front page to be edited, confirmed, and sent to print. I pitched my own stories and wrote in my off time about sports. Finally the editor said yes to an interview and profile piece on an Indian Formula 1 driver. I was delighted I had a paying job in journalism and excited to watch real reporters stream out of the office after morning meetings and back in the afternoon. To me they were rock stars, as I sat at my desk hoping to get moved up some day. That day came soon, and it was a remarkable break.

Six months into my stint editing the sports section, the paper's managing editor approached my desk. At first I thought he might be lost. "Are you able to travel tonight?" he asked. He needed last-minute coverage for a reporting trip to the United States. The Dubai government's global investment company, Dubai World, was buying a 50 percent stake in the iconic Miami Fontainebleau Hotel and re-launching it after a $1 billion renovation. The newspaper wanted to go big on the story for the business section, and *Tabloid* magazine wanted reporting from the Victoria's Secret fashion show, a Mariah Carey performance, and celebrity parties. Within hours I was on a flight to Florida on my first real assignment.

The managing editor was somewhat dubious about handing this assignment to a twenty-four-year-old ex-bartender. The ponytailed *Tabloid* editor was equally skeptical. No one seemed enthusiastic about my impending Big Break. It didn't matter to me, though; I had been underestimated my whole life. "I won't let you down!" I promised. *Tabloid* lady rolled her eyes.

I spent several days working nonstop in Miami. I ignored the jet lag and started attending events and sitting down for interviews. I never once left the resort—this never even occurred to me. The newspaper had asked for two stories. I filed five. Next to the hotel pool, I interviewed the Emirati CEO and his American partners, and then I raced back to my room overlooking the blue ocean framed by palm trees to write. I smiled out the window after clicking send on my stories.

At the Victoria's Secret fashion show, I sat alone in a dress and heels meant for Dubai nightclubs and watched Usher perform as the world's most beautiful women marched up and down in silk and lace underwear. Later that night Mariah Carey gave a concert to just a bar full of people. As I sang along and looked around the room, I thought of how I had been swimming in the warm waters off Soqotra island, naked as a fish, earlier that year, with no earthly idea where my life was going. My press pass felt like an identity. I had a job now, a label that helped me feel worthy of the life I was trying to lead.

When I returned to Dubai, the business editor offered me a full-time reporter position, my first ever real reporting job. I was to be a business features writer. I couldn't believe my luck.

Weeks later, the recession finally made its way to Dubai. The economy tanked seemingly overnight, and there was no shortage of news to cover. Half the city's construction projects—worth nearly $600 billion—had been put on hold or canceled. Oil money didn't save the countries in the Gulf—it devastated them. As the world's economy buckled, the price of oil had fallen from nearly $150 a barrel to below $40 in 2008. In a city where 80 percent of the residents were expatriate workers, when people lost their jobs, they simply went home. I was lucky I didn't have to.

Instead of poverty, what was left were abandoned cars, eerily quiet construction sites, and empty billboards by the highway. Thousands of expatriates just left their cars at the airport when fleeing the country, unable to meet their debts. I had moved with a friend to an apartment on the Palm Island, a palm-tree-shaped island built just before the recession closed in. Many of our neighbors were already leaving. One day after coming home from work, I walked out onto the balcony and lit a cigarette. Squinting through the late-afternoon sun at the beach-front apartment building across the street, I made out a man dressed in a bathrobe and slippers, standing in the street by the entrance, his arms crossed in front of his chest. In front of him a tow truck was carefully loading a red Ferrari. As I watched him, he just stood there silently staring at the car being repossessed.

I had a flood of important stories to cover. I wrote about Formula 1 car racing, the advertising industry, credit-card interest rates, grocery-store price wars, car sales—anything I could come up with. I was rapacious.

This was also the first time I noticed that my days felt easier the busier I became. Hard work was not hard to me. Between interviews all over the city, writing up stories, volunteering to stay late to oversee page edits and the layout of the business section, choosing photographs, and hunting for story ideas on the newswires, I had few opportunities to wonder why I was doing all this and if I was getting any closer to my real goals.

I bought a Porsche Boxster S from a colleague upgrading to a Porsche 911. Each day after work I would drive home with the top down, my hair blowing in the wind, smiling as I turned off onto the old coast road that took me to the island's bridge. As the sun hit the horizon, the haze was burnt orange. The sprinklers would come on and send a wet mist over the neat grassy verges. I turned up the radio and wished the journey was longer. My hands gripped the soft leather steering wheel of the sports car and I felt genuinely happy.

The day I bought the Porsche I called my father to brag. This was the sort of material advancement he would appreciate. When I hung up the phone, sitting on the tiled floor of my living room, I was quiet. I knew that I had clawed for his approval, that it still mattered to me. My parents hated that I'd gone to Yemen, but now I was star daughter for "making it" in Dubai. I felt a sense of emptiness after that call. I knew that needing his approval was a little betrayal of myself. I knew it meant I hadn't really broken free yet.

All through the busy first months of my life as a real journalist, a quiet voice inside reminded me, gently at first, that this was not the plan. It was only ever meant to be a stepping-stone—a way to get to the Middle East so I could try to get into news reporting there. I had slipped into my new life with relative ease, assuming this identity that now seemed uncomfortable. Sitting each day at my desk in the newsroom, I would look up at the TV screens fixed to the walls, playing CNN International and Al Jazeera English, their correspondents reporting from all over the world. For a second, I felt a sharp wave of panic in the pit of my stomach. I yearned to be out in the world, reporting with a team, broadcasting the most important stories of the day from across the Middle East, Africa, and Asia. The thought of it filled me with a fire no sea views or sports cars could put out.

One day I wandered over to a senior editor's desk and attempted to put forward casually a question I had been planning for weeks. Maybe they could assign me a foreign posting for the paper, like, say, Yemen? "Yemen?!" He laughed. "Why would you want to go there? Besides, we already have a contributor there." He returned to studying the newspaper on the desk in front of him.

On to Plan B then. News from Afghanistan had blared from the newsrooms' TV screens all day. The presidential election there, the country's first ever, was to be a major test of the new U.S.-imposed democracy that August. Widespread fraud turned it into a crisis as incumbent President Hamid Karzai, determined to remain for a second term, fought off rival Dr. Abdullah Abdullah. I bumped into an editor in the smokers' room, and we got chatting about the news. He offered to write me a letter of accreditation for the military if I applied to travel there.

Later that evening I met friends at a chic candlelit restaurant. We strained to hear one another over the loud music. I looked around at the faces in the room and wondered what it would be like to go on embed in Afghanistan with American forces. *Maybe I can just go there for a couple of weeks and see about finding a freelance post,* I thought, pushing chunks of blackened cod around on the plate in front of me with my chopsticks.

Two weeks later, I had a Moment. I was sitting on a folding chair inside a Mazda showroom among a group of about a dozen reporters and Japanese car executives, watching a promotional video for their latest car release. I had been tasked with grabbing one of the executives from the head office for a quick interview about their assessment of the industry in the Middle East. I had parked outside the showroom and clambered out of my sports car, so low to the ground I could hardly pull myself up in my high heels. I staggered across the dusty sand that had reclaimed the earth in place of paving, my black heels sinking into the hot, dry dust. In the insane summer heat, my hair stuck to the sweat on my face. I was utterly miserable and late, but stopped outside for a cigarette, nonetheless. *I don't want to be here,* I thought. A part of me felt deeply uncomfortable and uneasy that day and I just couldn't put my finger on why. I stubbed the cigarette butt into the sand with my shoe and accepted that I had to get on with it. The sooner I got it over with, the sooner I could go home, I reasoned.

I trotted into the air conditioning as executives turned to stare. The feeling of wasting time crept through me. *This spot is close to the airport,* I thought. Terminal two—that's where all the flights go to Yemen, Somalia, Iraq, Afghanistan.

After the presentation video was over, we were ushered into the main showroom and a silk covering was pulled off a "new and improved" version of a Mazda, to raucous clapping. It looked exactly the same as the other cars parked around us. I had read about people having these epiphanies, moments of clarity. But I always thought they occurred on mountaintops in Nepal or in hospital beds. For me, it was a Mazda car dealership in Dubai.

"What the fuck am I doing?" I asked myself, staring at the scene as though from a great distance. I couldn't hide from the reality that I was living a life I did not want to live anymore, and at the cost of what I considered to be my real life. I didn't want any of these things I had collected, lovely as they were. I wanted to be out on the road, telling stories that really mattered. I was supposed to be seeing more of the world than beaches and hotel bars. I knew with certainty that the industry wasn't going to hand me a job as a foreign correspondent. That if I didn't act this would be my life forever. I had to do something. It felt like I couldn't spare one more second of my life.

I decided to leave there and then, pushing the glass door open and stepping out into the hot air. I bundled myself into the Porsche I had pretended to love and cursed and yelled my way down the road to the airport. I had no plan. I just needed to act. I would figure out the rest once I had made this first bold move. Slamming the car door behind me, I strode into the airport to book a flight to Kabul, Afghanistan.

5

"Short Virgins Will Never Make
Good War Photographers"

I TRIED HARD TO LOOK relaxed as I stood in line for check-in to my flight to Kabul. Gazing around nervously, I felt like the entire queue was looking at me. They glanced away as soon as I caught their eye. I supposed they were wondering what I was doing there. *Join the club,* I thought.

The rest of those in line were mostly Afghans, as well as a few grizzled-looking American contractors. I leaned as nonchalantly as I could against my baggage cart, wearing an all-new wardrobe of combat pants, combat boots, and a scarf around my neck. Packed in the bag on my cart was a new flak jacket and helmet. I tried to exude calm confidence. Inside, though, I was nauseous.

The night before, wearing my new flak jacket and helmet, I had stood in front of a mirror in my Dubai apartment. I was excited and afraid. The jacket's thick black canvas vest reached from my shoulders to my hip bones and made my legs and arms look like thin poles. On the front and back of the vest were large rectangular pockets with Velcro flaps, each filled with heavy half-inch-thick protective plates. At the neck was a tall, stiff Kevlar-reinforced collar that grazed my cheeks. I looked like a war reporter, a newly minted one. The vest was too new, too pristine. I feared I'd be pegged immediately as a rookie.

After I had booked my flight to Afghanistan, I asked my Gulf News editor if I could take off several of the weeks I was owed. I never took time off, and it had simply accumulated. I would be going on my own dime to Afghanistan and would try my best to make connections enough there to maybe find a job or a regular freelance opportunity. I had no plan beyond that. Editors from the international section and the magazine had agreed to publish my pieces from the trip. *What will I write about? Where will I go?* I thought, stuffing panties into shoes with excessive force. *What if everyone laughs at me because I don't work for a paper anyone has heard of?* I dealt with that one by checking that each camera tape was inside its box and then neatly placing them back into the camera bag. Every doubtful thought that I couldn't block, I responded to with another task that pushed me toward leaving.

This was an apex moment in Afghanistan. The disastrous presidential election had turned the modern state of Afghanistan inside out. Afghans braved the worst violence their country had seen since the chaos of the civil war in the 1990s to make their voices heard and vote for a leader. Incumbent president Hamid Karzai had claimed victory, but his main challenger, Dr. Abdullah Abdullah, was contending, with staunch agreement from independent election observers, that widespread stuffing of the ballot box, bribery, and intimidation had made the election results fraudulent. Diplomats from Washington, D.C., to Brussels and beyond were working the phones between the two candidates to prevent the outright breakdown of whatever pretense of democracy the nation was holding on to, under the watchful eye of the U.S.-led military occupation. In the meantime, the Afghans who stood in line, risking their lives as the Taliban attacked polling stations, having the audacity to believe in the promises of democracy being made to them by the international community and their own leaders, watched the whole Western effort in their country to build a modern democratic state with a growing cynicism.

The Taliban were also growing in strength that summer, and the new general in charge of U.S.-led operations, Stanley McChrystal, had launched the largest operation of the war so far, in Helmand Province. Determined to retake parts of the Taliban stronghold, forty-one U.S. troops were killed in Afghanistan in July as they faced a ferociously talented insurgency. By the time my plane landed at the Kabul airport, McChrystal had written an extensive report for the White House calling for a massive military surge in Afghanistan—and it was about to be leaked to Bob Woodward.

The driver sent by the hotel pulled off the road abruptly and drew up outside a large dark green metal gate. There was no sign of any kind of hotel. Someone banged open a peephole and quickly slammed it shut before the gates swung open. We lurched into a small no-man's-land between two massive gates, where guards in uniforms used mirrors on sticks to check under the car, the same ones that they had used at checkpoints in Northern Ireland when I was a kid. Then the next gate swung open and the hotel grounds opened up before us.

The Gandamack Lodge was a guesthouse eternally described by journalists as "legendary" and "the only place to stay." An old two-story colonial-era house with sash windows, it had been converted into a small hotel, seemingly the last holdout of colonial Britain in Afghanistan. By the front door just before you climbed the stone stairs sat a small British cannon, rusting quietly as the grass sprouted up around it. As I walked down the entrance hallway, carrying my rucksack, I admired the ancient smooth stone floor, which dipped in the middle from centuries of foot traffic, and passed a row of antique wooden-handled rifles, also British, hanging on the wall. The British colonial legacy in Afghanistan was a bloody one, not least of all for the British. After attempting to control and subjugate the country and its people, for the first and only time in the history of the British military, its army was almost entirely wiped out, in a spectacularly bloody defeat at a place called the Gandamack outside the city. The reality was, any hint of kitschy nostalgia that lingered in the hotel also involved a great deal of irony.

The Gandamack's manager, Nawaz, shuffled through papers behind a small wooden desk and tapped violently into a calculator. It was early evening, and I could hear music playing through speakers in the garden and the hum of people chatting. The furniture was mostly wooden and antique, with well-worn Afghan rugs of auburn and burgundy spread across the floor. Most of the rooms were lit with small lamps adorned with old-fashioned tasseled shades.

Photos of smiling reporters hung on the walls. Across the room from the reception desk, a big machine sat inside a black cabinet with a glass door. Dozens of cables protruded from the machine, and it had some small, flashing lights. As I waited for Nawaz to check me in, a disheveled Englishman in old jeans and a T-shirt stormed in from the garden outside. Sweaty and angry-looking, he marched over to the machine and violently yanked at the cables, furiously pulling them out and reinserting them. "Nawaz, the fucking internet is down AGAIN!" he shouted over his shoulder. "I'm trying to send footage!"

I love it here, I thought.

Nawaz helped me carry my bags up the stairs to the bedrooms in the main house. On the landing at the top of the stairs was floor-to-ceiling shelving filled with flak jackets and helmets, shoved into open cupboards labeled by size. There were so many they spilled out and were scattered on the floor, all covered in varying degrees of dust. Not house dust. Outside dust. Afghanistan dust. They had been used by real journalists on real assignments. Nawaz fretted about how unsuitable my room was. "It's very, very small," he said, shaking his head. "It's perfect!" I beamed.

Peter Jouvenal and his wife, Hassina Syed, had owned and operated the Gandamack since journalists had first arrived in droves following the 2001 invasion of Afghanistan. Tall and charismatic, Peter smiled from beneath a thick strawberry-blond mustache. He had been a Royal Marine before becoming one of the BBC's top cameramen for dangerous assignments. Hassina, a businesswoman from a prominent Afghan family, was always dressed in a *shalwar kameez,* the traditional long shirt with loose trousers, usually pink or purple or floral, her hair tied back in a bun. Smiling, she clipped through the hotel in high-heeled shoes, a sea of chiffon scarf flowing in the air after her. Peter's connections with journalists and Hassina's business acumen made the hotel a massive success. They made it more than a hotel: it was a club for reporters, a place where connections and camaraderie came with a room. Everyone tolerated the high bar prices and lumpy mattresses because this place made journalists on the road, secretly lonely, feel like they belonged to something bigger, a community.

Later that evening, I was sitting in the hotel garden, an expanse of grass and trees below a small breakfast terrace off the reception area. In the far corner, a garden shed fashioned into a bar was staffed by Nawaz, who seemed to do every job at the hotel. My room may have been a bargain, but the bar prices reflected a "this is an Islamic republic, where alcohol is technically illegal, so pay up or get out" kind of attitude.

I sipped my beer and scanned the garden, noticing the small groups of journalists all drinking together and eating pizza. Real foreign correspondents, laughing and telling stories in the soft nighttime lamplight, enjoying Kabul's thin, dry air. It felt like I had been allowed into a special place I had only ever read about.

A tall American guy in chinos and a T-shirt approached me, smiling. He was in his early forties, with a few days' beard. He had kind eyes, dark, thinning hair, and that relaxed "end of a tough day at work doing the greatest job on the planet" sort of ease to him. "I'm Ben. Would you like another beer?" "No thanks," I replied. "I'm good." It was a compulsive answer, a knee-jerk, caught-off-guard no. As he walked away through the grass, I leaned back in my chair and swigged a mouthful of cold malty beer, surveying the scene of reporters from a safe distance. *No thank you indeed,* I thought. *I'm not here to flirt.*

The next morning I was sitting in the back seat of a taxi, leaning far over the armrest between the driver and a young male translator, straining to see the sky through the windscreen and holding on tight as we bounced along Kabul's potholed roads. We were searching for kites high above the city. Kabul's streets were a mixture of old seventies-era buildings, with glass and wood fronts; ten-foot-high concrete blast walls with razor wire at the top; and modern cement homes built in the post-9/11 era. Rows of trees clung to life where they could, planted beside the cement sidewalks. Soviet-era apartment blocks were the only tall buildings. Below these Kabul was a squat expanse of tiny homes cut through by alleys.

It was as if the Hindu Kush mountains held the city carefully cupped in their hands. Military helicopters would occasionally swoosh, slow and loud, over the rooftops. Tiny mud homes, each painted in a different bright color, dotted the mountainsides until the point where the incline became too steep. The poor of Kabul are like trees on a mountain, occupying the land up until they reach an altitude where there isn't enough soil and oxygen to sustain them. The humblest neighborhoods were high above the city on those slopes, and each little red, pink, or blue house had an old-fashioned TV antenna on the top, creating a wiry headpiece above each neat rectangular home.

In the streets, hawkers sold fruits and nuts out of carts, men squatted by wheelbarrows, waiting for casual labor gigs, and crowds of people made their way hither and thither, some weaving through on bicycles, hurrying to and from homes and open shopfronts and places unknown to me as yet. Beggars, mostly women in sky-blue burkas covering their entire body, stretched their hands out to the slow-moving traffic.

Cars roared through every street: yellow taxis and masses of old Toyota Corollas competed with big, rusty old buses packed with Kabulis. Wealthier Afghans, usually those affiliated with the government, and foreigners working for international charities all moved around in shiny 4×4s, many of them armor-plated. Military personnel and embassy staff also careened through the streets in armored 4×4s, their windows tinted too dark to see faces, a tall radio antenna affixed to the front bumper, swinging back and forth as drivers aggressively started and stopped their vehicles, impatient and fearful in the heavy traffic. Recently a suicide car bomber had tried to ram a car filled with Americans—the tarmac was scorched and the trees had been blown bare.

It was the Islamic holiday Eid al-Fitr, which meant the holy month of Ramadan, during which people fasted from sunrise to sunset, was over and celebrations had begun. It was a time for giving to charity, and the most desperately poor were out in force, hopeful that

Kabulis shopping for groceries and clothes were more likely to be charitable today. It struck me as astonishing that this place felt much, much poorer than Yemen, despite the billions of dollars that had been poured in by the Americans over the last seven years. I had never seen so many beggars or barefooted children in Sana'a.

For a story on Eid in Kabul, I was looking for children who happened to be flying traditional Afghan kites. The UN had handed out kites to children that year with white doves, the symbol of peace, on them. I had devoured the bestselling novel *The Kite Runner* earlier that year and was fascinated by the tradition. The book had been widely read in the West and had made the Afghan children's practice more widely known around the world. Readers, I thought, would connect with a lighter story on this for Ramadan.

It wasn't hard to find flying kites; many were dancing high above the city, like bright birds. Finding children flying them was our challenge. The driver suggested we head to Maranjan Hill, one of the main hilltops overlooking the city, for these princeling kite fliers. We pulled up a steep dirt road until the taxi couldn't move any farther.

Maranjan Hill is home to the mausoleum of Afghanistan's royal family. King Mohammed Zahir Shah was laid to rest there in 2007. Children were playing in the dusty ground next to the family's ancient crypt, its shiny new replacement under construction a hundred yards or so away. King Zahir Shah was the last of Afghanistan's monarchs until he was deposed by his cousin, with the help of military officers, and the monarchy was scrapped.

I had since college read books and articles on Afghanistan's dizzyingly complex and rich history, trying to understand the conflict, which involves layers and layers of backstory. Zahir Shah had wanted to build the country into a modern international state embraced by the global community, joining the League of Nations, the UN's precursor. He also championed women's rights and universal education, building the country's first university. He worked hard for years to maintain Afghanistan's independence and hedged his bets, refusing to take sides in World War II and during the initial years of the Cold War. That neutrality paid off when Afghanistan became one of the only countries in the world to accept aid money from both the United States and the Soviets. He said in an interview that he didn't want his country to "become the servants of Russia or China or the servant of any other place."

Ultimately, Afghanistan would lose that battle thanks to the Great Game, the global proxy war of diplomatic maneuverings and manipulations born out of the rivalry between Russia and Great Britain. The Soviet invasion in 1979 sparked ten years of repressive occupation and insurgency, when mujahideen fighters took to the mountains northeast of the city and fought the Soviets. Those mujahideen, religiously inspired guerrilla fighters, would attract young men from all over the Muslim world, fighting what they saw as a holy war against the abomination of secular communist rule in Muslim lands. With the help of U.S. funding and weapons, the mujahideen drove them out after a decade of slowly bleeding them, one helicopter downing, one convoy ambush, at a time. But then the mujahideen groups splintered and fought over the spoils. Throughout the early nineties, they hurled their remaining heavy weapons at one another, leading to countless civilian casualties. These bands of freedom fighters gave rise to modern jihadist groups, like the Taliban, which seized control of the country in 1996, while an exhausted public reluctantly welcomed the young religious nuts in place of criminal warlords and thugs.

But before long their rule proved to be two parts brutal, one part incompetent, and the Afghan people continued to suffer. Women were banished behind burkas and closed doors, and an obsession with killing and cutting in the name of God manifested itself in now-famous scenes of stoning, amputation, and public flogging. The economy collapsed, devastating poverty became the new normal, and Afghanistan slipped back into the nineteenth century. And as warring factions continued to fight, cause for yet another conflict arrived at its doorstep. Osama bin Laden and members of his group, Al Qaeda, were welcomed in by the Taliban. Bin Laden paid good money and had old connections from the mujahideen days. As a guest in Afghanistan, he secretly plotted and launched the 9/11 attacks.

The young boys in the scene before me knew none of this. They only looked up, straining their necks, squinting against the sun, concentrating. They worked in pairs. At this point there were only two pairs left in the game, each flying one kite between them, together. About half a dozen other boys stood by them, watching the flying battle in the skies above them.

The boy flying the winning kite was the smallest of the group by far, perhaps seven or eight. He wore a traditional gray shalwar kameez outfit of a long shirt and loose-fitting pants, and a neat waistcoat. His brown eyes focused on the sky with resolve as the older boys anticipated his victory, murmuring to one another while their eyes remained locked above. I was suddenly afraid I would distract the boy, ruining his chances. So far few of the kite fliers had noticed my translator and me shuffling over toward them. I could tell when the little boy won because his serious mien turned rapidly into a heartfelt smile. His older friends slapped him on the back and congratulated him. Downcast, the other boys slunk away. The losers took it hard—a knock to their fledgling masculinity.

On the way back to the Gandamack, we stopped by the Kite Bazaar. There, on a narrow road lined with shops, each with colorful handmade kites hung on the walls outside, patient children waited as store employees wound string around wooden spools. At one place a machine was gathering the thread, which looked like coarse fishing line. Many children in the street played with imported plastic toys, mostly replica AK-47 guns, chasing one another in morbid imitation games. Kites, however, are far from going out of fashion, one kite seller told us. So far business is good, he said, smiling agreeably in the golden afternoon sunlight.

I wrote up the piece for the newspaper that evening. I would need to embark on much more serious stories shortly. The war out there beyond the city's limits, in the villages and rural areas, was ramping up in the U.S.-led coalition's biggest military offensive since 9/11. It was getting even more violent just as the country was trying to hold a second round of elections. I could hear the low murmurs in the hotel garden bar beyond my balcony. The journalists down there had been working on those stories all day, I assumed.

The Taliban, which had initially melted away in "defeat" after the U.S.-led invasion of 2001, had regrouped and morphed into an effective insurgency. General McChrystal's leaked report posited that the war would be lost to an emboldened and ever-strengthening Taliban within a year unless a major surge of U.S. troops was deployed. The United States deployed 30,000 more troops in response.

I had to get near that story, but how? I had taped a map of the country on the wall above my desk to make sense of the news reports from the provinces and rural areas. Running fingers over its mountains and roads and cities, I longed to be out in those places. To actually talk to people. To visit the field hospitals and the soldiers and civilians. I wanted to see it all. The fighting, too.

Before leaving Dubai, I had reached out to the British military's press office in Afghanistan, on the off chance they would give me an embed with British forces in the south of the country, and I was waiting for a response. In the meantime, I had successfully pitched the Gulf News magazine a profile piece on British war photographer Tim Page. I had heard from other reporters at the hotel that Page was in town for a few weeks to train young Afghan photographers in workshops organized by the UN. I'd admired Page's work for some time, particularly his coverage of Vietnam, which made him famous. The UN's press officer in Kabul gladly arranged the interview.

My getting to it would be the hard part. I couldn't afford a private driver each day, and when it was time for me to leave, Kabul's secure taxi system was running behind. I lit a cigarette and paced outside the Gandamack, worrying quietly.

"Hi there!" boomed a voice over my shoulder. "Did your ride not show up?"

Walking down the stairs past me was the tall guy from the bar on my first night at the Gandamack. He was carrying bags and boxes of filming equipment with him.

"Need a ride?" he asked, smiling and breathless. He had a rugged in-country look and a deep tan on his face and forearms.

I thanked him repeatedly and stubbed out my cigarette. I clambered into the back of the Toyota Land Cruiser next to another younger reporter in neatly pressed chinos, smiling at me with bright white American teeth. *Must be on-camera,* I thought as we pulled out through the hotel's security gates. They were with an American TV news network. They had the entire 4×4 just to themselves, all the time, whenever they needed it. U.S. networks must have so much money, I marveled.

When we pulled up outside the UN's baby blue and white blast walls and I hopped out, he leaned out the window and handed me his business card. I thanked him and waved goodbye at the Land Cruiser as it roared away. "Ben Proust," read the card. "Producer."

Tim Page is Britain's Robert Capa. At eighteen, he left his home in England with his camera, eventually making his way to Southeast Asia, where he teamed up with friend Sean Flynn. The two of them worked the Vietnam War beat, sharing motorcycle rides, military contacts, and flophouse bunk beds, photographing the war for news outlets. In April 1970, Flynn, who had gone to Cambodia on assignment to examine the Vietnamese invasion, headed out on a motorcycle ride to take pictures of a Viet Cong checkpoint and was never seen again. Page never really got over it, and for the next twenty years, he searched in vain across Cambodia for Flynn's body. At the time of Flynn's disappearance, Page was in the United States recovering from a devastating head injury from a land mine.

"They say I lost an orange-sized piece of my brain in the end," he told me matter-of-factly, staring directly at me. "After that, everything in life seemed like 'extra time,' like I wasn't supposed to be alive." It wasn't clear if he was talking about the loss of Flynn or his own accident.

As one of the "wackies" in Vietnam—a journalist taking extraordinary risks to snap important lasting images of conflict—Page has been the inspiration for books, documentaries, and films for decades. His name is synonymous with risk-taking. Sitting across a table from me in the UN complex, Page looked like he had been dressed by a Hollywood wardrobe team for a movie on war reporters: dirty old scarf around his neck; crumpled, worn combat clothing; and a khaki shirt with the sleeves rolled up above his elbows, baring forearms that were burned brown, once very strong, like a retired soldier's. His clothes were creased exactly into the grooves of his sixty-something, lithe body. His face was long and sunken, like that of a high-class Englishman who hasn't eaten much more than the tobacco stuck under his fingernails as he traipses blithely across jungles and mountains. He had a thin layer of gray hair on his head. His long limbs and mannerisms exhibited an aristocratic boredom, yet his intense manner of speaking enthralled me.

Page crossed one long leg over the other and apologized for not having any marijuana for us to smoke. Then he leaned over the table to roll a cigarette between his elegant bony fingers, carefully gathering clumps of soft Golden Virginia tobacco from a green packet and arranging it into a rolling paper. The table was scattered with notebooks and empty coffee cups. He spoke about the Afghan students he'd been teaching while rich gray smoke rose from his lips. "Short virgins will never make good war photographers!" he mused. I giggled, nervous and unsure about how I was supposed to respond. I hated myself for it. He grumbled that the Afghan photographers the UN sent him to train were young and hadn't known enough of life's passions to capture them. But by and large, he admitted, they were very good students.

"The aim of it, I suppose, is to produce one jewel in the crown," he said. "Basically, Afghans should be doing the thing themselves. They should be interpreting their own country."

His weathered face was cynical and weary. He reserved most of his enthusiasm for an intelligent monologue critiquing post-9/11 reporting. Page was no adrenaline junkie. He was a relentless empath, demanding strong, piercing journalism. Because I knew he was the real thing, I was afraid he would see me only as a young woman with zero experience, a cub reporter trying to be like him one day. I listened more than I talked, letting him speak freely. He asked questions that had never occurred to me.

"Do we get inside the mental asylums? How many people in this country are completely and utterly gaga? I have no idea how many mental asylums there are in this country stuffed with shocked people," he said loudly, one arm folded across his chest and the other nonchalantly waving a crooked rolled-up cigarette, wafting a thin film of smoke around him. "Nobody has put a face on this war of the Afghan suffering."

Page was the first person who really talked to me about journalism— *real* journalism. Stories about the people, the places, the heart of it all. This war, Page complained, has been photographed only from military vehicles and bomb blast sites. The photographer is forced to work under new pressures from editors and stiff rules imposed by the military. I wondered whether the same was true for reporters.

"You don't really know what Afghans eat, how they sleep, how they conduct themselves, the wedding parlor syndrome—how much does it cost to get married?" he bellowed, now staring at me wide-eyed, as though looking for an answer. *No, I have no idea,* I thought. I was suddenly self-conscious, sitting in silence as he looked at me as though for an answer, one I didn't have to give him. *God, my kite story from the day before was so asinine,* I thought. Afghan families spent fortunes on their weddings, renting out beauty parlors and huge event halls at a cost they sometimes couldn't afford, often going into debt trying to keep up with their neighbors. Of course I didn't know that then, I just read the news reports about IEDs, the elections, the military surge. I realized at that moment that I hadn't been writing down what he had been saying for some time now.

I was beginning to understand this job by realizing what I absolutely did not know. I knew little about Afghanistan beyond this war—not much about its people, its culture, its diversity. And worst of all, I hadn't thought to ask. I had come to cover a war, not a country, a people. This obsession with being a war reporter was bullshit. It was a total distraction from the real work, which was capturing experiences of war. I felt a stab of embarrassment at how I had approached this trip, my longing to prove myself to the other reporters with war stories of my own. The stories of the war were those belonging to the millions of people around me living through it. I would never again approach this work without the kind of relentless humanist curiosity Page was demanding, almost shouting at me now through the smoke. The interview had become an outpouring of advice I hadn't known I needed. But he seemed to know I did.

I was not self-assured enough yet in front of veteran reporters like him to engage, fearful he would know instantly that I was a novice, or even worse, that he would judge me as a tourist. So I sat in silence, hanging on his every word, nodding and lighting a cigarette of my own.

"If you are going to get to the core of this country, you have got to put yourself on the line," said Page, his face serious once more. "This is not a picnic."

I was glad to hear him say this, the topic that news organizations weren't allowed to discuss but that I felt in my heart was the ugly truth. Risk is necessary. It must be taken for the right reasons. I nodded.

Media industry budget cuts, he explained, were the real reasons why images from the conflict that displayed the reality of what was happening in Afghanistan had been scant. Why all we saw were pictures of gunfire and bomb blasts. As editors come under pressure to save more space for advertisements and consumers want more entertainment, all there was room for was body counts and gun battles.

"I suppose the unfortunate part of that is it is what you put against [discussions about] how to fix your garden," said Page, now staring off into the distance. "Magazines want feel-good stories and shoot-'em-ups. This business is run by bean counters and men in gray suits. It's not run by imaginative editors."

That afternoon in that smoke-filled portable with Tim Page had more of an impact on the next decade of my life than I could ever have known. Page understood why it is important to do this work. To go deeper than the superficial images of war, to understand human beings as they are and not as we presume them to be. Here was a Vietnam wackie, a risk-taker, famous for his injuries and bravery, telling me to stop obsessing with the combat stuff. To go beyond the "bang bang." And if you get to the fighting, why are you doing it? Is it to tell a real story of what life is like for soldiers and civilians? Is it to capture the reality of fighting and camaraderie and loss and fear? It certainly shouldn't be for your own vanity.

I still had no idea how to become a foreign correspondent or a war correspondent, no clue how to cultivate contacts, build a team, form a narrative arc, weave characters and places and events into news pieces. That would come later. Instead, I walked away from that afternoon with Page with a clear mission statement: Be Brave and Tell the Truth. And to hell with the bean counters.

That night I joined a group of journalists for dinner in the garden. We sat by candlelight at a long table and talked about Afghanistan, the development effort, and the upcoming elections. A middle-aged Englishwoman called Linda joined us, a freelancer for radio stations and the British newspaper *The Telegraph*. She asked if I was going to the rally the next day for Dr. Abdullah, President Hamid Karzai's main opponent. Linda suggested we go together, share the costs of a driver, and watch each other's backs.

The next day I was standing in the local and international press corps, at the front of a large marquee filled with rows and rows of Afghan men. The tent held nearly a thousand people, most of them in smart traditional shalwar kameez shirts and pants, with suit jackets and waistcoats over these and turbans wrapped around their heads. The most senior men, those with long gray beards, sat at the front, listening intently to Dr. Abdullah as he spoke from the lectern on the makeshift stage in front of them. Some of the men in the rows nearest to me caressed prayer beads between their fingers, legs crossed, poised.

Dr. Abdullah had been expected to say something in English but stuck to traditional Pashto and Dari only. So when he finished and exited the stage, the pack of a dozen or so foreign reporters rushed outside after him and quickly surrounded him to ask questions, cameras over shoulders, sharp elbows in necks and faces, microphones sticking out, all to the sound of one irate reporter yelling, "This is MY interview!" The Al Jazeera English correspondent had been promised an exclusive and fumed when Abdullah turned to talk to all of us at once.

I held out my small audio recorder and braved a few questions. Linda grabbed my wrist and shoved it forward, pushing the Dictaphone closer to his face. "Get in there!" she scolded me for being so shy. I wrote up a small piece about the candidate's rally and his comments for Gulf News that night, grateful to Linda for pushing me to have more moxie in the media scrum. I would soon realize just how much it was needed when covering a war.

At breakfast on the hotel terrace the next morning I was happily munching toast and reading the article on my laptop when the Al Jazeera correspondent appeared, standing over my table. "Hello, I saw you at the rally yesterday. I'm Jane." I smiled, reaching out a hand. I couldn't have read the situation worse. She was furious. "Yes, I saw you," she fumed at me, her arms folded tight over her chest. She barked, "You really had no business being there." I sat in my chair in silence as she continued with her dressing-down. "You weren't invited, like we were," she spat. "And you were not dressed appropriately." She then turned and disappeared into the hotel.

My heart raced and I gritted my teeth. I glanced up to see if any of the other guests had heard. They were all reading papers and drinking coffee. I tried to keep from crying, at least until I could make my way upstairs to my room. I spent the rest of the day hiding there, terrified of the angry woman who I thought knew the truth: that I was an impostor.

The British army had reserved me a seat on a military flight to Kandahar the next day, and it couldn't have come soon enough to suit me. Being on an embed gave me a reason to be there, a role to play as a visitor to the military. Unlike scrambling around the streets of Kabul without connections, where the story, this war, this country, seemed such an intimidating behemoth to try to break down, reporting from an embed came with a welcome structure. No one could accuse me of having no business there.

Kandahar airfield, known as KAF by soldiers and journalists, was a vast complex, a mini city that housed the American and NATO soldiers, complete with gyms and a Wendy's and shops that sold Snapple and Hershey bars, all enclosed in a blastproof casing around the outer perimeter. Sitting in the sand just outside Kandahar city, in the province that the Taliban came from, it was as much a symbol of the failures of America's Afghanistan campaign as it was a functioning comfortable home for thousands. Outside the wire, America was losing the war against the Taliban. U.S. soldiers patrolled on foot at first and then in heavily armored Mad Max–style vehicles, as footpaths and roads exploded underneath them, boobytrapped by Taliban fighters with what the military called improvised explosive devices (IEDs). Crude bundles of explosives taped together with duct tape or wire, hidden underneath rocks or buried in the dirt, were slowly defeating the world's mightiest armies.

I stood near the perimeter of the base while a Canadian officer demonstrated how to de-mine an area. I stared into the haze far off into the horizon and daydreamed about seeing more of Afghanistan. The kind with Afghans in it. But the Taliban were kidnapping and attacking foreign reporters caught "outside the wire," and only those from news organizations who had hired the best-connected networks of local fixers, translators, and drivers could manage the odd trip reporting "unilaterally," as non-embedded reporting was called then.

The British military press officer who was hosting me was an athletic woman in fatigues and a dark green T-shirt, with her brown hair pulled into a tight bun at the back of her head. She displayed intense irritation when asked questions. So I kept mine to a minimum, which was not easy, given this was my job. Her approach to her work was not dissimilar to that of a prison warden.

When I asked gingerly if there was any chance of getting out on patrol beyond the base with some of the soldiers, she barked, "I told you on the phone that would not be possible!" At that moment, with comedic timing, a young English photographer came bursting in through the flimsy plastic door, breathless, sunburned, and smiling. He was thin and around my age, with a pale brown beard and shaggy hair. He dropped his camera bag and flak jacket on the floor and reached out a hand. He had just arrived back from patrol. I shot the press officer a questioning glance. For the first time since I had arrived the night before, the female press officer smiled. She was delighted to see "Tom, photographing for the Foreign Legion," and quickly made him a cup of tea. Tom got to go on patrol, but I would not be allowed to leave the base.

Later that day I was taken to interview young British soldiers in their small tented recreational area, which was furnished with old sofas and a TV. There were about two dozen of them milling around in their combat clothing and shirts, sleeves rolled high up their arms. They seemed shockingly young, even to a twenty-five-year-old like me. I felt like I had stepped into a boarding school common room.

The press officer marched between them, at times pulling one to the side roughly by the arm and sternly prepping him to speak with me. I couldn't hear what she was saying, but her face was serious as death. In the end they said very little other than the stock phrases of support for the mission: "happy to be out here doing important work" and "glad to be well supported and equipped." Despite the aggressive chaperoning, I felt a pang of anxiety about these young men—little more than boys—going beyond the wire, some of them so slight and young and shy.

British military press officers were trying to fight against the constant narrative that the Brits were incapable of controlling Helmand Province. It turned out they had remarkable power to do so. When I had rushed to fill out the paperwork to secure the visit, I had barely glanced at the clauses and agreements they wanted me to sign. As I typed up the story of my trip to KAF, a rather dull account of attempts by the Brits to mitigate the risk of IEDs, the female press officer lectured me about how she must see it before I emailed it. She then hovered stony-faced over my shoulder as I wrote. I was shocked that this was common practice. Not just common, universal. The British public had no idea that the reports they watched and read were completely censored by the military. Even TV reports were viewed first. In the years since, I have been asked by dictators and members of militant groups to see the final story before it airs or goes to print, and even they have asked with an impish smile, knowing the answer is of course no.

Tim Page was right: no one wanted the story about how bad it was out there for the soldiers or why it was. No one wanted to know a mission was flawed and their army was no longer a world power.

Back at the Gandamack a few days later, I was lying in my bed daydreaming that I lived there when an explosion shook my bedroom. It felt like a giant had just kicked the side of the building. For a split second I tensed under the blankets, afraid the thin windowpane above my head would smash. It didn't. The writing desk wobbled next to me.

What makes you know something was an explosion, most likely a bomb, and not just a very loud bang, is the force that rushes through your body. It's not dissimilar to when you stand up too quickly and your head swims and you catch yourself for a second to avoid falling. I knew instantly this was a bomb. The first one I had felt since I was a girl. It sounded very close.

I threw the blankets off and scuttled around in the cold air, quickly pulling on socks and jeans and grabbing my flak jacket. I stuffed some pens, a notepad, a camera, and a headscarf into a backpack and ran down the stairs, shoving my shirt into my jeans. My boots were untied. Journalists on the terrace were shoving the last morsels of breakfast into their mouths and drinking coffee while tapping on laptops and talking on the phone. "Bomb outside the Indian embassy," one of them said to me. That was just up the street from here. Then Ben appeared with his camera and tripod and serious work face. When he saw me, he came over and smiled, leaning down to give me a hug.

"You're not going over there yet, are you?" he asked when he saw me pulling on my flak jacket, his brows coming together with a slight furrow and his head tilted to the side. "Why not?" I replied. "You never go to the site of a bombing immediately afterward," he said, looking a little taken aback at having to explain this. "You should wait a while, maybe half an hour or so, in case of a secondary explosion."

I stared at him. "Yes, of course," I finally stammered. "I know, I know, I'm just getting ready." I'd had no idea. It had never occurred to me that a secondary explosion could be planned to kill first responders, police, journalists. I sat down at a table and poured some coffee, noticing my hands shaking a little. "Good." Ben smiled, wandering off. "Be careful out there!"

About fifteen minutes later I left the hotel with a small group of reporters gathered in the entrance hallway. My heart felt like it was thumping through my chest inside of my Kevlar. Still, there seemed to be safety in numbers. As we wandered up the street in a pack of around five people, I saw the parked dark green Afghan police Toyota trucks and a crowd of people stumbling around through the smoke and dust, which was still thick in the air. The ground was covered with the debris of smashed concrete and pieces of metal. As I walked through the chaos, I realized quickly that the other reporters were gone—we had all scattered as soon as we arrived. Dark burgundy-red splashes of blood were dotted along the street, soaking up the still-falling dust. The bomber had failed to enter the building full of Indian diplomats. He'd killed guards and civilians in the street outside instead.

There was a hospital across the street, and panicked people were gathering outside. My nerves eased as I settled into work. This was the ultimate distraction from the fear of being there, this close to death, to murder, anger, and grief. As I entered the hospital, sheepish and worried I would upset the staff, a nurse saw me and actually waved me into a tiled room filled with rusty metal beds. Among the patients there were two young teenage boys in beds next to each other, bandaged and in shock. The nurse, a young man, followed me and spoke in English, too, offering to translate if I asked questions. Unlike with the military, I was surprised to find that this nurse wanted me there. He was helping several journalists access victims to the bombing and asking their relatives if they minded us photographing and talking to them.

In the midst of the yelling and chaos, I got a few short descriptions of what had happened from the boys. They were brothers, both on one bicycle when the explosion knocked them off. They had dozens of small cuts across their faces and bandages on larger wounds on their arms and hands. The nurse had to lean in and shout his questions because their ears were still ringing from the blast. Both the boys were quiet, just staring around them, something that surprised me at the time. Before this point I had thought that blast victims would be irate, crying, shaking. I didn't recognize yet that it's much more common for people to be in shock, even with dreadful wounds. It's the relatives who scream.

I stepped back into the bright sunlight outside the hospital and felt a hand on my arm. Ben was rushing by with his camera held high, filming with his correspondent. "You okay?" he yelled over the noise of the crowd. "Yes, thank you!" I suddenly felt exhausted as the adrenaline and fear wore off. Weary, I walked back to the hotel and collapsed into my chair to write up some lines and quotes from the scene. Sweaty and dusty and exhausted, I was shocked by what I had seen, how raw and real it had felt. I had naively imagined more order, focused people moving around with purpose, helping and rescuing others. Instead, the confusion, the strange dreamlike quality of mass human shock, made less sense than the movie version of bomb blasts. People had stared, sat down, stumbled and fallen; others had wandered around in a daze. I had felt that I was stepping into waves of emotion and energy—anger, fear, and shock—from the crowd. Witnessing and encountering a tragedy so soon after it had happened was a raw and heavy experience.

As I hit send on my story and fell back into my chair, I exhaled fully for the first time that day. My room was a mess of half-eaten packets of biscuits and clothes across the floor. My flight back to Dubai was the next morning. I just couldn't picture myself back there. It felt like I had spent a year in Afghanistan.

I sat in the hotel bar that night with a group of other reporters and watched the doorway as people came and went. Each time my heart tugged a little and then dropped—no Ben. Finally he bounded in, well after midnight. He stood in the doorway and smiled across the busy, smoky bar. As he slipped an arm around me, I knew my rule from the first night would not hold. After that day, not even my own sense of self-preservation and instinct for isolation could deny that I needed the arms of another person. I felt more of a connection than one night could satisfy, but as I pulled off my clothes and slipped beneath his sheets, the flight out of there the next day was like a safety blanket, a neat off-ramp from the vulnerability of it all.

I woke up the next morning as sunlight slipped through a gap in the curtains. I watched Ben silhouetted in front of the window, his big shoulders leaning over tapes and camera equipment. I could hear chatter over breakfast being served on the terrace outside. I was emotionally exhausted. Yet in that moment, I felt a sense of belonging I couldn't quite explain. The more painful and shocking the reporting had been to do—the fast-paced drama of the bomb blast followed by Kabul's astonishingly swift recovery: roads swept, bloodstains hosed into drains—the more I understood the need for the solidarity of a place like this hotel and for the bonds between the journalists within it. I watched Ben as he worked and knew that something set apart from my work had also begun. As I entered a world of much violence and cruelty, love, too, was finding its way into my life.

6

No Openings

A THICK BLACK ENVELOPE WITH gold writing was waiting on my desk at Gulf News when I returned from Afghanistan. The letters CNN were embossed on the corner. I tore it open without sitting down. CNN were opening a major new bureau in Abu Dhabi, the UAE's capital city, which was about 148 kilometers, a drive of less than an hour and a half, from where I was standing; this was an invitation to the grand opening. The feeling of providence was undeniable. Just the day before I had been sitting in Kabul's airport departure lounge, dreading going back to my job in Dubai. Now that I knew how it felt to be inspired by an assignment, I couldn't possibly go back.

At the CNN launch, I attended the press conference, where the president of CNN International spoke of their excitement concerning the new bureau. As soon as the presentation was over, I marched up to him and held out my hand. I was a hardworking, experienced Middle East–based journalist who spoke Arabic and would love to talk to him about any opportunities, I declared with my widest smile.

"He's the one you need to talk to," the president replied, nodding in the direction of another executive chatting to journalists at the other end of the stage.

His colleague was tall and slim, with faintly graying floppy hair. He seemed a little surprised to be asked for a job at a press conference, but graciously handed me a business card and said I should call him. A few days later I sat in Tom Fenton's brand-new office in Abu Dhabi, fidgeting with my hair. A large poster from Nelson Mandela's 1994 presidential campaign in South Africa hung on one wall. Another wall was all glass, the bright sun pouring in from outside. A huge world atlas sat on the shelf within reach of where Tom sat at his desk. Tom was American, with an accent that sounded like an old Hollywood movie star.

He took my résumé and placed it to the side of his desk without looking at it. He explained he really had no openings because all positions had been filled by CNN staff who had come from other bureaus. I assured him I would do any job going. I would work as a desk assistant or an executive assistant or a receptionist. "I'll open mail and park cars," I said, looking him straight in the eye.

I had no idea how this was *supposed* to be done. You were actually meant to have an agent, who would place you with talent executives at network headquarters. I didn't even know TV reporters had agents. Tom humored me because he could see I really was a journalist. And I was hungry. Hungrier than anyone he had ever met.

Suddenly I heard myself blurt out, "What about doing some freelance work for you?" I was thinking on my feet now he had been very clear about not being able to give me a job parking cars. "I could report from Yemen, if you like . . ." Tom stopped for a moment, and his face showed interest. He was intrigued. At the time, a small and relatively circumscribed conflict had been developing in Yemen's northern tribal lands between the central government in Sana'a and a local movement called the Houthi rebels. I would report on this story for CNN, I told Tom with total confidence.

When I brought the story back, he would not have to air it, of course, but if he would just agree to look at it, that was enough for me. "I would be happy to look at your story, Jane," Tom said as he got up to show me the door. He continued to smile as he waved me off, most likely chuckling to himself and fully expecting never to see me again. I knew Tom thought this strange young woman was never going to be able to deliver on her promise, just as assuredly as I knew I would astonish him.

Some weeks after I left Afghanistan, Ben had visited Dubai en route home from assignment. For a couple of days stolen here and there, in hotel rooms and over room service in bathrobes, we were starting to feel like a couple. I called him excitedly from the street outside the Gulf News building and told him all about my meeting with Tom, how I planned to wow him with a story from Yemen's communities impacted by the war in the north of the country, a hidden war that only a handful of aid agencies were accessing. He was silent. Finally he spoke up. "Maybe you should do a lighter feature on women there instead," he said.

I felt a rush of disappointment and anger. How could it be okay for him to report from the front line of the war in Afghanistan and not okay for me to do dangerous work also? As we spoke, Ben was planning a trip to Helmand, where he would be at the very front of McChrystal's new surge. I pointed out the immense double standard. Ben promised to never tell me to do women's stories ever again. I dropped it and moved on, but privately, the secret wound of it added pressure to my trip to Sana'a—the kind of pressure every woman striving to prove herself to the doubters, even the ones who love her, knows.

Days later I was back in my beloved Sana'a's Old City. I had booked a couple of days off from my Gulf News job and brought along Ashraf, the British Egyptian cameraman who had been doing online digital video work at the paper. In his early thirties, Ashraf was fun and passionate about getting out and doing more regional stories of importance, but he was unconvinced this trip was a good idea. When I told him it would be fine, he laughed and said, "I'm not sure, Jane, but yeah, all right."

Both he and I had sworn each other to secrecy about the trip. If Gulf News found out, I would be fired, and my visa for Dubai would be canceled. My entire fledgling career was riding on this trip. A Yemeni journalist also linked to Gulf News had agreed to connect me with a good local reporter who could work as a fixer for us, the industry term for someone who has the connections to get us to where we need to be. As the plane landed in Sana'a, I looked down on the red-brown city of ancient structures under the plane and beamed. This city felt as close to home as anywhere in my life then, even though I had lived in Dubai for eighteen months now.

But my joy abated quickly on our first day as it became apparent the Sana'a I knew from two years ago had changed. Reports of growing Al Qaeda threats had seemed unfounded when I had read about them in the news, but the atmosphere in Sana'a now was tense, the political scene more radical. Walking through the Old City with Ashraf toward the bread market I commented about how exciting it was to be back. How we could sit in the small square and eat kebabs cooked over the coals and fresh bread and hot sweet milky tea, just like I had before.

We hadn't made it to the market before we came across a severe-looking imam, waving and shouting. He wore a Saudi-style headdress and his thobe was high above his ankles, a sure sign he was an adherent of the fundamentalist traditional Islamic sect, Wahhabism. Wahhabis interpret the Prophet Muhammad's dress and behavior very literally, including that trousers below the ankle are sinful. A form of extremist Sunni Islam, Wahhabism is not indigenous to Sana'a or much of Yemen. After having only ever experienced kindness and smiles and friendly greetings in these streets, I was stopped in my tracks by this man's angry stare.

Ashraf was, too. We shuffled past, shooting glances at each other, and decided to head back to our small hotel, where we were asked if we were married. Another red flag. We moved to the Sheraton, one of the last international hotels still open in Sana'a. I sat on the end of my bed and pulled off my boots. I texted Ben to say we had made it and all was well. I didn't tell him about the imam or the uncomfortable feeling around town.

The next morning we met up with Sami Al Ansi, our fixer at Bab al-Yemen, the Old City's ancient gate. Even for a Yemeni he seemed remarkably happy to see us. Sami's enthusiasm for life exuded from him: his smile was huge, his listening face an intense frown of concentration, and when he showed surprise, his eyes widened like a child's. He was in his early twenties, rail thin, his cheekbones prominent in his face.

Ashraf, Sami, and I talked through the latest developments in the conflict and our plan to understand its civilian toll. It felt good working as a team, even having the simple camaraderie of making plans. It felt like anything was possible.

The Houthi rebels had clashed with President Ali Abdullah Saleh for years, demanding that he recognize their religious political movement. The Houthis were marginalized and their communities often punished by indiscriminate military action and deprived of even the most basic services. The Saleh government doled out access to water, decent roads, and health clinics according to how obedient a group was, and the Houthis were anything but. This latest violence threatened to carry with it a regional and international dimension. The rebels were pushing north across the border and into Saudi Arabia, onto land they historically claimed as their own. The Houthis are revivalists of Zaidiism, a branch of Islam aligned more closely with Shiism. The combination of Shia Islam mixed with a social justice agenda alarmed the House of Saud even more than the Sana'a government. For the first time in the long history of the conflict, the Saudis were sending fighter jets across the border to attack the Houthis.

I had secured permission from the UN refugee agency to visit the displacement camps in the north, in a place called Mazraq, where people were fleeing when the fighting reached their villages. The journey took several hours on winding roads north of Sana'a. The countryside was familiar: the gray and red mountains outside the city; the low stone walls on the edges of some of the steepest drops; and the broadening out to plains farmed with goats and oxen. There were very few cars on the road, even fewer going the direction we were. When we arrived, several uniformed soldiers at a simple military checkpoint directed us off the road to an expanse of makeshift huts, some being erected as we walked among them. This was the first time I had ever been in a camp of people displaced by war, but definitely not the last. I didn't know then that millions would be forced from their homes across the region over the next dozen years.

Every detail was a stark, shocking tragedy I tried not to stare at. Women washed their clothes outside huts they had erected with branches and straw, tied together with old rope. Squares of white and blue tarpaulin stretched between sticks and dirt, the UN High Commissioner for Refugees (UNHCR) logo peppered over each little temporary home. Many people had brought their livestock with them, a few goats or chickens or a donkey, the key to their survival. I approached one elderly woman in an emerald-green dress as she scattered straw among a few goats outside her hut. She said her name was Fatima Al Sabani. Her husband shuffled over from inside their hut to talk to us. He was blind, his eyes shut but eyelids fluttering, and he had almost no teeth. "There were air strikes on our home," he told me. "We were inside our house. We ran away following the other villagers."

They were both frail and terrifyingly old, alone here with nothing but their livestock. As I asked them questions, I was struck by how little I could do to help them. I was asking them to tell me what had happened, what had made them flee. They, like everyone else we spoke to that day, lamented air strikes they said were indiscriminate, falling on the fragile mud homes in which they had lived their whole lives, villages that had been reliable, safe places to live for generations. This was a personal catastrophe for each person I spoke with that day. In the background the sound of muffled thumps accompanied a slight shake of the earth beneath our feet. Government forces were shelling Houthi positions, and these people's villages, nearby.

As Ashraf and I walked among the tents, there appeared to be some activity buzzing around the gate to the camp. Several huge black 4×4s with tinted windows pulled in at high speed, bouncing over the dirt and grinding to a halt. Soldiers jumped out of a small truck, clutching AK-47s, their berets neatly folded on one side. They pushed back a growing crowd of Yemenis and aid workers.

"The vice president," announced one of the UNHCR staffers. Abd Rabbu Mansour Hadi had been dictator Ali Abdullah Saleh's number two for years. He was charged now with visiting the front line and being photographed with those displaced. He got out of his vehicle and, surrounded by bodyguards, walked through the space cleared by the soldiers. I watched him make his way toward us and told Ashraf to be ready.

I slipped under the barrel of a soldier's gun and strode over toward the vice president. I put on my least-threatening face and extended my hand. The soldiers looked at one another and didn't know what to do. Hadi stopped, looked at me with shock, and then shook my hand. He began walking again, and while I got in as many questions as I could, Ashraf, like a pro, filmed while walking backward in front of us.

"Iran is helping them," Hadi said, referring to the Houthis. "By money." The Yemeni and Saudi governments had long accused Iran of stoking the conflict by funding the Houthis. What he couldn't have known on that afternoon was that in five years those same Houthis would sweep south into the capital and he would flee for his life.

The displaced Yemenis looked on at the commotion created by Hadi and his armed entourage with a mixture of weary curiosity and indifference. He stayed approximately five minutes in the vicinity, shaking the thin hands of some exhausted refugees—"working the line," as politicians in the United States term it—before hopping back into his SUV and careening off in a cloud of dust, his photo op finished. The thousands of displaced Yemenis turned back to their tents to prepare simple meals for their children.

Reporting on Yemen, I saw the truth in Tim Page's advice. These civilians, who had no part in the bad blood between the Houthis and Saleh, were essential to the story of that conflict. I had no idea that in only a couple of years this one refugee camp would pale in comparison to the massive humanitarian catastrophe that would unfold as war consumed the entire country.

Back home in Dubai, I wrote a TV news script based on our interviews to voice over Ashraf's footage. I had never written anything like it before. I had studied TV foreign news reports for years, listening and transcribing the words of the narrator, watching how they structured pieces at places like CNN and the BBC. TV writing is different from newspaper journalism, all short, stark sentences, easy for viewers to digest. Ashraf and I edited the piece after work hours in a small room off the Gulf News newsroom. We were both taking a huge risk. We knew that. But my loyalty was to myself, not to Gulf News. I knew they would never give me this opportunity. I had to make it happen for myself.

A few days later Tom called. "I think it's very good, Jane," he said. My heart was in my mouth. "What would you like to do with it?"

"Would you be interested in buying it and airing it?" I asked, as calmly as I could manage.

"Yes, I would, Jane. How does $1,500 sound?"

Wait, not only were they going to air my story, with me, a non-CNN reporter, a nobody who had never ever been on air before, but they were going to *pay* me? This was incredible!

The night the story aired, I was in my apartment in Dubai. I stood in front of the TV screen with my hands covering my face, listening to my voice and the voices of the Yemenis we spoke with. I was so consumed with fear and excitement I could barely stand to watch.

Most TV reporters hate seeing themselves on air. They wince at every little turn to the camera, the shots they don't like, a way of speaking that suddenly feels silly. My first time was more intense than it has ever been since. My stand-up—the section where I speak directly to the camera—still makes me laugh when I think of it today. I walk slowly past a donkey and crouch down next to a tent for absolutely no reason. But none of that could dampen my satisfaction.

When I stepped out of the elevator in the Gulf News building the next day, my colleague Derek was standing there, in the foyer just outside the entrance to the newsroom. "Jane! Fuck, man, you were on CNN last night!!" He beamed.

"Shhh!" I said, looking over my shoulder. "Do you think anyone will have noticed?"

Derek roared with laughter, his raspy voice bellowing through the corridors. "Jane, you were on CNN! Of course they are going to notice!" he gasped. "Who cares? Fuck these guys. Good for you, that's huge!"

I walked into the newsroom, and much of the usual commotion settled in seconds as I was shot the kinds of stares from booths and desks a high school kid in serious trouble could expect. As soon as I reached my desk, my phone rang, and I was summoned to Human Resources. They had already prepared the letter for my termination. It sat on a coffee table with three chairs around it for me; the head of HR, who seemed embarrassed and uncomfortable with the firing; and the newspaper's managing editor, a South African who was so apoplectic he struggled to speak. I had been deceptive, he told me. I was being investigated, I was dishonest, I had appeared on a competing news organization's outlet. At times he would have to stop himself and look away, so disgusted he appeared to be with the very sight of me.

I sat in silence and mustered all my strength to remain calm, polite, and professional. Underneath, I was trembling. When I picked up the pen to sign the letter, my hands shook, and I hoped they didn't notice. I found it all terrifying—not because I was no longer going to be working there, but because, for the first time in my life, I was in trouble. Me, the good girl. The first in class. The varsity field hockey player. The first with her hand in the air with an answer in school had just been fired from her first-ever job in journalism. *Who does she think she is?* echoed quietly in the back of my mind.

The HR manager escorted me back to the newsroom in front of all my colleagues to collect my things from my desk. I was given a small cardboard box and filled it with old newspaper clippings and stationery. Moments later, I was outside on the sidewalk holding my cardboard box. As I placed it in the trunk of my car and drove away, I realized amid all the fear and shame and embarrassment, I was proud of myself.

7

Cross Fire

AFTER THE INITIAL EXCITEMENT OF my reporting from Yemen and my angry divorce from Gulf News, I had a less-than-dazzling freelance career at CNN. A story on a camel beauty contest in the desert outside Dubai was a "soft piece," meant to be fun, uplifting, and quirky. But I was determined to be a serious foreign news reporter. A friend visiting from Kabul after the camel piece aired declared me CNN's camel correspondent. I laughed and smiled along with the joke, privately in absolute agony. I needed a more serious story.

I'd been following a crisis in Somalia, where the Al Qaeda–linked group Al-Shabaab was gaining ground, with dire civilian casualties. I pitched a story on the African Union's resistance efforts in Mogadishu to Tom. He was supportive; Tom believed deeply in old-fashioned field reporting. But the network would never take on the legal liability of sending a freelancer into places like Yemen or Somalia. I was on my own.

Most networks were avoiding Somalia coverage not only because the dangers were so great but also because the story was not considered important enough to spend the money on private security guards for their teams of staff reporters. Four months before I went to Somalia, a Canadian and an Australian freelance reporter were released after being kidnapped in Mogadishu just two days after they arrived. They were brutalized for fifteen months before their ransom was met. In 2005 an experienced Africa producer for the BBC who had flown in from Johannesburg was shot dead in the street just outside her hotel hours after she arrived. No TV network had sent non-Somali staff reporters since.

Yet it was an important story for global security. Al-Shabaab, which controlled almost the entire country, save for tiny carve-outs the government clung to, had pledged allegiance to Al Qaeda the year before, adding an international component to their threat. With swaths of wild country open to the group, Somalia was on the verge of becoming an Al Qaeda training ground. The West had heard little to nothing about Al-Shabaab's grip on Somalia, but their tactics were familiar: recruiting child soldiers and brutally punishing civilians for perceived insults to Islam.

By the fall of 2010 African Union (AU) soldiers would be deep into the Battle of Mogadishu, an offensive to finally push the armed Al-Shabaab out of the city. A messy mixture of soldiers from France and other EU advisors, and from American security companies were circling in and out of Mogadishu helping to train and support them.

I began covering the war in Somalia that spring, a solo, self-shooting, one-woman band, selling my stories to CNN International. In March, the city was gripped by a tense stalemate, with AU forces held down, clinging to few positions beyond the coastal airport. On my first trip to the city, all I had to go on was an email from the African Union's press office in Nairobi saying that there would be someone to meet me at the airport and escort me onto the military base next door.

As I stepped off an African Express plane onto Mogadishu International's tarmac, I was so relieved to see him I thought I might throw my arms around him. His jungle-green fatigues were well pressed enough to show he was not one of the regulars. A matching green beret was tilted over a face mostly covered with his aviator sunglasses. Weighed down by my camera bag, I waved furiously. He smiled back—a huge grin, white teeth vivid against dark brown Ugandan skin. Major Ba-Hoku Baryigye—granted his consent, you may call him BB—was the African Union's spokesman in Mogadishu, charged with looking after the few foreign journalists who ever came here. So far, it had mostly been a trickle of grizzled freelance photographers flying in from Nairobi.

BB stood with his hand outstretched, seemingly delighted to have another visitor. He was about my height, around five-five, but his expressiveness belied his size. He could be laughing with me and then turn the next second to bark orders at a soldier. This was not what I expected from a military embed with soldiers under such enormous pressure.

The African Union, something like the United Nations of Africa, is a coalition of African states, and in Mogadishu they had a small contingent of peacekeeping soldiers, most of them from Uganda and Burundi. They were meant to be supporting a Somali national army of the new Transitional Federal Government in Mogadishu, but this army was in reality a completely underfunded group of clan fighters in flip-flops who regularly abandoned their posts and sold their AK-47s. In 2010, the city was a no-go zone for any Westerners not "embedded" with the African Union troops. Few foreign reporters had spent the night in any hotel in the city for years because of assassinations and kidnappings. Small parts of the city purported to be under the "control" of the internationally backed government, but in reality the city was controlled by the militant Islamist terror group Al-Shabaab.

I felt a private sense of joy at this small victory. I had made it here. Thankfully, BB had not asked me for a letter of accreditation from any news organization. I had no commission at all. I was traveling on the last of my rent money.

Somalia had been in crisis since the rule of dictator Mohamed Siad Barre had collapsed in 1991, resulting in uninterrupted bloodshed as various warlords tried to seize control. During a humanitarian intervention by American forces under a UN mandate in 1993, eighteen U.S. soldiers were killed in battle against Somali militiamen loyal to warlord Mohamed Farrah Aidid. The three days of bloody street battles, which killed and injured an untold number of Somalis, would be remembered in the book and subsequent film *Black Hawk Down*. The

United States pulled out in 1994 and the United Nations followed a year later. The entire international community had abandoned the country. By 2010, Somalia had long been synonymous with bloody civil war. No clearer example of a failed state existed. The violence sparked an enormous diaspora as millions of Somalis fled the violence any way they could.

The African Union peacekeepers controlled the military base next to the airport, pressed up against the Arabian Sea, and a few blocks of abandoned, smashed homes surrounding it, as well as the presidential palace in town. Everything else was controlled by Al-Shabaab. The country had no foreign embassies, no Western aid agencies, and no United Nations offices or staff. The Ugandans held on to the airport landing strip and building, allowing a few commercial flights to land every week, but other than that, the country was still largely cut off from the outside world.

BB and I sped off the airport grounds in a pickup truck, heading out through a rusty gate into what looked like scrub. The AU base was a maze of sandy dirt roads, trees, and khaki tents. As we bounced down the tracks between thick, thorny trees, BB's phone beeped with a message, and he let out a chuckle, showing it to me. It was from the militants. "We will kill you all," it read in English.

"They are crazy!" BB laughed. "Always watching, silly fools." They had seen us at the airport. I sank a little lower in my seat.

Before leaving home in Dubai, I had spent the week with friends and fellow journalists warning me against the dangers of the trip. The African Union fighters couldn't be trusted, they said. They were poorly disciplined, they were mercenaries, they wouldn't look after you well. They would abandon you in town, sell you to Al-Shabaab, or simply be slaughtered if they were attacked.

When I arrived at the AU camp, fear of my hosts quickly fell away. As we pulled up in the pickup to a clearing in the base's forest of trees, Ugandan soldiers peered out of tents, smiling and waving. An officer showed me to the old porta-cabin I would share with a fe-male officer. Tall and strong, my roommate was quiet and tidy—even her cornrows exhibited a military precision. She was polite but never smiled. "It's hot in here, eh?" I tried. Silence. "Does that ever turn on?" I ventured, pointing at a rickety air conditioner hanging on the wall above the door. "Generator is off," she replied. Her automatic rifle was propped against the plastic wall of the cabin next to the head of her bed. Our cots each had a mosquito net just large enough to cover the bed hanging from the ceiling above. A jerrican of water and a plastic bucket, my day's washing ration, were left outside for me to use and refilled each morning.

I was sorting through my filming gear when a soldier wandered over and gently tapped the open door. I looked up. "I have a spare bar of soap, madam," he said with a thick Ugandan accent, smiling and waving a pink bar in the air. "If you would like it, I will leave it here by your washbasin." He sat it on top of my jerrican outside and ambled off. Yes, perhaps not so terrifying after all.

That night my roommate was shaking her head and tutting at my scattered belongings, which had been flung all over the floor as I rummaged to the bottom of my rucksack for my toothbrush. "You should put them away—especially the soap, because there's a rat who comes in that corner." She pointed to a big hole in the floor near my bed. "He'll eat your things." Her contempt for my slovenly civilian mess was palpable.

Sure enough, in the dead of night I was woken by scurrying and screeching. The rat padded around my corner of the cabin, as predicted. I was too tired to think of anything useful to do about it and lay panting in the heat.

I thought about an American photographer I'd met at the airport in Nairobi. We were two of only three non-Somalis on the plane. Crumpled and dusty and entirely relaxed, he looked like he had been on assignment for several months already. He'd been injured in the Congo recently, he said. "My guides just sewed it up with a piece of string." He planted his boot on a rock and pulled up his pant leg. True enough, he had a three-inch gash down the center of his shin, which had been stitched up with the thickest, filthiest string I have ever seen. This rat wouldn't make for half as good a story.

The aforementioned rat sounded more midsize mammal as it waddled about. My officer roommate slept on, out cold. I heard the rodent come closer to the pillow end of my bed and sat up, reaching for the small flashlight beside me.

Suddenly, as I sat up, the rat went berserk, running screeching to the bottom of the bed. It was so dark I could hardly see anything. Then to my absolute horror, it jumped right onto the end of the bed, landing on my feet. All that lay between us was a mosquito net, and its massive bulk felt more like that of a Labrador puppy than a rat. I leapt out of bed and thumped the creature with my flashlight, only to find I was tangled in the net, flailing around in a panic. I was certain my roommate would wake up and start firing that AK-47 at any moment. She could be forgiven for presuming militants were in our cabin given my hysterics.

The next morning, I woke to find my roommate's bed neatly made and the contents of my rucksack strewn all over the floor. My washbag was in tatters, almost entirely devoured, and most of its contents gone. The rat had eaten my bar of soap and dragged things like my shampoo, toothpaste, and hairbrush through the hole in the bottom of the cabin, flinging them across the rocky ground outside. I never found my hairbrush.

Getting around Mogadishu with the African Union meant traveling in their armored vehicles, which are called Casspirs. Picture a cross between a small truck and a tractor, with no suspension. In the back is a kind of long, cylindrical container with tiny bulletproof windows along the sides. It's like a mobile oven packed with about twelve soldiers strung along the sides facing one another. A gunner at the center stands on boxes of ammunition, and we could see only his legs as he swiveled around, ready to react to any attack. We sat with our backs against the outer casing, bouncing around. The engine roared so loudly we couldn't hear each other speak. Sweat rolled down from beneath my helmet, and my hands became so slippery that I struggled to hold the camera.

I peered out of the tiny, cracked glass windows, grubby and several inches thick to withstand bullets and bombs, and marveled at how close and yet far away this place seemed. I longed to walk around, and of course I was also deeply fearful of it. Instead I filmed from a perch on the ammo boxes, desperately trying to keep the camera still as the truck rocked beneath me.

Mogadishu is unmistakably beautiful, even with all the bullet holes and destruction. No matter how hot the city gets, there is always a strong breeze coming off the ocean, and the stark quality of the sunlight only brightens the colors everywhere. Palm trees rise up from the rubble, swaying in the wind, and giant heaps of pink bougainvillea lean over whitewashed walls, drawing your eye away from the ruins like a defiant smile. Vegetation had begun to reclaim some abandoned parts of the city, as creepers and trees spread through homes and backyards and peeling, abandoned swimming pools in once-bougie neighborhoods. It was like walking through someone else's memories.

Somali culture is distinctive in many ways. That's why Mogadishu looks like nowhere else. The Somali language wasn't formally written down until the 1970s, and instead for thousands of years oral traditions thrived, like passing on news and history in songs and poems. Somalis were largely a nomadic people, surviving by herding cattle and camels, and as such, out of necessity shared news when they came upon one another, molding stories into poems handed down through the generations. They also conveyed information through paintings on buildings instead of words, lending a sort of artistic, decorative effect to the city. As we careened through the streets, whitewashed shop walls hand-painted with pictures of their goods flew by. Whole chickens, bottles of bleach, and notebooks were set against a brilliant blue sky.

Meanwhile across the "government-controlled" area of the city, an uneasy stalemate prevailed. The African Union soldiers were sticking to their peacekeeping mandate and only counterattacked, meaning they could not expand beyond the few small blocks they had a loose control over. Al-Shabaab insurgents were free to continue running most of the city and country as their own.

I had never filmed anything myself before this trip and was terrified of making a mistake. I was using a Sony Z1 camera and would feed in small tapes, which I could then log and review later in the evening on the camera's own viewfinder, provided I could charge my batteries in the precious few hours that the generator was turned on at the base.

I refreshed my understanding of how to use my camera each morning. I left a small notepad on the floor by my camp cot, next to my contact lenses, so it would be the first thing I saw in the morning. *Hold camera still! Hold the shots longer! Clean the lens!* all yelled at me in my own handwriting the moment I woke up.

Each morning I emptied my ration of water from the jerrican into the bucket and, kneeling in the dirt, scooped cool water over my sweaty, sleepy head. Having clean hair every morning was the one thing I thought would keep me looking decent on-camera. Because there were no showers at the camp, I had nowhere to really wash my body in private, so I used baby wipes for that. A short stroll down a dirt path between the trees led to the toilet, a hut of corrugated metal positioned over a hole in the ground. I don't know how many soldiers shared it, but it was too many. The smell made my eyes water. As I batted the swarming flies away from my face, I thought of something Martha Gellhorn wrote when she was traveling in Chad: "The latrine broke my lion heart."

In the afternoon, AU fighters slaughtered and plucked chickens, chopped them up, and cooked the pieces over a fire, serving either traditional East African polenta or mashed potatoes on the side. Boiled cabbage or tinned vegetables were also offered and, to my joy, sweet, soft, squishy canned pears. Nothing teaches you to appreciate the simple joys of food like the life of a solider on a forward operating base, with so few comforts that second helpings of boiled cabbage feel like a birthday treat.

Having seen Mogadishu from the perspective of the AU soldiers, I knew I needed to meet Somali civilians and understand theirs. My encounters with them were frustratingly rare. My first opportunity came on a sad morning at the edges of the military base. The AU had set up a makeshift hospital ward there. The need for it was overwhelming. By eight a.m. hundreds of people were already crammed against the barbed wire and thorny branches that had been piled up as a crude barrier around the base. Old men and women with sick babies were pushing and shoving against the barrier and one another, as local Somali fighters pushed them back. Occasionally the soldiers fired warning shots to keep the crowd back. It was already hot and there was no shade if you wanted to stay in line. The old men wore neat short-sleeved shirts and long wraparound skirts in patterned fabrics. They bent forward, bony hands clutching the top of walking sticks and beards dyed bright orange with the traditional henna. The women seemed more panicked. They used the ends of their headscarves to swat flies away from their babies. A Somali fighter held up a metal detector in his hand, scanning each person before they were allowed into the hospital ward of the camp.

"We cannot stay long," warned BB, who had taken me there as a favor after I grumbled about the lack of access to Somalis on my trip. "Al-Shabaab can send suicide bombers here." These people had taken a risk by coming here. They could be attacked simply for trying to access medical treatment from the African Union soldiers. Due to the preceding two decades of chaos, war, and a complete lack of state institutions, Somalis had no access to any decent healthcare in the city.

The medical facilities inside the camp were designated for the African Union soldiers, but did open on certain days of the week for Somalis to be treated by Ugandan military doctors. Inside a dirt courtyard between a few cement buildings, large white tents were erected as wards. One was for sick babies, and each bed had a fearful mother sitting on the end and a tiny bundle of cloth in the center. From the moment babies in Somalia are born, they must fight to survive some of the toughest challenges in the world. One in seven children under the age of five dies. Diseases like malaria kill many, but malnutrition and lack of treatment mean that most often children die from infectious diarrhea.

As I walked between the metal framed beds in that miserable excuse for a hospital I was learning that the official casualty rates of war zones are vastly understated. There are always so many more who suffer and die due to the unintended consequences of conflict: the collapse of economies and governments, and with these failures, the chances for any decent public health—sanitation, nutrition, or medical care.

I approached one bundle on a bed, lifting my camera up and making eye contact with the mother sitting beside it. She gently nodded and I started filming. The doctor had come through the ward before me to tell the patients a journalist from CNN would be filming and that they could tell me if they didn't want to be filmed. The cot held a baby boy lying on his back, the blanket around him open like his tiny mouth, gently struggling to bring in air. His mother watched him with downcast eyes, her own frail frame and hunched shoulders covered in a dark green dress. He was barely blinking. A doctor in a white coat came over to check the drip. I asked what was wrong with him. "Diarrhea," he said, and walked away.

The little boy was silently slipping away. His mother sat motionless, a small crease between her brows the only outward sign of her pain. I was suddenly horribly aware that I was witnessing one of the worst moments any human can endure: the loss of a child. This baby was not long for this world, and I was filming perhaps his very last moments. Beneath it all, I felt a flash of shame.

To stand in a hospital with a camera and not a stethoscope, to offer no tangible help to the person suffering in front of you, to voyeuristically witness their suffering—all of this is grotesque. This was my first such experience. I had an overwhelming sense of futility at what I was doing, pointing a camera.

I firmly believe that journalism, TV in particular, plays a crucial role in showing the rest of the world its own reality. I still believe that. But sometimes the peering at suffering and documenting it, chasing the "powerful nature" of images of others' pain, is guilt-ridden work. War reporters see a lot of pain and ask if it's okay to capture it. It is such a delicate, sensitive balancing act—especially for a twenty-five-year-old working alone with no other colleagues—and all we can do is be as compassionate and respectful as possible. To do that, you must allow yourself to be vulnerable. In those moments where I am witnessing the profound vulnerability of someone else, I also feel laid bare. You can only really get through it by sending as much love to the person you are filming as you can. People recognize real empathy. It is the only decent behavior in war reporting. As a little girl poring over *National Geographic* images of suffering old ladies in Bosnia, I wondered why the photographer had not helped them. I understood now that a part of that photographer wondered this as well.

I got word that the Somali president had agreed to give an interview to me and two photographers embedded with the AU. We clambered back into the oven-like vehicles and bounced across the city's potholes to Villa Somalia, the presidential palace. The presidential compound was hardly flashy, but it stood in stark contrast to the ruined city around it. Neatly maintained flower beds filled the space between whitewashed walls. There was the usual sound of gunfire from beyond those walls, and we had to dash from the Casspirs and through the door into the building quickly to avoid the one spot where snipers could still sneak a bullet. But as I waited for the president to be ready for our interview, I happily sat on my flak jacket and leaned my head against the wall behind me while watching the sea in the distance. This may not have been Kim Jong Il or Barack Obama, but it was my first ever interview with a state leader and I was excited. Sharif Sheikh Ahmed was previously a leader of the Union of Islamic Courts, the fairly extreme ruling group that ran Somalia before Al-Shabaab broke off.

Finally we were shown into the president's office. The others were just taking photographs and I was to record his responses to a few quick questions. I would film and ask questions at the same time, as

I had been doing for the whole trip. The office was small, with yellow curtains pulled shut, leaving the room looking like the inside of an orange. Sheikh Ahmed hadn't arrived yet, and I marched over to the window behind his desk to pull the curtains back, my rucksack still on my back, as the president entered. I whipped around and my rucksack swung directly across his ornate table, taking every object on it with me. Awards, official trophies, and a huge brass plate crashed onto the floor. The plate rolled and rolled and rolled for an eternity as I stood dumbfounded.

"Cover your hair!" barked a presidential aide as I struggled to pick up the paperweights and pen holders from the floor. "Sorry, sorry, I'm so sorry!!" I cringed, piling objects back onto the desk and covering my head with a scarf. One of the photographers smirked. The president stood there and watched, a faint bemused smile on his face. He was gracious during the interview, slowly answering questions with a sober dignity. We discussed the threat of Al-Shabaab to the Somali civilian population and efforts to build up the Somali national army, which was the only way to protect any territorial gains by the African Union if and when their soldiers moved forward.

And soon they did. When I returned to Mogadishu for the second time, things had changed dramatically. Now it was an all-out offensive urban war. In July 2010, just a few months after my initial embed with Ugandan forces, Al-Shabaab had attacked the Ugandan capital Kampala with several suicide bombers, killing over seventy people as they watched the World Cup final in outdoor cafés. The following month the African Union agreed to change its mission mandate inside Mogadishu to an offensive one. They were not there to keep peace anymore—in reality there was no peace to keep anyway. They were now to take the entire city, pushing Al-Shabaab out, street by street. The second Battle of Mogadishu had begun. The fighting was intense, and it was my first front-line combat work. On this trip, I worked alone once again, filming everything myself. It would be a baptism of very dangerous fire.

I followed AU fighters on foot as they exchanged fire with Al-Shabaab's fighters, including, according to Ugandan officers at the front, foreigners from Chechnya, the Arab world, and Pakistan. It was, I admit, thrilling to be given such a privileged spot to watch and observe and crouch and run alongside soldiers as they fought. I crawled on my belly next to Somali militia fighters who had recently struck a deal to join the AU troops in fighting Al-Shabaab. I was as focused as I've ever been, the initial fear having long given way to adrenaline and the determination to do the work. I thought, *I can do this, I AM doing this*. Crouching behind a lump of concrete in a laneway overgrown with vegetation, I reached a front-line position where the militia fighters were firing madly down the crumbling concrete road and then jumping for cover into the trees. BB had agreed to drive me to these positions to witness the fighting, but the militia fighters were moving in and out of the trees and back and forth along the road, and at times I found them flanking me, firing from behind and over my head, toward Al-Shabaab positions.

This was the first time I heard the whistle of bullets flying over my head, the unmistakable buzz of slower bullets, and the crack of high-velocity rounds. I managed to steady myself long enough to film the fighting from whatever vantage point I could crawl to. The AU were advancing. The Ugandan troops had by now smashed holes in walls between houses, and as we raced along, new rabbit runs gave them some semblance of cover as they pushed forward. Snipers remained a threat, as is the case for any advancing force in urban warfare. The defensive group always holds the vantage points and has time to prepare. So we stayed low and ran quickly from place to place. BB took me to a rooftop where Ugandan troops were firing mortars toward the hillside in the distance. The firing of each mortar produced an almighty, terrifying explosion. I was not yet experienced enough to know to bring foam earplugs to the front lines. Since that trip I never travel without them.

Over the coming months the Ugandan and Somali forces would push Al-Shabaab from the city, providing enough of a foothold for the internationally recognized Somali government to somewhat operate. The militants became insurgents and continued to menace the city with suicide bombings and assassinations, but the international community took note of the progress. The UN, who had packed up and left over seventeen years earlier, returned and provided aid to people who needed it. The Battle of Mogadishu was a turning point for the country, and while a multitude of challenges did and still do continue—including more frequent droughts due to climate change, pushing young herders to join militant groups like Al-Shabaab—Mogadishu came back to life. In the coming years, some members of the Somali diaspora would return there to start small businesses or contribute their professional skills toward building a vibrant society.

After my final trip to Somalia that year, I sat at an outdoor café in the Nairobi airport and drank a cold Kenyan beer in the shade while I waited for an Emirates plane back to Dubai. As I watched the travelers come and go through the carpark and terminal doors, I felt the adrenaline and stress and fear and excitement drain away. I had just had my first-ever experiences of covering real combat, and I had been given an intimate glimpse of myself in a role I had long only imagined. I had a heightened sense of fear when under fire, my heart racing and breath heavy, but my hands didn't shake and I could continue doing my job. I was jubilant to find that I could manage. My filming was not great, but I was not paralyzed by fear. And for one of the first times in my life, I felt a true satisfaction with and fulfillment in my work. Not because it would earn praise or prizes, but because I had done this hard work well, and I knew it, and that was enough. I wasn't performing for someone else. For a brief moment, I was not trying to make others proud of me. I was proud of myself.

I would later learn that fear is a great ally, a way to stay alive and make smart choices. It's most important to avoid panic. I would learn to respect the presence of fear, making it a kind of colleague in the field. Gritting my teeth, taking deep breaths, and getting on with filming while deafening .50-caliber guns are fired or I'm running with the troops as they retreat or advance—this was something I figured out first in Somalia. The truth is, those physical effects of fear I experienced under fire—heart racing, sweating, heavy breathing, and a sense of unease deep inside—are almost exactly the same sensations experienced by anyone who has had chronic anxiety. I was getting better at living with these.

I bounced into the CNN bureau, as I had done frequently for a year and a half, my face slightly sunburned. I was fresh off a trip to Sudan reporting on its upcoming split in two and went on at length about the conditions there for displaced people, what I had filmed, what it was like on the UN flights. My money had mostly run out, and I was looking forward to getting paid. Tom arrived and waved me into his glass office.

I chatted excitedly about the trip, happy to see him again. "Jane, we need to talk," Tom finally interjected. Normally he would be all ears for stories from the road, a former field producer turned manager now listening wistfully from his gilded cage of an office. He looked stressed and tired. "I am being laid off," he said, shrugging his shoulders in disbelief. After twenty-five years at CNN, Tom was being pushed out. As we spoke, his replacement was on a plane to Abu Dhabi. He was losing his job. I was losing my only connection to the career I had dreamed of.

On paper, my career was doing fantastically well. I was the youngest foreign correspondent on air for CNN, reporting from high-risk war zones in Yemen, Sudan, and Somalia. But I wasn't staff and I was very far from in the club. Tom was able to give me a small monthly retainer, whereby I had to give CNN right of first refusal on my stories. But it still wasn't enough. I got $2,500 a story, paid in brown envelopes of cash out of the bureau safe. The math was simple: if I sold one story, I would likely break even; if I sold two, I made some money to live on for a while. No longer able to afford rent, I had been sleeping on the sofa at the home of some kind friends between assignments.

I was often deeply ashamed of my inability to make a living at what I did, and being forced to lurk in other people's spaces made me feel as though I barely existed, as if I were a ghost that floated between bookshelves and dining tables and kitchen counters. Yet those moments only propelled me to keep heading out on assignment whenever I could. In the back of my mind was a cautionary voice reminding me there was a time limit on how long I could survive.

When I was on the road, everything about my life felt right. I had a sense of purpose, consumed as I was in the travel and the task of working in challenging environments and pursuing stories the world needed to hear. The work could be dangerous, but that was the point. I was covering the parts of the world CNN staffers were not, because the balance of risk to reward was considered too high. I could travel to the black holes of coverage areas and report from there cheaply for the network.

The grind made me a remarkably adept field reporter and producer. Need an interview with that general in Yemen leading operations against Al Qaeda? I would find a way to him. Give me a week, and I would be sitting at his kitchen table chatting with his wife as his daughter played the piano nearby. Need American Special Forces training militaries from sub-Saharan nations in counterterrorism operations? I'm there, filming at the shooting range in Senegal. I could get almost anywhere, figure out visas, access, and the right people, risk life and limb, and I could do it on a shoestring budget. Solitary as the work often was, Tom was my ally.

Now I stood across from Tom in his office as he prepared to pack up. "Don't worry about me, Jane, I'll be okay," he said. "I thought this might be coming and have other options." But he looked shaken. I felt such sadness for him and was at a complete loss for words. His replacement was coming to the office the next day and I should, between my edits of the Sudan work, try to get a meeting with her, he said. Tom was worried for my future. In retrospect, he knew a lot more about corporate culture than I did. I'm sure she will be very nice, I told myself as I left the office that day. She wasn't. She wanted little to do with anyone associated with her predecessor, promptly canceling my monthly retainer and having her deputy email me to tell me to stop coming to the bureau.

I was in a tailspin and had no idea what to do about it. This career I had built, however fledgling, seemed to be coming entirely apart and there was nothing I could do. "I am not dropping you, Jane," Tom's replacement snapped at me through the phone when I appealed for answers. "I'm simply returning you to the market."

I had about $3,000 left in my bank account, and my future seemed a bleak horizon of failure. I internalized the rejection. It stung just as harshly at twenty-six as it had when I was six. I couldn't yet pry the two women apart, little me and bigger me.

I went for a drink with a media consultant friend I was staying with in Dubai and worried aloud about what to do. I knew I had been naive about office politics and major news organizations. "Well," he said, before taking a long gulp of beer, "you are no Lara Logan, that's for sure. So it's going to be much harder for you, Janie." He said it sternly, as a warning. He meant it not as an insult but to somehow prepare me for the business, a kind of tough love.

Staring out at the dark night-time beach, the waves rolling in the distance, I sniffed back my tears and hoped no one noticed. It was an agonizing moment that cut through me like a quick, sharp stab. At this point, Lara Logan's career had been an unparalleled, sweeping ascent to the top since she had begun covering conflict in Afghanistan and Iraq after 9/11. Lara was brave, like me. She was good-looking, unlike me. Her beauty and flirtatious on-camera style were celebrated and rewarded with swift promotions at CBS. *I will never be known for my beauty,* I thought. I was faced with one ineluctable thing I couldn't change about myself.

Until this moment my looks had never entered my consciousness when it came to work. It hadn't occurred to me to wear makeup, certainly not in war zones, and most times I was in the studio I looked pale and nervous. I thought back on the women I had grown up reading about: Martha Gellhorn, Gertrude Bell, and Dervla Murphy. I admired them for their toughness, their courage and tenacity. Now I also wondered, what if they hadn't also been beautiful?

My imagination ran away with me. Perhaps this was why no one had hired me. I felt I was forever marked: too ugly for TV.

I read once that when you feel absolutely broken and defeated, when you have failed at something and the undeniable truth hits you, you should take one full day to mourn and feel unabashed self-pity. One day only, and then get back to the drawing board. I knew I shouldn't allow myself to feel low for long. I feared slipping into a hole I couldn't crawl out of. My mental healthcare was my self-preservation. I was not compassionate with myself, but I was strong. I took more than one day to stop spinning in tearful self-pity and hurt about my CNN dismissal, but only a couple more. When an email came through from *The New York Times* bureau chief in East Africa, Jeffrey Gettleman, I knew that was my way forward.

I had met Jeffrey in South Sudan. Now he wanted to go to southern Somalia and asked to share the costs of the trip, he as a print reporter and me as a TV correspondent. He had his sights set on an interview with the country's most powerful warlord, Ahmed Madobe, who had recently teamed up with Kenyan forces to fight against Al-Shabaab. I was absolutely in. I packed my bag and flew back to Nairobi with the last of my cash in the world.

Part II

8

"Our Correspondent We Are Not Naming
for Security Reasons"

OUD MUSIC BLARED THROUGH THE streets of Sana'a as rice and meat sizzled on outdoor gas stoves and crowds of laughing and chatting men and women wandered between makeshift tents. On the sides of the tents hung slogans and paintings, all calling for political change, all criticizing the dictator Ali Abdullah Saleh.

It was November 2011, eleven months since Tunisian street fruit vendor Mohamed Bouazizi poured gasoline over himself and lit a match, sparking waves of anti-dictatorship protests across the Arab world, ten months after those protests in Cairo removed Egyptian dictator Hosni Mubarak, and just a few weeks since Libyan dictator Muammar Gaddafi was brutally murdered in the street by armed militiamen. With Gaddafi and Mubarak gone, Saleh was now the longest-serving dictator left in the Arab world—a risky role to play.

Ali Abdullah Saleh had been Yemen's dictator since the country was unified in 1990. He joined the Yemeni military when he was just a boy, took part in the revolutionary coup of 1962 that removed the last Yemeni king, and rode a wave of Arab nationalism and anti-colonialism up through military ranks and into the presidential palace.

Now a new wave—the most groundbreaking in the Arab world since the end of British occupation in Egypt—threatened to end his rule.

Fevered calls for freedom were heard all along the Red Sea and across Yemen's highlands to Sana'a's youth movements, universities, and dinner tables. Around "Change Square," as activists had dubbed the streets they now occupied outside Sana'a University, a new Yemen seemed to have poured out of homes and into the light.

Sami Al Ansi walked with me through the tents, filming the scenes around us and occasionally embracing friends, old college classmates, and fellow Yemeni reporters with his usual wide smile. I had called Sami from Dubai when I learned I could get a rare visa. It had been two years since he had helped me reach the refugee camps in Yemen's north, for my TV debut. Now I was on assignment for Al Jazeera English.

In the wake of my devastating split from CNN, I'd reached out to the new "voice of the global south," and they bought the freelance story from Somalia about the warlord Madobe and his fighters. That had kept me from thinking myself an utter failure. Al Jazeera was the undisputed leader of reporting about the Arab Spring. In 2011, freelancing for Al Jazeera meant working for the big boys of international news.

President Saleh's nephew was a general in the army with a habit of making his own rules. He felt journalists should be allowed into the country, whatever the story. I had interviewed him for a CNN piece on Al Qaeda the year before and when I reached out to him again to help me get back into the country he put me in touch with the head of the tourism union, Mohammed Saif, who helped me get a visa, find accommodations, and even arranged for me to use his trusted driver, Fuad Al Yadoumi. I didn't know it yet, but Mohammed, Fuad, and I would work together for years, long after the Salehs left the country. They were my team, men I trusted with my life, time and time again. I also didn't know how lucky I was. This sort of welcome would soon be a rarity for foreign press in the Middle East.

To Saleh's government, now fighting for their survival, Al Jazeera was an existential threat. Arab world dictators and royalty saw their journalists as a mouthpiece for revolution, carrying the messages of young revolutionaries into millions of homes. When Mohammed realized my affiliation, he did me the favor of not asking questions.

I was proud to be an Al Jazeera journalist. They paid my expenses and insurance, and I filed stories each night. It was my first ever real commission. The only catch was that I could not appear on-camera. I would have to voice the stories and keep myself out of Sami's footage, in case I was discovered and arrested by the government. I understood why this was necessary. Saleh's own men were responsible for many attacks on the press.

I set aside my fears. This was a huge break. I needed this. I had no apartment, no home base, and no money. I had promised Laura I would come home for Christmas but couldn't afford the flight. She had given birth to her first baby a few weeks before. I was playing all or nothing with my life and career. I was caught between excitement and overwhelm, desperately trying to impress the network executives while not getting shot.

As had always been the case, the Yemeni Ministry of Information assigned me an escort, functionaries known in the press as ministry men. On the one hand, this person would be able to smooth my passage through security force checkpoints and watch my back in case of attacks or kidnappings. This ministry man would also be able to report back on what I was doing and whom I was talking to. But they were rarely much of a threat to journalism. Most were paid $50 a day for their trouble, a fortune in Yemen. As the Yemeni government spiraled in crisis, these staffers were simply trying to keep their jobs. In an ironic dance, they didn't ask too many questions about my work so they could justify keeping theirs.

For this trip I was lucky to be appointed Mohammed Al Qahdi. He showed up in my hotel lobby on my first morning. A stout, balding thirty-something man with a kind, smiling, but at times anxious face, Mohammed wore a suit without a tie. When he shook my hand, he seemed a little nervous. He had trained to be a journalist, he told me, but as a family man, he couldn't turn down a government job with a reliable salary. I always felt, deep down, Mohammed Al Qahdi was rooting for the reporters above all else.

Fridays were the busiest day of the week for protests throughout the Arab world during this time, and in Yemen the protesters spilled out of the university and surrounding streets to block off the main ring road around the city, Sixtieth Street. On our first Friday of filming, I was amazed at the size and energy of the crowds. Tens of thousands of people gathered in Change Square, frisked by volunteers on the way in to check for weapons, women on one side and men on the other. Even General Ali Mohsen al-Ahmar, a senior commander and former loyalist to the president, called for Saleh to step down. It was a politically opportunistic move, but it meant that his troops bolstered the protests, and tanks surrounded the square.

We heard Friday prayers and then political speeches calling for Saleh to step down, before uproarious chants—the Arab world's refrain back then from Libya to Egypt to Syria to Yemen was *Ash-shab yurid isqat an-nizam!* or "The people want the downfall of the regime!" The roar from the crowd was an incredible force, as though it was trying to reach across the city to the presidential palace itself. People were jubilant, feeling as though this time, providence was on their side. Change was inevitable. As Sami held the camera over his head and filmed the crowds unfurling a huge Yemeni flag, I looked behind me to where Mohammed was waiting patiently and caught his eye. He was smiling.

The hopeful atmosphere didn't last. The next week, protesters returned to the square to face gunfire. The gunmen were thought to be a mixture of tribesmen loyal to President Saleh and the security forces. I rushed through the hotel lobby to drive there with Fuad and Sami and tried to appear calm. Lounging on couches by the sliding doors of the hotel were Yemeni intelligence officials. Their job was an old, paranoid Ba'athist throwback, watching who came and went in the only remaining large hotel left open. They wore suits from the 1970s and '80s, with wide lapels and pants, smoked constantly, and usually had thick mustaches and quiet stares. I was painfully aware that they could, if half decent at their jobs, look out for my reports, even without video footage of me. An American lawyer I met in Kabul had emailed me the day before. "Just listening to Al Jaz in Kabul and I think you are the mystery gal in Yemen," she wrote. "Hard to cover up that accent!"

I walked past the officers as casually as I could. Once in the area of the protests, Sami and I jumped out of the car and headed toward the crowds. The shooting appeared to be over. People were walking fast between buildings, looking over their shoulders. Occasional cars used as makeshift ambulances honked their horns and careened through the streets. Sami led me into a warehouse just off the street, a wide-open storeroom that people were rushing into and out of. Shouts echoed off the cement walls inside.

I smelled antiseptic and blood as my eyes adjusted to the light. This was a makeshift field hospital, treating those who had just been shot. Injured protesters were too afraid to go to the main hospitals in case they were arrested. Female nurses, volunteering as part of the revolutionary effort, rushed from gurney to gurney in the center of this otherwise bare warehouse. Several skinny men were splayed on their backs, arms out by their sides, while nurses hastily bandaged gunshot wounds to their torsos. Their faces were twisted in agony.

Sami got to work without hesitation. I stood in shock, initially paralyzed by the scene. I had never seen a person who had been shot before. Someone yelled at me to get out of the way as an injured man was being carried in by a group of protesters, rushing and shouting. Gunshots once again ripped through the street outside.

Two men standing next to a bed, their faces stony with anger, looked at me. To my surprise, they began waving me over. These men saw a reporter, and they wanted to speak. I rushed over. "It was Saleh supporters who shot at us," mumbled the man in the bed. His voice pulled me from my paralysis and returned me to the job I had to do.

When we left the scene and found Fuad with the car, he was on edge. He asked Sami and me what we had seen. I could see horror and anxiety in his face in the rearview mirror as we told him. Fuad settled back into the driver's seat with a sigh and brooded.

Sami and I edited the story in my hotel room through the evening, constantly fearful of being discovered by the security officials in the lobby. The gunshots and blood periodically flashed back into my mind. This was deadly serious work. Sami checked the hallway outside my room before I dove under the bedcovers to record my voice-over. At the top of each hour, I went live on the phone. The Al Jazeera news anchor introduced me as "our correspondent we are not naming for security reasons." Anyone passing our room could match the loud female voice (speaking in English) to the one on Al Jazeera's feed.

Sami and I often laughed at our predicament. The internet in my room was too slow to send our video to Doha, so we would head down to the lobby where it was a little faster, sit on sofas near the security suits, and drink tea as casually as possible while waiting for the footage to load.

I ran on coffee and cigarettes and a sense that if I kept moving, I would not have to think about what I was doing and what the risks were. When I did slow down, I sat on the end of my bed and tried, with mixed results, to meditate, aware my mind was walking a tight-rope of paranoia. I was afraid of being arrested. Exhausted, I escaped from my harrowing day of reporting before sleep by watching *Keeping Up with the Kardashians* on the small TV in my hotel room. I slipped under the covers of my bed, exhausted and covered in sweat and stale smoke from my day of reporting, and I was transported to a life in L.A. completely contrary to my current reality.

The mood at Change Square was never quite the same after the shootings. It seemed Saleh would not leave peacefully. People were nervous beyond anything I had seen before: crowds would panic en masse as rumors of advancing gunmen spread through the streets. While out reporting one day, I popped into a small traditional grocery to grab snacks for the team. Outside the store, a soldier fired his gun in the air in anger at a car that got in his way. Hundreds of people rushed away from the gunfire. I felt my heart beat fast and hard in my chest. Sami was filming down the street outside. We had a rough plan for meeting up back at the main square entrance if we lost each other and our phones. I had no idea how to get there now.

Dozens of panicked people rushed into the shop, sending neat stacks of food and dry goods flying. The metal gates of the shop door were slammed shut with a bang so loud it sounded like a gunshot fired near my head. Suddenly the lights went out, and we were all crammed inside, trapped, in pitch-darkness. I could hear the crowds outside shouting, some banging on the metal door. I pulled a lighter from my pocket and with trembling hands flicked it on. The faces around me glowed, men staring fearfully, women clutching their children, terrified that the soldiers were coming back to open fire on them.

Calm soon returned outside, and we were able to leave, but I was frazzled. It was a reminder that at any moment things could spin out of control around me. I was in a crowd, yet completely alone.

Yemen was headed toward war. The country was awash with guns, tribal unity delicately managed and manipulated for decades by Saleh was fraying, and protesters lacked the leadership or institutions to move forward with elections.

"It's a very dangerous time," Fuad told me one day when we were alone in the car. Worry flashed across his normally stoic face. Yemenis like Fuad were fearful the situation was unraveling, as it had in Libya. During all my conversations with Fuad, he never once expressed a political view. He saw these things through a moral lens, steeped in Islam. It was wrong to shoot unarmed protesters, just as it was wrong to try to kill Saleh.

On our last day in Sana'a, Fuad drove me back to Mohammed Saif's home office and I sat with Mohammed under the trees in his garden. We drank sweet tea in glasses and ate butter cookies his wife had made, the birds chirping around us as he pointed out his coffee plants and fruit trees, all encased within the tall walls of his compound. In the Middle East, and especially in the politest Arab countries like Yemen, it is customary to make small talk before discussing business, but our chat on this day felt like more than just a nicety. We needed a refuge from the chaos of everything outside his walls.

Mohammed had built this home with the money he had made as a tourism travel agent. The walls of his office were covered in photographs of travelers from everywhere—all over Europe, Japan, Canada, the United States—riding camels in the desert, hiking in the mountains, visiting historic sites like the seat of the ancient Queen of Sheba in Marib. Mohammed walked around his office, as always in a perfectly pressed suit and tie, showing me old maps and telling me who everyone was in the photos. His office was full of memories fading in the sunlight. No tourists were coming to Yemen now or were likely to come any time soon.

I felt a deep sadness and guilt as he told me about the business he had built, all the people he had connected with. I was free to return to my life just as his was spinning out of control. I may have had very little of a home life, but it was only too plain to me in that moment just how free from chaos and danger it was. This would always be the case, on the road, with my local teammates. I would never know what was really at stake like they would.

Mohammed and I settled the bill for my expenses. At least paying him in dollars could help him keep the lights on, I thought, and vowed to make sure I shared his information with other reporters. We talked vaguely about my work and stared at the floor, careful to avoid the subject of Al Jazeera. When we said our goodbyes, he gripped my hand firmly and smiled.

I was determined not to break my promise to my sister Laura that I would be home for Christmas, for the first time in years. It would be weeks before Al Jazeera's accounting department sorted through my Yemeni receipts and paid me, so I took what was left in my bank account and traveled to London, then got on a bus, then took a ferry over the Irish Sea. I sat on the deck, shivering into my coat, and looked out across the dark waters around me. A part of me held a secret fear. *My assignments are getting more dangerous,* I thought.

Shortly before I left Yemen, I got a call from an executive producer at Al Jazeera in Qatar. "Jane, would you be willing to go to Syria for us? We might have a way to get you in."

9

Homs

I MET MY CONTACTS IN a bar in Beirut. They were young men, activists from Syria tasked with helping the first journalists access the insurrection leading to revolution inside the country. They told me when and where to meet a car the next morning in Beirut's bustling streets. It would take me to the Syrian border.

After a day and night of driving along rural Lebanese roads, avoiding government checkpoints, the men in the car told me to get out and walk with them. A thick fog surrounded us. I followed my hosts across several muddy plowed fields, struggling to keep my balance, my rucksack slung over one shoulder. Inside it was a video camera and the ten thousand dollars Al Jazeera managers had given me in Doha. I was still wearing my flak jacket. It was getting dark now. At one point my foot slipped completely from underneath me and I tumbled into the mud with a cartoonish thump. Everyone quietly laughed, the tension broken for one merciful moment.

A figure stepped out of the darkness, and the first thing I noticed was the outline of a gun. My hosts walking next to me didn't flinch, so I presumed this was a rebel from the Free Syrian Army (FSA). The gunman waved us toward him in silence. Staying low, we crept across laneways and followed a row of poplar trees. We reached a wire fence, which the gunman pulled up so we could creep underneath.

"This is now Syria," someone whispered. We had crossed.

Syria's revolution was sparked with the words *It's your turn next,*

Doctor scrawled on a school wall by teenage boys in the southern city of Daraa in February 2011. Several dozen boys, believed to be between ten and fifteen, had been watching the revolutions spread across the Arab world on TV screens, from Tunisia to Egypt, broadcast live on Al Jazeera Arabic. Emboldened by what they saw, the boys wrote revolutionary slogans one night on the walls of a government building in the small city.

The word *Doctor* was a reference to Syrian president Bashar al-Assad, who had trained as an ophthalmologist. But this wasn't Tunisia or Egypt. This was Syria. The boys were arrested in the middle of the night, handcuffed in front of their parents, and taken away. When they were released weeks later, bloodied and badly beaten by regime torturers, their families gathered in front of the governor's office to protest. The security forces opened fire, killing several people. Daraa, as with much of southern Syria, is a heavily tribal culture dominated by large, strong families. The regime had started a blood feud. Protests swelled in the weeks that followed.

Assad sent in the army's Fourth Division, led by his own brother Maher, to quell the protests. Hundreds were arrested, including more children. Hamza Ali al-Khateeb was thirteen years old when he attended one of the protests and was arrested by security forces. A month later his body was returned to his mother and father. His jaw was smashed, and he was covered in burns, from cigarettes and electric cables. His kneecaps were broken. He had been beaten so badly he was black with bruises. He had one gunshot wound through each of his upper arms. His penis has been severed. Hamza's parents allowed activists to film his body. This footage and photos, evidence of the child's agonizing, tortured final days, spread across the country and wider world. The barbarism was beyond words; only pictures could convey it.

Assad was using torture as a tool to frighten, to get inside the head of anyone who, in the quiet of their homes, was thinking about taking to the streets to call for his removal. The psychological impact of his security forces' actions, the stories of torture that came from the prisons when inmates were deliberately released alive to disperse them, the threats written in wounds on the bodies of those returned to families for burial, reverberated across the country. But it wasn't enough. This time, the anger was even stronger than the fear.

At the border fence, I thanked my escorts and climbed into a car with an unnamed driver. We drove through the winter-weary Syrian countryside of orchards and farmland for half an hour until we reached a remote farmhouse surrounded by an orchard of fruit trees. The only sign of life was woodsmoke from the chimney.

I pushed open the farmhouse door and found dozens of muddy boots in the hallway. The faces of ten men turned toward me as I entered a small adjacent room. They were all young, with stubbly beards, big brown eyes, and smiles. The room was deliciously warm from the woodburning stove in the center, and the smell of cigarette smoke, coffee, and damp clothes drifted around us.

AK-47s hung on the walls above the rebels' heads. But for the presence of a few satellite phones and cell phones charging in the corner, the scene could have been taken straight from the Spanish Civil War, eighty years earlier—bands of young men working in groups across rural areas to rebel against their own repressive government. They beckoned me to come and sit with them.

I was exhausted and hungry. Sweet coffee and cigarettes had sustained me for most of the journey. The rebels noticed me falling asleep and brought a blanket. I drifted off to the sound of their chattering in Arabic and the hiss of wet sticks on the fire.

I woke the next morning to riotous laughter. One broad-chested rebel was attempting to put on my flak jacket as the others fell about in hysterics. These men didn't have any such luxury. To them, my jacket seemed an absurd weight to carry around. The fighters were already ready to go as they tied their boots on for the day at the front door. A blanket a few feet from me stirred, and a bearded face emerged. He must have come in the night and fallen asleep after I arrived. After sleepy hellos he explained he was the commander of this rabble of farmhouse rebels, tasked with holding the immediately surrounding area. It was an impossible mission, and his mood seemed fitting. He would not give me his real name and would not allow me to film him. His only duty here, as he saw it, was to give me a safe place to stay for the night.

He got up and headed outside to the front of the house. I followed him. The men stood around, bouncing to stay warm, having cigarettes and freshly brewed coffee for breakfast. The morning felt grim. A thick gray fog lingered, and I noticed a peculiar lack of birdsong for a rural dawn. Out of the fog, between the fruit trees, figures began appearing—returning rebels who must have been on night duty. They came like ghosts walking toward us through the mist, as though they had already died in the fighting and returned nonetheless to report to their commander. Pulling a smudged notebook from his pocket, the commander called the roll and then rubbed his upper lip. Not everyone had come back.

Fear began to creep into my mind. The rebels were arranging my ride from here to the last stop before Homs city. I wanted to stay here with them and the farmhouse and the fire and the blankets.

It took two more days to get into Homs, 60 kilometers (roughly 37 miles) from the border with Lebanon and the first significant rebel stronghold in Syria. For one stretch of the rural journey, we traveled in a beaten-up car so packed with defected soldiers they had to hang their AK-47s out the window to fit us all in. I climbed in and perched as delicately as I could on the knee of one young defector, red-faced with embarrassment as his comrades laughed and joked. At that point I was thrilled to be careening around the misty countryside with this band of rebels. The feeling didn't last.

Suddenly we came to a slow crawl. The driver had spotted a government military checkpoint up ahead. We did a swift three-point turn in the mud at the middle of the road and sped off in the other direction. I was certain they would spot us and fire on the vehicle. I was coming to understand that the rebels had little real control over anything around here. It was clear that the front lines between the government and these renegade troops were fluid. This assignment already felt more dangerous than I could have imagined.

The rebels chuckled and bantered among themselves when it seemed we were in the clear, beyond sight of the checkpoint. I felt a kind of foreboding in the pit of my stomach. Their readiness to die had a sort of recklessness to it. In Syria, people disappeared all the time.

Of all the brutal dictatorships in the Arab world, Bashar al-Assad's regime was the most extreme—more sadistic even than Colonel Gaddafi's in Libya. Bashar had inherited the presidency from his father, Hafez al-Assad, after his unexpected death in June 2000.

Bashar was not meant to inherit power. That was his older brother Bassel's presumed destiny. A tough young military man, groomed in the image of his father, the thirty-one-year-old Bassel died in a car crash in 1994. The tall, thin Bashar, chinless and lacking in charisma, seemed an unlikely Arab strongman. It turned out he had a dangerous affinity for power. He speaks quietly. This only made him appear all the more sinister as the world learned about his mass torture chambers and vast executions. He is no traditional Arab dictator, like the hulking figure of Saddam Hussein railing against the West, or the flamboyant Gaddafi. Those men were bullies. Bashar is a monster.

While the region's other dictators would fall and flee or be trapped and killed, Bashar would sooner crush the entire country of Syria, drag it into a war that would last over a decade, kill more than half a million people, and displace millions more, than give up his power.

Shortly after the protests began in Syria in 2011, journalists were banned from the country, and the risk of being arrested or killed was high. This story was perfect for a reporter like me: willing, tough, and with mettle just hearty enough to exceed my fear. This was a time in my life when I thought all I could offer the world was my courage. I wanted to do it. Besides, this felt like history happening. In these early days of the Arab Spring, there was still so much hope, and many believed the Arab world's youth were rising up to claim a better future and revolutionize the political landscape of the entire region. I didn't want to miss seeing it up close.

Al Jazeera wanted to send one person alone as a test. A few months earlier they had attempted to send my colleague Dorothy, a print reporter and dual Iranian American passport holder, flying into the airport in Damascus. She was arrested on arrival and deported to Tehran, where she was held in the notorious Evin Prison and interrogated for weeks before her release. Undeterred, Al Jazeera had been in contact with the activists while I was in Yemen, and they had promised a way in for me. A better-known journalist would be at a greater risk. I was perfect for the job. I was instructed to film stand-ups alongside all my reporting and smuggle the footage out with me, broadcasting the stories once I was safely out of the country.

The Assad regime was seizing, torturing, and murdering journalists from everywhere. The risks were enormous. Sending me, a freelancer, was a smart move for Al Jazeera. It gave them a little more deniability if anything were to happen to me. I assured the Al Jazeera executives I was more than comfortable taking on this important work. But I had been confident in the boardrooms of glittering Persian Gulf glass towers. Now I was inside Assad's Syria, alone in the mud and rain and being handed from one group of anti-Assad activists and rebels to another, a human cargo, trying hard to keep moving in order to forget what could happen to me if I got caught.

Homs was still controlled by the Syrian regime, save for the Baba Amr neighborhood, which had risen up against Bashar al-Assad's rule. Government checkpoints attempted to seal off Baba Amr from rebellious rural areas like Qusayr. Smugglers and activists dodged snipers to get in and out. Smuggling reporters in had been going on for only a matter of weeks.

Alone again, I was driven to Qusayr along small roads to keep us from government eyes. On arrival I was ushered into another safe house to meet the lead activist for Baba Amr, known only to me as Nasser, likely not his real name. Mostly bald, in his mid-thirties, and dressed in a sweatsuit, he looked at me with a friendly but doubting face. "You are a lot younger than the journalists we're used to here," he said with a thick British accent. He didn't mean it as a compliment. "We've had people from Sky News here and the BBC," he remarked as we sat down. "They are great reporters. You look very young." He seemed distinctly disappointed that Arab media giant Al Jazeera would send a tiny Irishwoman in her mid-twenties, traveling with no crew and a camera slung over her shoulder. It hurt my pride.

Nasser told me the plan for getting me into Baba Amr: I was to simply drive into Homs and hope for the best. I was horrified, but completely at the mercy of my hosts. All I could do was as I was told. I would spend the night at Nasser's house in Qusayr town and leave the next morning. His shy, smiling wife welcomed me warmly and we ate supper together on the living room floor. I spent a sleepless few hours lying on the floor of their living room until a pickup arrived. I had breakfast with Nasser and his family in silence. Eating hummus, salad, and bread, I felt sick to my stomach with fear.

The driver, who we agreed would not tell me his name in case we were caught and tortured, waited at the front door. Here we will call him Ahmed. As I stepped out on the tiny porch to meet him, Nasser's wife came running after me. Smiling, she threw her arms around my neck and then, leaning back and looking me straight in the eye, finally spoke a few words of English. "You are a hero!" she declared. It took everything inside me not to throw up on my feet. I had never been misunderstood so spectacularly. My fear was all-consuming. I felt trapped and alone inside this corner of a country in crisis, with these strangers. A swelling of tears stuck in my throat before I pushed it away. I walked over to the pickup, got in, slammed the door, and lit a cigarette.

Ahmed and I drove from Qusayr up a tiny laneway until we reached the large beltway that surrounds the city of Homs. He parked just thirty feet from it and went on foot to make sure there weren't any checkpoints that could see us. Qusayr town was largely opposition controlled, with a few gunmen lingering on street corners, but that seemed to end at its outskirts and the main roads were still under the control of the regime. The areas in between would be the riskiest for us to pass through.

When he was satisfied, Ahmed walked back to the car and drove up onto the freeway—gunning to the other side and swinging a left to bring us in line with the moving traffic. His face was deadly serious as he checked his rearview mirror to see if anyone had noticed a vehicle darting onto the highway from the direction of rebel territory. All clear. We were driving down the road, almost like any other married couple of the Syrian Arab Republic. My hair was covered with a headscarf and I had my flak jacket on under my overcoat. I kept my gaze low throughout the terrifying drive. I slowed my breathing as best I could. It was the only thing I had any control over as minutes ticked by slowly. Minutes that could change or end a life forever.

Syrian soldiers dressed in fatigues were waving traffic to the side of the highway at random to check the vehicles and drivers. They seemed to be stopping mostly the larger trucks, but some cars, too. My driver and I did not look at each other or speak throughout the twenty minutes it took to get through the area. Several times a soldier would wave at us to pull over—my heart would beat like it wanted to be out of my body—and the driver would nonchalantly slow until they could see a woman in the car. Then the soldier would signal us to continue.

Finally, we jumped off the road and started slipping through tiny streets deeper in the city. We turned onto a road guarded by a ragtag bunch of rebel fighters. The front line here, it seemed, was being held by about four young men in part sweatsuits, part military fatigues, holding AK-47s. Some rebels, the most recent defectors, wore uniforms, but most wore a mixture of fatigues and civilian sports clothing. It was raining gently now, and as we slowly approached, they were huddled over a barrel burning rubbish. A torn piece of blue tarpaulin had been strung as shelter over part of the barricade, and a few large tires blocked the road. Two of the men came to the driver's car window and waved us through into Syria's first rebel-held neighborhood.

While Daraa city had hosted the country's first protests, Homs was the first city to witness armed and organized insurrection. It came to be known as the home of the Syrian revolution. And it was the Baba Amr neighborhood where it all began. Conservative, poor Sunni Muslims lived there, most opposed to the dictatorship of Bashar al-Assad. Buildings made up of family apartments on each floor were on either side of the small, winding streets. As I arrived, rubble and debris were scattered across the streets. Shelling from tanks into the small stronghold had increased in recent weeks. The rain came down in a soft drizzle from a sad gray sky.

I was taken to the main activists' center for the revolution, in a nondescript concrete apartment building down one of the narrow streets. Around half a dozen activists were in the apartment when I arrived, sitting cross-legged around a tiny living room, leaning over their laptops. Each looked up and smiled and waved as I walked in. I beamed back at them, adrenaline draining from my body and relief rushing in. I had made it. I spotted Nasser and threw my arms around him in a hug, as the other young men—for they were all men—chuckled and teased him. He had traveled into the city on a route he wouldn't reveal.

The activists' headquarters were equipped with a Broadband Global Area Network, or BGAN, link, they bragged. Small portable satellite terminals about the size of a briefcase, BGANs, when working properly on a rooftop or open area, provide a strong internet signal. Journalists have used them for years. When you need to send footage back to home base you can bypass slow hotel internet connections and get a speedy one of your own. But war reporters also knew that many governments and militaries can track BGAN satellite signals and can drop a bomb on the very building from which it was detected. Some journalists in such circumstances tried to take the BGAN to a different area to send footage and then leave immediately. Nasser seemed unconcerned when I asked if they worried about the satellite. The activists' main task was to film the bombardment of the Baba Amr neighborhood as well as any protest rallies taking place. They wanted the rest of the world to know, and help.

With the area surrounded, and only a few international journalists being smuggled in when they could manage it, they had been forced to take the conflict online. Activists were trying to prove beyond a doubt to the international community that civilian areas were being unfairly targeted, and a media war was raging on YouTube. They had a small collection of various items for filming on, from handheld cameras to iPhones. Laptops were passed from one knee to another, sharing footage. The atmosphere had the same balance of camaraderie and competitiveness as any newspaper newsroom I had been in.

In this small flat, a remarkable shift in how wars, rebellions, and insurgencies are fought was underway. This was an early information war. The activists were all volunteers, and clearly driven by a personal commitment to the Syrian revolution. Their tools were simple, but their voices reached the entire world.

Initially I had hoped to stay in Syria at least a week, but having seen the front line held together by a few tires and AK-47s, I knew everyone here was likely to die. They knew it, too. The level of nihilism amongst the activists shocked me. I inwardly winced when Nasser announced, almost proudly, "We are entirely surrounded and expecting the army to come in and raid the neighborhood at any time."

"Don't worry, Jane," one activist whispered later that day as we crouched amidst incoming gunfire. "If you die, I will die with you."

Part of me felt dangerously duped. The activists Al Jazeera producers met with had depicted the rebel stronghold as stronger than this. I had an uneasy feeling that their cause would be given a boost should a Western reporter be killed by government forces raiding the neighborhood. That afternoon I chased after the activists along the edges of the rebel-held area down streets we knew a sniper's bullet could reach. We couldn't avoid driving in full view of the sniper positions the government army had set up all around the restive neighborhood. The crack of incoming bullets sent me sinking deeper into the car seat. I closed my eyes in terrified anticipation. The activists roared with laughter at me. "Welcome to Syria!!" one joked as we drove along in the rain. "It's lovely!"

We were trying to get to the very outskirts of Baba Amr to film regime tanks and positions surrounding it. It was important to be able to show how the Syrian army had surrounded this neighborhood and were bombarding it. Avoiding the notice of the very troops we were trying to film felt like an impossible task. Once we managed to get to the spot we wanted to visit, we would leap out of the car and race into a building or behind a wall for cover. We were well within range of regime bullets now.

One of our first stops was at an abandoned school, now nothing more than the frame of a two-story building pockmarked by shelling and bullets. The rubble crunched loudly underfoot. The team of three activist cameramen raced up the stairs, with me running along behind. On the stairway was a rebel sniper peering through a jagged hole in the wall. He fired his gun as I scrambled past him. The noise was deafening. My heart raced and I panted for breath. For the first time in days my mind was clear and focused: follow the others, stay low, keep filming. When we reached the roof, the sound of incoming tank shells was increasing. The rebel soldiers seemed to be firing back with small arms. One wall on the side of the roof of the building facing the army onslaught was still standing. A shell would blast through it as if it were a cobweb. But the media activists I was with raced up to the wall, pressed their faces against it, and positioned their cameras in any small holes that had been blown through. They peered through at the government army, the enemy, focusing their camera sights on tank positions. All just to film the scene. The crazy bravery of this rabble of cameramen shamed me into creeping forward and filming the very same way.

I gave my camera to Nasser to hold and spoke into the lens with the viewfinder turned around to make sure I was framed correctly. In the piece caught on-camera I'm wearing a huge black coat over a flak jacket and a red headscarf. I look startled. *It will have to do,* I thought.

I couldn't shake the feeling that I was being watched. *The regime must know,* I told myself. People in the neighborhood saw me, the activists all knew. The feeling of something or someone behind me stayed with me each moment I was in Syria. It seemed impossible to ignore the reality that getting out of there would be even riskier than getting in, given the likelihood they—the monsters—would know of my presence. In reality, you cannot trust everyone in war zones, not even those closest to you. I worried about the activists' BGAN. If I couldn't go live on air for my own safety, I shouldn't linger around their satellite signal, either.

Still, I was grateful for the internet when I managed to skype Ben on my second day inside. His voice coming through my laptop as I crouched over it in the activists' apartment left me weak with relief. "It's so much worse here than we thought," I told him, steadying my voice as best I could. "Do you think I am letting everyone down if I leave after a few days rather than a full week?"

"Get what you can and get out alive," he replied calmly. "You have done incredible work already."

I was equally scared of not doing a good job. This assignment was a privilege, and I was mindful every moment of the precious spot I had taken, the risks the activists had taken to get me in, and the several senior correspondents in the newsroom, those I looked upon with awe, who had wanted the assignment. I knew I was there because I was disposable and brave—my two greatest assets so far at this point in my career. This story was so much bigger than me and my career ambitions. I was at the center of something enormous, with millions of lives at stake.

I could feel it physically. During times of extreme danger, fear left a cold, metallic taste in my mouth, but shame would push me forward when I stopped and the activists rushed across a road within a sniper's sights. The line between cowardice and carelessness was too blurry. It was like I was running through a storm.

Down the street from the activists' media center was a field hospital. The makeshift facility made for grim filming. In a ground-floor apartment, walls had been knocked in and replaced with hospital dividing screens. A young female nurse was treating civilians and fighters for shrapnel and bullet wounds. "They come here, but we have only simple medical equipment," she told me, covering her face with a scarf to hide her identity. No one from this neighborhood would dare present themselves at a government hospital.

At a nearby home, I discovered why. The young man's mother's sobs filled their small apartment. She gasped for breath between wails. Her family gathered around her as she wept, trying to comfort her. A small photograph of her son was clutched between her index and forefingers as she rocked back and forth in a vain attempt to sooth her grief. He was twenty-eight years old. The family told me he had gone out to buy cooking gas and never returned. They heard from others that he had been shot in the leg and taken to a government hospital. Days before I had arrived, they were told to come and collect his body, which was horribly mutilated, showing signs of torture. With tears running down her cheeks, Ahmed's mother cursed Syria's president. "I hope Bashar al-Assad sees all his children slaughtered to pieces," she cried.

The undertaker was busy in Baba Amr. The activists took me to see him at work, in the rooms where bodies were cleaned and swathed in white shrouds. In the courtyard outside, scraps of flat Arabic bread sat on old rugs, drying in the sun. People were starting to fear hunger. It was a prescient, intuitive kind of fear. As the war raged several years later, rebellious neighborhoods would be surrounded and starved into a cease-fire by government troops. Once inside, I waited for my eyes to adjust to the darkness before I saw three men of fighting age lay in shrouds, neatly placed on the floor. As is customary, they had thick wads of cotton wool in their mouths, leaving their jaws open wide in astonishment. Their faces looked like silent screams.

Mosques broadcast the need for blood types from their minarets between their usual calls to prayer. When a patient was taken to the field hospital in need of blood, calls asking people to donate blood would go out over the loudspeakers. So off we would race to the hospital again. We developed a routine: from the front line to the hospital, to the undertaker, to the bakeries, to grieving mothers' living rooms.

If there was a thrill to any of this, it was the warm contentedness of arriving back at headquarters to find that all of us had made it out unscathed. I was greeted by a feast of rice, kibbeh (Syrian meatballs covered in bulgur wheat), hummus, and fresh bread laid out on the floor. There was little food to be had in Baba Amr, but this was still the Arab world, and I was their guest. Tradition dictated that any visitor be given a meal no matter the circumstances.

After dinner, Nasser said I must sleep in the apartment down the street with women who would host me. "No way," I protested. "If there is going to be a raid by government troops, I want to be in here with you guys." Only these guys knew the way out. The activists grumbled for a few minutes about sleeping with a lone woman in the apartment. I ignored them, dragged my small bag of belongings, camera, and flak jacket into the room next door, lay down on the carpet, and fell asleep instantly.

The next day, my hosts escorted me to an abandoned building to meet rebel commanders. I found a group of men mostly in plain clothes, smart suits with woolen overcoats and trimmed beards, and a few in military fatigues, sitting in a circle muttering. I asked one commander off-camera what the Free Syrian Army wanted if they did overthrow the Assad government, in terms of a power structure in Syria. "Justice" was his one-word answer.

Another commander had defected from Assad's forces only weeks before. With striking blue eyes and a short beard, he looked stressed. The rebels needed NATO to declare a no-fly zone, he explained, so that others like him would be moved to join the revolution. Only when the Assad regime could not use the skies would his troops feel the balance had truly tipped in favor of the revolution.

The year before, as the Libyan civil war escalated, NATO forces had imposed a no-fly zone, grounding Muammar Gaddafi's air forces and ruling out aerial attacks on Libyan civilians. The measure was credited with winning the battle for the Libyan rebels and enabling Gaddafi's fall. Now Syria's rebels demanded the same support, marking the beginning of the end for Bashar al-Assad.

But the White House and the UN were more cautious with Syria.

Those advocating Western noninterference would point to Libya's descent into fractious civil war, while hawks pushing for interference would criticize Obama for inaction. Back at the activists' apartment, everyone settled on the floor around the tiny TV to catch updates on the UN Security Council debates over a resolution to call for a cease-fire in Syria by the Assad regime. I looked around the room at the hopeful faces and knew they would never get the resolution passed. Russia and China would veto it. In the end, their only hope would be action by the Obama White House.

I also knew I needed to get out. In the days since I had sneaked into Baba Amr, the perimeter formed by the government troops had tightened. An assault on the area was close, and the rebels knew they would have trouble escaping themselves when it came. I tried to keep my nerves in check and arranged for the driver who had smuggled me into Homs to take me back out. As I prepared to leave, the activists called me little sister and told me I was very brave. Part of me felt ashamed for leaving. I couldn't quite meet their eyes. People seemed to have a habit of telling me I was very brave just when my courage was failing me. My hands were shaking as I left the small concrete apartment building and climbed into the truck.

The driver told me we would be in Lebanon in an hour and a half. We left shortly after lunchtime. Three hours later we were still bouncing down mud tracks in fields. It was pitch-dark outside. Neither of us spoke, except for every fifteen minutes when I would nervously ask in Arabic, "Are we close? How much longer?" Eventually a thin line of twinkling lights appeared on the horizon. "Lebanon," said the driver.

When I had the nerve to glance left at his face, I noticed it was becoming increasingly lined and hardened along the journey. He had leaned over the steering wheel, shoving his face closer to the glass, searching for possible signs of danger. Now he drove with the headlights off so we could avoid being spotted. I looked down at my phone. No signal out here. If I could just hold on until those lights in the distance were upon us, then we are free.

Finally, through the dark we could see the small, abandoned

farmyard where we were scheduled to meet our Lebanese contacts, who would escort me to Beirut. We had made it. Rain was falling on the windscreen and the mud became thicker as we slowly bounced toward the gray buildings.

Suddenly two men with guns appeared from behind bushes. They seemed huge as they moved toward us in slow motion. Panic poured through me. We had been spotted. Surely they were Assad's secret police. The driver fell silent, stopped the car, and wound down the window as they approached. I sat frozen in the seat next to him, my head down. I thought of my camera and footage inside my rucksack at my feet.

The driver was told to get out of the car. He climbed out and offered the men cigarettes. They declined. This seemed like confirmation we were going to be arrested. I sat there in the passenger seat and stared at the buildings ahead of me, knowing I was a short dash—maybe a hundred yards—from the border. My thoughts were clear and sharp. I had a decision to make. I could make a run for it. But then Ahmed would instantly be arrested and probably tortured and killed. I remembered my producer's instruction back in Doha: "If they catch you, make sure you demand to be taken to a commanding officer. Tell them you are a foreign journalist."

No phone signal, either, so no way to say goodbye to Ben. I quickly thought of those in my life who would struggle most with the news of my disappearance and death. I didn't feel panic anymore. This was the first and only time in my career since that I felt quite certain I would die. I accepted the fact quickly. I was not filled with self-pity or anger. I felt sadness. *Laura will never get over this,* I thought. *Lesley will be devastated; she's too fragile for this.* For Ben, this would be a wound that would never really heal. I felt an ache in my heart at the thought of how this would stay with them for the rest of their lives.

The driver opened the car door and reached over to pretend to be getting something out of the glove box, whispering to me to get out and say nothing. With shaking hands, I opened the vehicle door and clambered out into the mud and rain. It was a miserable night of dampness and shadows. *A shitty fucking night to die,* I thought. He walked to the front of the truck and I joined him. My rucksack swung over my shoulder. The two gunmen remained by the car as the driver reached down and took my hand and started walking toward the farmhouse. I walked next to him in silence, clutching his hand tightly and struggling to stay on my feet in the mud. My heart was thumping against my chest. I had no idea what was happening but was prepared to be shot in the back. I braced for a gun's crack with every step that I took. The shot never came. We reached the house and walked behind it and into freedom. I looked up at the driver, almost afraid to ask what happened. His nose was bleeding from the stress. Red streaks raced down his chin as he turned his face upward, shut his eyes, and mouthed a prayer.

It seemed the gunmen had not noticed that I was a foreigner and that he was a driver for the opposition. They instead appeared interested only in stealing the truck. We had been saved. Soon I was bumping down the road back to Beirut, covered in drying mud up to my thighs, silent with disbelief. Fear rang through my body like a silent alarm. And as I left Syria, the fear didn't lessen.

10

A Killing

I COULDN'T SLEEP. SYRIAN AGENTS could be in my room. I turned the light out, yanked the covers up over my exhausted body, and closed my eyes. My head was full of racing thoughts. Throwing the covers off, I climbed out of bed and turned the light back on. I could hear my heart beating fast. I tiptoed to the wardrobe of the hotel room—nothing inside, just the usual safe, bathrobe, and empty hangers. I had a creeping feeling someone was in the bathroom. Pushing open the door and turning on the light, I squinted and blinked into the bright light. Nothing but white tiles, a porcelain bathtub, and my reflection in the mirror. My face was white, too, wide-eyed and terrified.

I called Ben at home in London. "I'm not okay," I said. "I need to get away for a while. Can you meet me in Istanbul?"

When I made it back from Syria, I walked into the Al Jazeera newsroom in Doha and was heralded a hero. People I had never met smiled and nodded at me in hallways, turning to look back once they passed me. Others glanced up from their desks and whispered to one another. Producers vied to work on the edits of my stories and anchors vied to have me on their shows, shaking my hand and asking if I needed anything at all, anything, maybe a coffee? Someone get her a coffee!

Here I was, belonging, leading the network's coverage on the biggest story of the year. We had scooped CNN International and the

BBC, our main rivals, and had proven to other networks nervous about sending teams into Syria that it was possible.

The UN Security Council was finally voting on the resolution to call for a cease-fire. This was the most crucial time for diplomats, politicians, and the public to get some idea of what was going on inside Syria. I watched on one of the dozens of TV screens attached to desks across the huge open-plan newsroom and studio as Syria's ambassador to the UN, Bashar Jaafari, called the rebels and activists "terrorists." The day I was first on set, hair and makeup done up for studio reporting, the Security Council resolution failed to pass, after a veto from China and Russia. Two weeks later the UN's General Assembly passed a resolution calling for a cease-fire by the Assad government, but with no real implementation powers, the resolution had no teeth. The Syrian uprising was on its own.

A producer and I edited my footage and interviews into three stories, focusing on life inside Baba Amr, the activists' allegations of torture by Assad's regime, and the activists themselves. I spent hours in edit suites putting together the pieces, insistent that we profile the Syrian activists. These were some of the world's first citizen journalists documenting war and rebellion. They put out videos of themselves all over YouTube, but no one had profiled them in person as they worked. Their work would democratize journalism, the use of social media, and the coverage of major events around the world. I knew they were the heroes of the story, these brave, wild young men. Employing the video images and voice-overs and news headlines, I wanted to send them a nod, and from deep in my heart, an apology, for not being as brave as they were.

People were treating me like a star. This moment was what I had always wanted. But I felt like a fraud. Staring at my reflection in the mirror as a staffer blew out my hair, I was haunted by questions. If I had stayed longer, perhaps done more stories, would it have made a difference to the UN vote? Did the activists, polite and friendly as I hugged them goodbye at their door, deep down wish someone else had come? Did I take this assignment for my career or as a way to tell this story? Maybe it was just vanity and foolhardiness that sent me into Syria. What if I was not the right person? What if a better, braver reporter had gone in and stayed longer?

All the while, I continued to feel fear physically. In the frantic swirl of edits, hair and makeup, on-set appearances, and meetings with management, I vibrated with fear. I had yet to come down from the adrenaline, and I knew that after several days, this was not normal. *PTSD is flashbacks, psychosis,* I thought. *This is not that.*

I perched on a desk in an unused meeting room, and easing my sore feet out of high heels, I dialed the number for Al Jazeera's tele-therapist service. "Do you feel suicidal at all?" chirped a female voice on the other end. "No, I don't," I answered. "I am not really getting much sleep." She told me to rest up and call back if it didn't go away. Even in 2012, the thin line between *fine* and *suicidal* in front-line journalists was not something news organizations were ready to contend with.

One senior manager offered a cautionary note: "I wouldn't want to alarm you, Jane, but it might be a good idea to alter your routine a little; it's always wise to get in the car at a different time each day, you know." Would I ever feel safe again?

While I was in the back of a taxi returning to my hotel that night, my gaze darted around at the cars surrounding me. Was someone looking at me? Do those men look like Syrians? For a few moments, I was back in the truck in Syria, trundling over the dirt roads in the night, trying to reach Lebanon. Gripped with paranoia, I checked the rearview mirror again and again. As soon as I was finished editing in Doha, I flew to Istanbul. I bought the British *Sunday Times* in the airport and saw a double-page dispatch from Homs by Marie Colvin, their senior reporter. She must have been smuggled in by Nasser, I thought, with the same group of activists, the next journalist in after I left. She described women and children trapped, homes smashed by the incoming shelling, the same desperate field hospital I had stood in days earlier.

Ben and I walked along Istanbul's cobbled streets, watching the pigeons fly over the domed rooftops of its ancient mosques. It was cold and damp and free of tourists in February, leaving empty restaurants and cafés filled with bored waiters. The stunning city center felt like a movie set between scenes, waiting for the actors to emerge. With the place to ourselves, we sat huddled in our coats in a café on a beautiful old street. Over many glasses of sweet, strong Turkish tea I told Ben about every moment of the trip. It felt like a confession. I realized while I was going on that fear had never followed me out of a war zone like this. At twenty-seven, I wasn't aware that not all fear was simply to be overcome.

Ben held my hand and listened. I walked around the city, window-shopping for carpets and petting Istanbul's army of stray dogs and cats, and began to feel like myself again. I pulled my boots off and entered the famous Blue Mosque, built in the seventeenth century. Under a spectacular domed roof, it was decorated inside with an ocean of delicate blue tiles and lit with low-hanging chandeliers. I looked up at the ceiling and my heart swelled with gratitude and relief that I was alive.

I was also grateful to have Ben at my side. His presence in my life was a loving, supportive one, albeit held at a very long distance. We didn't have a life together. I ran decisions by him, coveted his council, and opened up when I doubted myself. Ben was kind and patient. His love felt uncomplicated and nonjudgmental. It made me feel less alone.

Later that evening, at our little hotel, Ben was taking a shower before we headed out to dinner. I sat at the bedroom's desk on my laptop, following Twitter updates from Syria. The news had broken online that Marie Colvin had been killed. She had died when government shelling made a direct hit on the activists' apartment in Baba Amr in Homs, destroying the entire floor. I stared at the screen in disbelief. Were any of the activists killed? I felt a growing panic and confusion. Marie Colvin was a well-known veteran reporter. She was fearless and invincible. The eye patch she wore after losing an eye covering a government crackdown on the Tamil Tiger rebels in Sri Lanka proved it.

I read on. After I had left Syria, Marie was next to be smuggled in by the activists. They brought her in with a CNN team through a large underground water drainage tunnel to avoid government checkpoints around Baba Amr. Marie had stayed on after the CNN team left, continuing to do TV and radio interviews for British and American broadcasters as the crackdown on Baba Amr intensified. She had used Nasser's internet, provided through the BGAN. The regime must have used the BGAN signal to locate the office she was working from with the activists, I thought. As I tried to focus on the words swimming in front of me on my computer, the sharp ring of a Skype call made me jump. It was Nasser, calling from Baba Amr.

"They hit the building," he said, sounding shocked and confused. "I don't know what to do. I cannot believe I got an internet signal here. It's all gone."

"Tell me what to do, Nasser. Tell me how to help you!" I pleaded. A fine rain fell on the windowpane in front of me.

"I have Marie's body." His voice started to crack. "I don't know what to do. Can you call *The Times*?" He started to cry. "I always thought of you as a little sister, Jane. You know that?"

"I'm so, so sorry," I said several times over, at a loss for better words, as he sniffed away tears. After I hung up, I called *The Times* of London, getting through to their foreign desk and alerting them to turn on Skype and speak with Nasser. Still reeling, I hung up and stared out the window at a gray night in Istanbul.

I wondered why Nasser had called me in that moment of panic. It's possible my number was the first on his Skype call list from the week before. A selfish part of me wondered whether I came to mind also because he, too, felt awkward about my decision to leave earlier than I'd planned. I had thought I was a failure because of how afraid I had been in Syria. That feeling in my gut I had mistaken as weakness was a survival instinct I hadn't understood.

I was never able to get in touch with Nasser after that call and do not know if he survived the war.

Six years later, I was reading the news in my home office in Beirut, the Mediterranean sun pouring in through balcony doors, when a story popped up about the trial against the Syrian regime for the murder of

Doing homework at the kitchen table in the early 1990s.

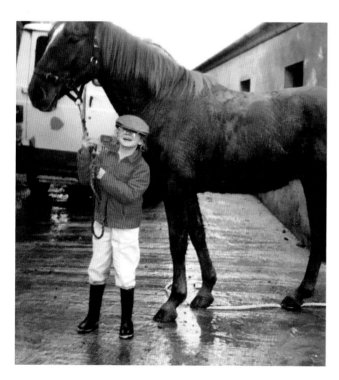

On the farm in Markethill, Northern Ireland.

All images are courtesy of the author unless otherwise noted.

Hiking in the mountains of northern Yemen in 2008. Between Arabic classes, I went on weekend trips into rural, ancient villages perched on mountaintops at some of the highest altitudes in the Middle East.

CNN's new camel correspondent, posing for a picture at a camel beauty contest in the desert outside Abu Dhabi, UAE, in 2010. Shortly after my first on-air appearance for CNN, reporting from Yemen, I was desperate for another assignment.

Embedded with African Union (AU) forces in the second Battle for Mogadishu, 2010. I was one of the first TV reporters ever to embed with the AU troops. The soldiers brought me to front-line positions to capture intense battles as they, alongside Somali fighters, pushed the militant terror group Al-Shabaab from the city. It was my first time near active combat.

Filming at the notorious K4 Junction in Mogadishu, a flashpoint between AU peacekeeping forces and the Al-Shabaab militants. I worked alone on these embeds, and learning on the job, filming with a borrowed Sony Z1 camera. *Courtesy of the UN*

On assignment for CNN in June 2011, filming displaced people on the soon-to-be border between Sudan and South Sudan. These children were taking shelter in the schoolhouse of a nearby village and were mesmerized by the viewfinder on my camera, through which they could see what I was filming. *Pete Muller*

The United Nations was conducting food drops in Abyie to those who had fled the fighting. Thousands of people had arrived with nothing but their children and the clothes they were wearing.

Pete Muller

Sana'a, Yemen, December 2011. Protests had erupted as the Arab Spring had reached Yemen. At one of the largest Friday protests, a massive Yemeni flag was unfurled over the crowd. Dictator Ali Abdullah Saleh's regime had banned Al Jazeera staffers from the country, so the network concealed my identity on air.

Traveling through the mountains in northern Yemen, where coffee, grains, vegetables, and qat, the local, chewable (mildly narcotic) leaves grew in ancient terraces. After all my years of travel, Yemen remains one of the most beautiful places on earth to me.

Cairo, Egypt, August 14, 2013. A mosque served as a makeshift morgue for slain protesters. Hours earlier, they had been staging a sit-in for the reinstatement of President Morsi when they were shot by Egyptian security forces. That day remains one of the most shocking in my life.

A snowy Kabul military airport in the winter of 2013. The Hindu Kush mountains surrounding the Afghan city provide a spectacular backdrop on clear days.

Going live on location in northern Afghanistan for Al Jazeera English, October 2013.

Celebrating my twenty-ninth birthday in the garden at the Gandamack Lodge with Qais, Abdullah, Nadir, and other colleagues. Afghanistan was the first place I had a close-knit team, and they came to feel like family.

Traveling through rural Baghlan province, Afghanistan 2014. I snapped this picture from our car as we drove behind Afghan security forces in U.S.-made Humvees.

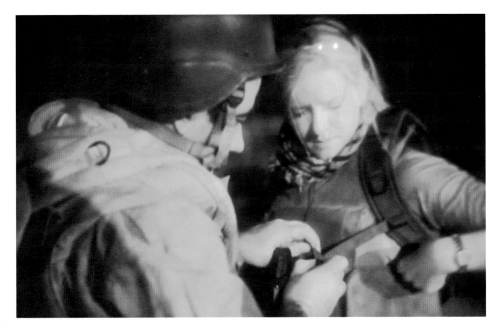

Qais helps me with my gear as we prepare to board a chopper on embed with Afghan special forces.

Reporting live from Gaza in 2014 for Al Jazeera English. Three Israeli students were kidnapped and murdered by Hamas fighters in the West Bank earlier that summer, sparking months of violence. After Hamas rocket fire from Gaza into Israel, Israeli strikes on the Gaza Strip intensified, killing more than 2,000 Palestinians and injuring 10,000. *Wissam Nassar*

Talking to families sheltering in United Nations–run schools in Gaza during the war of 2014. Coordinates of the schools were provided to the Israeli military and declared safe zones, so families camped out in them for weeks hoping to find shelter and safety.
Karim Haddad

One of my first reporting trips for *PBS NewsHour* took me to Iraq as it prepared to escalate its war with ISIS in September 2016. Here, I visit Kurdish positions north of Mosul city on the edge of Iraqi territory, with ISIS positions in the distance.

Major Ziad Al Ghobary guides a sniper at a front-line position in Mosul in November 2016. Iraqi forces were pushing ISIS from the city, with help from a U.S.-led coalition.

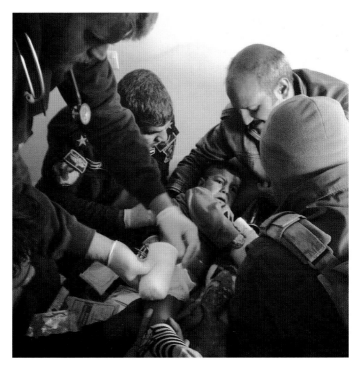

American Marine veteran and volunteer Pete Reed bandages five-year-old Karam at a makeshift front-line medical center in Mosul, December 2016. Pete and his friend Derek (*far right*) traveled to Iraq to join the fight against ISIS, and they quickly learned the Iraqis didn't need fighters but medics. They set up a triage center close to the front line in Mosul, saving countless lives.

Back in Mosul in January 2017, the city was carved in two, between ISIS-controlled areas and the Iraqi military. On the front, crossing streets meant running fast to avoid snipers.
Nish Nalbandian

Talking to kids who live a few streets back from front-line positions in Mosul in January 2017. Most of them had lived under ISIS rule for years. *Nish Nalbandian*

The Old City of Mosul, on the west bank of the Tigris River, where ISIS militants retreated. An untold number of civilians, many hiding in basements or being used as human shields by the terror group, were killed.

Adiba Qasim in her home village in the Yazidi homeland of Sinjar, western Iraq, December 2017. Adiba worked with us as a fixer and translator, helping us talk to women within the community who had escaped or returned from ISIS captivity, many of them having experienced horrific trauma.

Graffiti on a wall in Hodeidah, Yemen, in December 2018. Iran-allied Houthi rebels controlled the city, and anti-U.S., anti-Saudi propaganda proliferated. Here, then President Donald Trump milks the Saudi king for dollars.

Driving out of Kabul, south toward Taliban territory in November 2019. I wore a burka to get through government intelligence and military checkpoints and into Taliban-controlled areas.

In Somalia in early 2018, visiting a female-led African Union tank battalion outside Mogadishu.

The Taliban's red units, their version of special forces, in Wardak province, November 2019. These men were my escorts for the day and were charged with my safety. Grooming was important to them. Before I took this picture, the man with the red bandana across his forehead pulled a small, pink pocket mirror and matching comb out of his fatigues and brushed his hair.

While in Wardak, I met with the Taliban's commander of the area and his closest fighters. They arrived in a humble car flanked by motorcycles, bouncing along in the mud, as heavy fighting roared beyond the trees.

Preparing to head out with Afghan security forces outside Kabul in January 2021. Taliban gains threatened the city's security, and the Afghan forces were under pressure to show they could secure Kabul city. Still, areas just outside the city were so dangerous now that full body armor and Humvees with gunners were necessary to visit checkpoints.

With Ahmad Massoud, son of famed Tajik mujahideen commander Ahmad Shah Massoud, in the Panjshir Valley, June 2021. He told me he was training his forces to fight like guerrillas, not an army, as Afghanistan's Western allies had done, and that's why they were the only ones who could face the Taliban. *Roya Heydari*

Interviewing new recruits to local militia forces in the Panjshir Valley of northern Afghanistan in June 2021. The young recruits were green and thin, struggling to march in formation. Many of them were young farmers' sons and carried old hunting rifles.

"AUS, WE HAVE VISA." As Kabul fell to the Taliban in August 2021, thousands of desperate Afghans swarmed the airport. Many of them had worked with the U.S. and its allies on the battlefield or in development projects. Systems for checking and processing visas for those who had them collapsed in the chaos, and they faced a desperate scramble to get inside the airport compound.

August 22, 2021, a British paratrooper watches as Afghans plead for access to the Kabul airport several days after the city fell to the Taliban. The cement ditch in front of him was where many of the Afghan victims of the ISIS suicide blast were killed four days later.

Onboard the U.S. military evacuation flight from Kabul to Doha, Qatar, on August 25, 2021. These huge C-17s were flying packed with Afghans sitting on the metal floor, clinging to one another. They were not allowed to bring any luggage at all to their new lives, just a small purse for paperwork. Small mountains of luggage lay abandoned in piles at the airport behind them. They flew out of Afghanistan with nothing but each other, most bound for the U.S. eventually.

The Baron Eight, the few reporters who remained at Kabul airport throughout the evacuations, take a picture before we leave for good. *Left to right:* me, Kim Sengupta from the British newspaper *The Independent,* Eric O'Connor, Simi Jan from Danish TV2, Dominique van Heerden, Stuart Ramsay, Martin Vowles, and Toby Nash—all of British Sky News.

Marie Colvin. In 2016 Marie's sister Cathleen Colvin and other family members had filed a suit in the U.S. District Court for the District of Columbia, which included a trove of leaked documents and eyewitness accounts from Syrian regime defectors. The most famous of them, known as Ulysses, confirmed that Assad's regime monitored broadcasts coming out of the Baba Amr media center and worked to locate their sources. "Tracking down these journalists became a top priority," he said.

"Senior military and intelligence officials were overseeing a campaign to surveil, target, and kill journalists in Homs," Ulysses testified. "This campaign resulted in the assassination of Marie Colvin by Syrian government forces."

The New York Times report that day read: "One document shows how military and security forces intercepted communications between journalists and the activists. Intelligence officers passed on information about a journalist for Al Jazeera to a military special forces unit with the instruction 'Take the necessary measures.'"

I would never ignore my instincts again.

The apartment was high up in one of the towers in Dubai's marina district. Sparkling waters lapped between the buildings, and boats were moored in the yacht club across the way. The moment I stepped into the apartment, I knew I would take it. The smell of the wood floors mixed with the sunlight pouring in through all that glass made me smile. It was beautiful. *Surely Ben will love it,* I told myself, leaning over the balcony in the early summer heat.

For the first time in my TV career I was making good money, so I could afford to rent this beautiful space. *I'll do anything to make this work,* I thought. *I'll create a home so lovely Ben will adore it here. He'll hardly even think about London.*

I treated making this home for us as a life-or-death ordeal. I rushed to the real estate agent clutching fat brown envelopes from the bank, afraid that everything could slip away at the last minute. A strange, subtle sense of fragility and fear hung in the air as I hunted for furniture. I created picture boards of color schemes and sofas and beds and soft furnishings. My laptop, usually full of articles and TV scripts, was now overflowing with images of bed throws and crockery and dining chairs and matching napkins. The things nice, normal people have in their homes. *I'll have a normal, happy life,* I decided. Between my assignments, of course.

When Ben first arrived, we were delirious with joy. I made green curry, his favorite dish, and as the furniture had yet to arrive, we ate sitting on the wooden floor, chuckling at our little dinner picnic in such a luxurious setting. The city's lights below sparkled with such promise. I stared out the massive wall of glass. Ben hung back.

"Come on over, darling," I called over my shoulder. "The view is incredible."

"I don't really like heights," he replied, his voice a little flat. "I'm sure I'll get used to it, but just give me some time."

I had no idea Ben was afraid of heights. He would adjust, I thought. He would embrace the newness just like I had when I first arrived. Then, as though on cue, my phone rang.

Al Jazeera needed a correspondent in Jerusalem as soon as possible. A planning editor from the headquarters in Doha asked if I was available to go first thing in the morning for a week, maybe more. Some of the worst violence in a decade had broken out in the Old City and the occupied West Bank between Palestinians and the Israeli Defense Forces. Hundreds of civilians had been injured in clashes. Palestinian leaders were pushing for prisoner releases from Israeli jails and a halt to the ongoing expansion in the West Bank. Tensions were already high due to an uptick in Hamas rocket fire from Gaza into Israel and ongoing evictions of Palestinians from homes claimed by Israeli settlers. President Obama had signaled earlier in 2013 that the White House wanted to reignite U.S.-sponsored peace prospects. Secretary of State John Kerry was flying in and out regularly, shuttling between both sides. There was much at stake.

"Absolutely," I said down the phone. "I'll go." I balanced my phone on my shoulder as I opened my laptop to check for emails I had missed during dinner. "How do I get there?"

The United Arab Emirates did not formally recognize Israel at the time because of its occupation of the West Bank, and direct flights there were banned. In thrilled autopilot, I worked through the logistics on the phone and searched around in bags and boxes for my passport. To be sent to Jerusalem when serious news was developing was a step up for me. Al Jazeera was not choosing me for my disposability this time. Of all the many other journalists they could have sent, they wanted me.

Ben seemed disappointed as we said our hurried goodbyes the next morning. I was too focused on the work ahead to read into his response and too inexperienced at creating any form of balance between my work and personal life to understand the significance. The truth is, before now I had never had a personal life to balance. Days later, I woke in my room at Jerusalem's American Colony Hotel ready for a morning of live reporting.

I paused my preparations for the day to quickly check my emails and saw a message from Ben, sent at 1:50 a.m.: "I really want to talk to you. Please call me." Then at 2:00 a.m.: "I really need you. I can't do this anymore. Everything here in the flat is fucked and I'm lonely, bored, and broke. I really need your help."

My heart dropped. I reached for my phone. No missed calls. The UAE doesn't allow phone calls from its territory to Israel or occupied Palestine. Ben couldn't get through. Barefoot in my bathrobe I leaned over the room's writing desk and struggled to pull my Israeli SIM card out of my old Nokia phone and insert my Dubai one. *I can't do this anymore,* rattled around in my head.

When I finally managed to get the phone to work, Ben explained that the air conditioning unit in the living room was not working and the stove top would not turn on. He wanted me to come home or he was going to move back to London. I worked to calm him down. A knot of panic gathered in my chest. My driver would be here in half an hour to drive me to the bureau. I pleaded for Ben to calm down and assured him I'd call the landlady to make the repairs. Disheveled and without having read the morning's updates on the conflict, I swayed around Jerusalem's winding roads in the back of a car, on the phone to my landlady and taking instructions down in my reporter's notepad about how to reset the stove top.

Ben calmed down and apologized. He sounded embarrassed. I was so relieved he wasn't gone that I assured him everything was fine. I was the one who had left immediately after he arrived. I was the one who should be apologizing, right? *Please don't leave me,* I thought. Another part of me stung. He had threatened to leave if I didn't come home. That thought hung in the air.

By the time I returned from Jerusalem, Ben had gone on assignment himself. I dropped my rucksack on the floor and looked out over the city. In a deeper, quiet part of me, I was relieved Ben was gone. I poured myself a glass of wine and walked out to the balcony for a cigarette.

I had thought I could have it both ways—my life on the road and a happy partner at home. I was stunned by Ben's resentment at my travel. I couldn't recognize how much he was struggling to cope with this new life. We never talked about it. I felt as though I was forbidden to strive for the only thing I had ever dreamed of, as though I was selfish for wanting important assignments. Succeeding in one part of my life meant failing in another. I wanted so much to have a real, loving relationship, but it seemed to come at a cost. By now I knew what men, especially older, more romantic ones, thought when they looked at young female war reporters. I could see it in their mesmerized faces. They love the idea, but not the reality.

I felt misunderstood. Anyone who would ask me to stop traveling, working, and reporting couldn't possibly know me. I had a sinking feeling that I had not found my person. That maybe they don't exist.

I lit another cigarette, stared at the traffic below, and thought about my sisters. I couldn't talk about any of this with them. But I desperately craved a closer relationship, wanted to be able to turn to them, especially at times like these. The summer before, I'd stood on the rocky beach outside Fanny's cottage on a rare sunny day and wept as I watched her ashes being scattered from a small rowboat out in the bay. I wished more than anything that I was sitting by the fire with her right then. That sinking feeling followed me around after Ben returned from assignment. I covered it up with new furniture and the novelty of long, leisurely breakfasts.

I had stumbled out of Syria nearly eighteen months ago and had barely stopped moving since then. Al Jazeera management were delighted with me. I rushed from protests in Jordan to the humanitarian crisis in Yemen and the trials of war criminals in Bangladesh. I spent Christmas Eve 2012 reporting live from the square outside the Church of the Nativity in Bethlehem. It was exhilarating.

Yet I felt far from secure. I heaped pressure on myself. There was no room to become complacent, no reason to presume Al Jazeera would continue to send me to major stories. The head of Al Jazeera English, Salah Negm, had always had a Machiavellian approach to running a news organization. After my triumph in Syria, Salah had called me into his office, congratulated me, and said with a sly smile, "Jane, we want to make you the face of our coverage of Syria." A few hours later, I sat at a desk in the open-plan newsroom, as a much more senior correspondent emerged beaming from Salah's office. "Salah wants me to be the face of the Syria coverage," he told a colleague, as I sat nearby.

An email arrived from Al Jazeera's executive producer for South Asia asking if we could talk. They wanted me to head to Afghanistan and work out of the Kabul bureau for a while. For the next few months, I would spend six weeks reporting from there, followed by two weeks off. I would keep Dubai as my official home base, but would spend most of my time in Kabul. I could barely contain my excitement. "Yes, yes, yes!" was my answer, loudly. I did a little victorious wiggle where I was sitting. For a moment the executive's tone changed. "Let's see how it goes, Jane, first," he said at the end, delivering carefully chosen words tactfully. "It can be a difficult bureau to work in, some very big personalities, and I need to make sure you all get along." "Sure, sure," I replied, "of course!"

This was huge for me. Al Jazeera took Afghanistan very seriously, and the correspondents who had held the position previously went on to be the network's most senior international correspondents. Plus, Afghanistan was the Vietnam of our era—a conflict impacting tens of millions of people on the ground, encapsulating the intractable dilemmas of post-9/11 counterterrorism. I could help shape how the world saw it. I could hardly believe it. I would finally have my own beat.

I never for a moment thought to ask Ben if he would mind. I had never asked anyone for permission to do anything in my life—not out of selfishness, but because I had never belonged anywhere, to any place or group or family. I had figured out how to use this trait as a strength. I could do whatever I wanted. I could move to Afghanistan at the end of the week.

11

Helicopters Under a Full Moon

THE DRIVER PICKED ME UP at Kabul airport and drove me straight to the Al Jazeera bureau, a three-story house surrounded by tall walls, with a covered parking area next to a small, neat rose garden. It was a gorgeous sunny morning. On the way, I wound the window down and smiled as the city rushed by. I had last been in Kabul three and a half years ago, on my first-ever trip as a print reporter, trying to find a footing as a foreign correspondent. The smell of dry, dusty air was unmistakably Kabul. My heart warmed.

I bounced into the office, a small newsroom with desks facing one another and TVs on the wall airing the three main international broadcasters: Al Jazeera English, BBC, and CNN. The bureau was staffed with young Afghan men—there were very few female Afghan media workers then—all hunched over their desks. I waved an enthusiastic hello. After years of covering breaking news, I was excited to settle into this place, to get under the skin of the place, as Tim Page had instructed me to do years earlier in this very city.

This was a vital time for Afghanistan. The United States and its NATO allies were working harder than ever to wind down the war and were handing over combat duties to the Afghan military. President Obama's surge of 2009, which had added an additional 30,000 U.S. troops, had not worked. The Taliban remained a strong force across Afghanistan, and NATO's Plan B was to formally hand the fight over to the Afghan military. Within days of my arrival in Kabul,

NATO leadership and President Hamid Karzai would announce the fight was now being led by Afghan security forces.

Arguably even more important, the country's next presidential election would be held in a year—spring 2014. Karzai's second term was ending, and in a great test to Afghanistan's democracy, a democratic transition of power would theoretically take place. It was the ultimate trial of America's project in Afghanistan since the invasion after 9/11: a test of the country's democratic institutions.

Several members of the Al Jazeera team looked up from their desks and smiled at me. Mahmoud, the cameraman, stood to shake my hand. Over six feet tall, he towered over me. He was about my age, spoke with a slight lisp, and was one of the most affable, friendly people I had ever worked with. He wore pressed chinos, collared shirts, and tweed or tan suit jackets most days. We all teased him about being the best-dressed cameraman in the business. We knew he enjoyed it. Nadir, the engineer, waved and smiled from his seat. He was stout and shy, with reddish hair and pale skin. When he wasn't tinkering with satellite equipment to make sure we were on the air each day, he stared at his computer and avoided much of the office banter and chat.

Abdullah was the second producer. His floppy brown hair framed a chubby face. Abdullah was more traditionally dressed, always in an Afghan shalwar kameez and always on his phone and smoking. Qais Azimy was the undisputed leader of the pack and my new partner in crime. Shorter even than me, round faced and balding, with thick eyebrows and a deeply expressive face, Qais was, in the Al Jazeera bureau, a king in his own court.

He was the only one not smiling at me. He paced up and down the room with his phone between his shoulder and ear, talking. When finished, he walked past me and sighed. "There has been an explosion outside the supreme court," he said over his shoulder, reaching for a cigarette. "Mahmoud, let's go."

"I'll come! Just let me get my stuff," I said, reaching for my rucksack at my feet.

"No, we will go," he shot back at me, before stopping in the doorway and looking back at me with disapproval. "You are not ready."

He walked out and Mahmoud went after him, shooting me an apologetic smile. I looked at Abdullah and Nadir. They leaned lower over their computers and avoided my eye. Every single member of the staff at the bureau had been handpicked and trained by Qais. He was known to be brilliant, the best-connected producer in Kabul, whether it was to the Afghan government or the Taliban leaders, the bravest TV pro, and a leader among all the Afghan producers with international broadcasters. And he was famously difficult and obstinate. I would learn later that week that Al Jazeera had sent me to replace another reporter he had clashed with. Qais I would have to win over.

I spent the rest of the week covering the fallout from the Taliban's bombing of the supreme court. Seventeen people had been killed, almost all of them clerical workers for the court on their way to work. The next day Qais suggested a visit to the family of one of the victims. This time I was invited along. The house was in the outer reaches of the city in a poor area where squat single-story homes of traditional mud and cinder block are connected by narrow laneways. The area was known to have a Taliban presence, and Qais advised me as we climbed out of the car that we should not stay long.

I could hear the wailing the moment the wooden door to the backyard was opened. The family had gathered, and women sat on the floor while men walked around in deep shock and sorrow. Children wandered barefooted and wide-eyed, overwhelmed by the commotion and pain the adults were displaying. The loss of a breadwinner to a family like this in Afghanistan is devastating, endangering the ability of dozens of people to feed themselves. These violent civilian deaths were profoundly unjust, meted out by a war that cared nothing about a man walking to work. I pulled a scarf over my head and steeled myself against the grief.

Standing quietly to the side, I let Qais mumble inquiries and offer his respects to the men in the yard. The wailing grew as another news crew, this one from local TV station TOLO, interviewed a woman. I watched, unable to understand their Farsi. Yet I was aware of the only thing there was to know: the wound this loss had forced her to endure. She wore a green shawl and sat on a simple wooden seat, crying. My breath quickened and my throat tightened as I watched her. I wiped a tear away with my shawl and tried to compose myself. I saw Qais staring at me, and when I looked back, something between us clicked. There was a knowledge in his face, like a puzzle had been solved. Maybe Qais had wanted to know if I cared enough to cover the country he loved. He had heard that I was brave: tales of my work in Syria had impressed many at the network, and local bureaus competed for the most swashbuckling of correspondents. But bravery doesn't equate care. It mattered to Qais that I gave a damn. After that day, we were inseparable.

Al Jazeera had rented me a spot at the Gandamack Lodge, which I was delighted to find just as it was several years prior. When I saw Nawaz, the manager, I threw my arms around him with great excitement. He laughed and noted I had a better room this time. It looked like the inside of a faded old English country home, with huge sash windows and chintz furnishings. Metal springs poked out of the mattress and the boiler over the bathtub bequeathed a minute and a half of scalding hot water before turning ice cold. In a strange way, I felt at home.

Still, the enormous changes during the intervening years since my last visit were unmistakable. Audacious bomb blasts and attacks on international targets in the city were on the rise, and an economic downturn loomed as the NATO allies prepared to leave. Afghanistan was already the longest war in U.S. history, and the Afghans' ability to take on the fight against the Taliban, to keep Al Qaeda at bay, and to maintain the security of the new, democratic Afghan state was the U.S.'s only realistic off-ramp. The American TV media had already left.

The team and I were set to attend the ceremony at the National Defense University formalizing their handover of combat duties to the Afghan security forces. Nadir and Qais arrived early to set up the satellite truck, and Mahmoud and I went by chopper from the main U.S. base in Kabul alongside NATO commanders and a dozen other reporters.

As our helicopter lifted off from a grassy field inside the main U.S. mission's headquarters, the screaming rotor blades of the aircraft threw up hot dust around us. This was a Chinook helicopter, I realized. The same ones that used to land on my father's fields in Northern Ireland, from which the camouflaged British soldiers emerged and disappeared into the green countryside.

At the ceremony and press conference that followed, NATO secretary general Anders Fogh Rasmussen announced the start of the final phase of the drawdown of foreign forces in Afghanistan. Within eighteen months the United States and its military might and all coalition forces would be out of Afghanistan. After the failure of the surge, the Pentagon had pivoted to recruiting, training, and arming the 350,000-strong Afghan security forces. President Obama wanted an end to the war, and this was how it would happen. There were still around 100,000 international forces in Afghanistan, and two-thirds of these were Americans. Questions around how the Afghans would fare without them lingered.

We spent the day going live from the event on the hour every hour. I was connected to the studio through an earpiece and a microphone placed in front of me. Qais sat in the truck, watching me on one small screen and the ongoing speeches on other screens at the same time. Between live shots on air, I would climb in next to him, out of the sweltering sun and dust, and read the notes he had taken, take pointers, and discuss my script as I balanced a laptop on my knee. This was the first time I had ever worked with a producer on a big story. My previous strategy was just to figure it out myself as I went along. Working with a producer as skilled and helpful as Qais was deeply rewarding. I loved it.

Later on, over a drink in the Gandamack's garden bar, Qais lit a slim cigarette and thought out loud, one foot thrown over the opposite knee. The Afghan security forces were going to struggle against the

Taliban without the Americans, he said. He was certain. The Afghan special forces were the only real hope for the government in Kabul. But there was no real way of knowing how those elite units were doing, either. They had never had a journalist embed with them, Qais said. They strictly forbade even Afghan reporters from coming along on missions. At this, Qais stared off into the distance and said, "Yep," to nothing and no one in particular. He had a habit of doing this, I was coming to learn, when he was cooking up something, finding a way around obstacles.

Qais and I would continue to have this conversation for weeks, while he went out each evening to socialize with government officials and military figures. Over tea in the bureau each morning, we stood on the front terrace by the rose garden and discussed the night before. Dinner with the minister of the interior, drinks with special forces commanders. I begged Qais to take me along, but he always reminded me that the presence of a woman would completely change the dynamic.

"You don't understand," Qais would say, shaking his head. Afghan society gossiped like it was an Olympic sport, and I had to keep a favorable reputation. As much as I reminded Qais that I was a professional Western woman and told him that I didn't give a flying fuck what anyone thought of my moral compass, he insisted I leave the socializing to him. I bristled at the thought of male colleagues who'd come before me and the socializing with Afghan officials that they'd been allowed.

After my first trip, I flew back to Dubai for my two weeks off to find that Ben still hated Dubai and spent most of his time inside hiding from the intense heat. We were out for drinks at the yacht club one evening when my phone rang. It was Qais. "I got the access," he said. We could embed with the Afghan special forces. I could hear Qais smiling through the phone. In my cocktail dress and heels, I smiled, too, preparing to transport myself back into my other world, as if through a wardrobe of coats into Narnia.

Within days I was running across the tarmac of Kabul's military airport's helicopter flight line, through midnight darkness save for some orange light coming from the nearby hangars, toward a helicopter readying for takeoff. I wore a flak jacket, a helmet, and a hydration pack for the lengthy hike ahead. I climbed up the back ramp and Mahmoud followed. The pilots were pulling on levers and pushing buttons up front. The gunners behind them held on to massive automatic weapons pointed out open doorways. The Afghan special forces sat on either side of me, our backs to the outer sides of the chopper. They wore the most advanced kits American dollars could buy, from body armor to night-vision goggles, and held automatic rifles.

With a roar, the chopper rose over the lights of Kabul. The moon was full that night, and as we swooped over the jagged peaks surrounding the city, I looked out and watched them turn silver under its light. Three other helicopters flew alongside. This flight into Taliban territory, the screaming howl of the aircraft rushing through the dark night's sky, was the culmination of twelve years of American-led efforts to create a force in its own image. I looked around at these fighters, packed in shoulder to shoulder, and thought about their prospects without the support of the United States.

Suddenly the sharp clack of automatic weapons snapped me back into the moment. Flashes of light sparked, and ammunition belts jolted as the gunners opened fire. I jumped in my seat and grabbed the sides of my bowed head. The commander of this unit laughed and nudged the soldiers next to him. They all chuckled while I forced my shaking hands onto my lap and laughed, too. The gunners routinely opened fire after takeoff, I would later learn, to make sure their weapons were working and hadn't jammed, should the helicopter come under attack or a threat from above be spotted.

When I had walked into the commander's office the week before, he had stood up and reached out a huge, strong hand. As he shook my hand firmly and locked eyes with me, I felt, to my own shock, underneath the khakis and combat boots, a fundamental sense of my own femininity. I had erased this part of myself from my professional life. Major Farzad Nasrallah was the commander of the unit we were going to be spending time with, and a young rising star within the ranks of the Afghan security forces. He was just over six foot tall, with hazel-brown eyes, a chiseled jawline, and a deep dimple at the center of his chin. He was, like me, twenty-eight. He was also, unlike me, filled with confidence. "He seems rather pleased with himself," was Qais's withering assessment.

Major Nasrallah and I agreed we would join his regiment on night raids in Taliban territory and discuss the Afghan special forces' ability to take on the fight against the Taliban without U.S. and NATO soldiers. The Afghan government and military brass were trying to persuade the Americans not to pull out entirely—to keep providing intelligence, reconnaissance, and air support for the Afghans. Even now this elite unit was still being trained and mentored by NATO forces. Ordering air strikes when they came under fire still required NATO permission.

As Qais and I discussed the issue of operational security with the major, what types of classified equipment we couldn't film, and how their raids operate, my phone rang and I excused myself and wandered off to the other end of the enormous office. As I paced up and down, looking out the window and carrying on a conversation with producers in Doha, Nasrallah barely pretended to talk to Qais. Instead, his eyes followed me around the room. He was not afraid to catch my eye and hold it. His attention felt like an overwhelming weight, unlike anything I had ever experienced before. I was suddenly awkward, laughing too loudly at his jokes, painfully aware that a younger version of me I had long ago left behind had reentered the room. Qais looked at me, then at Nasrallah, then back at me, and frowned.

The chopper descended to land, and the soldiers pulled their night-vision goggles down over their eyes. I thought of what an Afghan pilot had told me earlier in the night: The moonlight helps make the landing more visible to the pilot. "But it also makes it easier for the Taliban to spot you landing," he said.

As soon as we rushed off the helicopter and crouched in the dirt nearby, it took off, disappearing into the black sky. The others followed, and soon we were just a group of several dozen fighters and three journalists, standing in a field at night. My ears rang as the screech of the helicopter engine was suddenly replaced by a heavy, thick silence. We were to hike several miles to a small farm compound, where the target for arrest, a Taliban commander, was believed to be inside. My eyes adjusted as we walked in single file along fields, occasionally clambering down and over deep ditches. I was grateful for the moonlight. With no night-vision goggles, I myself would otherwise have barely been able to see at all.

Finally we reached the house. The fighters scanned the hills with their firearms' red laser beams while Mahmoud filmed. In the absence of a night-vision camera lens back in the bureau, the unit had lent us a small scope and helped Mahmoud duct-tape it to the end of the camera. A few muffled instructions and the soldiers were ready to move in.

"You stay here," Qais whispered, holding a small camera and torch. "I'll call up and tell you it's okay."

"No way!" I hissed back. "I did not come down here to wait in the back!"

A voice in the darkness shushed us. Over Qais's shoulder I could just make out the first few soldiers starting to run down the small mud pathway toward the home's metal gate. We ran after them, Qais holding his camera up over my shoulder. The soldiers gathered around either side of the gate. There was no more whispering now, just silent hand gestures. Suddenly one of the soldiers shouted in Pashtu and banged on the metal doors. After a few moments they kicked the door in and ran inside. It was a typical rural Afghan home, a mud building within high walls surrounding a courtyard. Chickens squawked and jumped as we all crashed through the entrance and the soldiers started securing all the exits.

The soldiers searched the home and brought a few men out to the courtyard, their hands zip-tied in front of them. The NATO forces set up a small computer system in the corner of the yard to process fingerprints and iris scans. As I lifted a phone to film them, one of the

Europeans looked up and shouted at me to stop. The intelligence-gathering equipment was out of bounds for us. I noticed that at no point was an Afghan soldier near the intelligence-gathering equipment, either.

As the soldiers worked their way through the house they came upon a larger room with women and children inside. "Don't be afraid," a soldier shouted in Pashtu when shrieks were heard from the other side of the door. "We have wives and mothers and sisters," Qais translated for me. This was meant to calm any fears the women and children would be mistreated and, Qais suspected, to put on a show of respect for the cameras. In Afghanistan's deeply conservative cultures, entering a home with women inside was a grievous affront to the male head of the household. The men kneeling in the straw outside, blindfolded with their wrists tied, surely burned with rage no matter what the soldier declared.

A Western female special forces soldier entered the room first, followed by the men. The women attempted to cover their faces. They crouched and backed away toward the wall, terrified. The room had no furniture in it, just rugs, cushions, and blankets spread out on the floor. The female soldier was there to frisk them and search the room for weapons. As this happened, I could see Qais's face harden. The male Afghan soldiers quickly looked around under cushions and left, satisfied.

A baby who had been sleeping in a small hammock hung from the wooden rafters woke up and began to cry. The Western female soldier insisted on checking inside the hammock and began rummaging through the blankets. An Afghan woman walked over and stood pleading with the soldier. Qais was unable to stay quiet. "There's just a baby in there!" he shouted at the soldier. "Let me do my job," she snapped, furious. I was shocked at Qais's sudden flash of anger, his sense that this raid was an affront to these people. But as we flew back to the capital, bouncing along once more in the helicopter's faint green light, it occurred to me that Qais's own children were sleeping in their beds just a few hours' drive from here. This was his country, and regardless of ethnic differences and perspectives on the war, these were his people. However much I came to love, understand, and empathize with Afghans, I would never do so like he does. For me, this was still a foreign war.

Qais and I spent the next few days burrowed in the Kabul bureau's edit suite, a small room with the walls covered in black foam for sound insulation, furnished with a large desk holding computer screens and editing equipment. A sofa against the wall was largely for anyone who came to work with a hangover from a night at the Gandamack Lodge bar, cheap boxed wine still coursing through their head. But this time we were all focused, delighted with the footage, debating the best sound bites to pull from the interviews with the country's former intelligence chief Amrullah Saleh and with Nasrallah and his troops. We knew we had something very rare and special, the first embed with the very soldiers responsible for holding back the Taliban when the NATO allies departed. As Qais and Mahmoud and I marveled proudly at our work, I got a call from Doha.

"Jane, we need to you get to Cairo right now," the producer said. "Things are getting very serious there."

12

A Massacre in Cairo

I LIT A CIGARETTE AND wandered through the small street, squinting under the baking sun of Cairo's summer afternoon while my cameraman, Tom, filmed the scenes around us. Sweat started to seep through my blue shirt and I looked for a shady spot up ahead.

At the end of the makeshift road was the main entrance to the camp at a place called Rabaa Square. Supporters of the Muslim Brotherhood had built the encampment to host protests against a recent military coup that had forced elected President Mohamed Morsi from office and into jail. Morsi was the head of the Muslim Brotherhood, a secretive eighty-five-year-old organization pushing for political Sunni Islamic rule. Following the 2011 revolution in Egypt, the Muslim Brotherhood had emerged as the only truly organized institution, despite being banned for years, and had run for and won the nation's first-ever elections.

A large yellow bouncy castle had been placed in Rabaa Square underneath a tarpaulin. Beyond it was a clearing of cement and cars and the small roads leading into the protest area of makeshift tents. This was the vulnerable outer perimeter. I could see the bouncy castle's yellow sides moving up and down and heard the sounds of a few dozen small children squealing and laughing inside. Pictures of Mohamed Morsi printed out on crumpled paper had been stuck haphazardly to the sides of the castle, from where he nodded, smiling and glassy-eyed, to the rhythms of the moving castle. The camp's children had been placed in the path of the up-coming assault.

I approached a man as he was looking on, clutching his two-year-old boy dressed in a T-shirt with Morsi's face on it, and asked what he thought about the impending violence. "If my son dies, then it was God's decision," he answered, smiling.

Tom kept on filming and I sat down on a nearby chair in the shade and thought about what I should say in my stand-up. Russ, our security adviser, sat down on a plastic chair next to me, silent. He carefully sprinkled Golden Virginia tobacco onto a white cigarette paper and looked around. I had known him for a matter of hours, but I knew what he was thinking. "Pretty fucked up, eh?" I said. "Yep," he said, nodding and gripping his unlit rollie between his lips.

We filmed a stand-up for the story, a simple update on the mood inside the protest, outside the tent. Then we headed to the mosque at the center of the square, the epicenter for the Muslim Brotherhood organizers of the protest, the Morsi supporters. He languished in jail while these groups tried to build a movement to somehow undo the coup, by their own blood if need be. Inside, people milled around chatting to the press.

Yet it was tough to get a usable sound bite from an interview. This was partly because the Muslim Brotherhood didn't like to talk about the Muslim Brotherhood. They preferred to talk about the Egyptian revolution more broadly and wanted to be viewed as the representatives of the entire protest movement that had ousted long-time Egyptian dictator Hosni Mubarak in 2011 after massive protests. The Egyptian revolution of 2011 had become a symbol of the Arab Spring and had been broadcast around the world. Egyptians from all walks of life took to Cairo's Tahrir Square to call for more freedoms and dignity under a representative government. The Muslim Brotherhood supporters wanted their current protest movement to be seen as a continuation of that optimistic, heady time of revolution. Getting them to talk about real politics was a chore.

Our local producer, Ahmed, pulled me to the side. He was an

Egyptian journalist working for Al Jazeera. In his mid-twenties, he seemed younger. He was tall and thin, all long limbs. Though he seemed awkward and shy, he was also bright-eyed and kind. "I got a call from Jamal Elshayyal," Baher told me as we stood in the baking heat at the steps of the mosque. "It was a bit weird. He asked me what you were reporting on and told me to keep a close eye on you." He looked down at his feet, confused and defensive. "I'm telling you because I don't want you to find out about this later and think I would ever spy on you, Jane."

Jamal Elshayyal was a young correspondent who was becoming more prominent at Al Jazeera English. As another reporter, he had no authority over me. Yet he seemed answerable only to those at the very top and was rarely managed or given assignments through the usual executive and senior producers. My sense was that he was concerned I was not pro-Muslim Brotherhood enough.

My career at Al Jazeera was starting to crumble. It seemed to me that this news organization was using my work—my mettle and grit and smarts and everything I was pouring into my reporting—as a propaganda tool. As someone who had given everything I ever had to journalism, I felt personally betrayed and deeply wounded. Reporting was the only way I could feel worthy in this life, and now it felt far from noble.

I felt hot tears coming and sniffed them back as I smoked and watched people cross Rabaa Square, fighting their own battles, living through their own much bigger crises. As I sat quietly smoldering, my team stood around and looked at their feet, unsure of what to do.

My phone rang again, and I crouched close to a wall to make out the voice on the other end. It was Qais. The stories of the special forces battling the Taliban had aired. Afghan president Hamid Karzai had requested a viewing in the palace. He was appalled. Karzai had been calling the Taliban his "brothers" and had been trying to ban night raids because they were so unpopular in Pashtun areas. He gave Major Nasrallah a severe dressing-down and suspended him indefinitely. "Christ alive!" I yelled into the phone at Qais. "Yeah, but what can you do about it?" Qais responded.

As my plane landed in Cairo, I had thought of how Major Nas-rallah's presence, his gaze, felt like respite from the chaos outside. His brown eyes, his wide smile, and the deep dimple in the center of his chin would flash into my mind at times when it shouldn't. He came to the hotel garden bar for a beer with me and the guys before I left. But the guys didn't show up that night. I leaned over and picked a leaf out of his soft black hair. "Call me Farzad," he had said, and had smiled at me in a way he shouldn't have.

Ben and I spoke on the phone on my first night in Cairo. "When are you coming home?" he asked again. I felt a pang of guilt about more than being away for work. I felt greedy for wanting this life. "You are such a selfish girl," my mother used to say to me when I was little. "So selfish."

A call from Russ, the security adviser, woke me the next day. I looked at my watch before I answered: 7:14 a.m. I heard people screaming and gunfire in the background before I could make out his words. "Do not come down to the square!! Whatever happens, do not come here, Jane!" he roared. "It started!"

Then, a phone call from the Cairo bureau chief: "Jane, we want you to go into the square. Can you get there?" he asked, slow and serious.

Russ shot me a disapproving look when we arrived. Crowds of people were running in the opposite direction, panicked and scream-ing. Russ, Tom, and I pushed our way against them toward the main opening of the square and halted in the chaos. Gunfire rang out everywhere, automatic bursts of the army's assault rifles vying with single shots of smaller fire.

Men occasionally rushed past us toward the square, moving against the throngs of those running for their lives. They were carrying plastic gas canisters. It was impossible to know how much time passed before thick black smoke billowed down the street. The crowd now seemed to emerge from the cloud. "The mosque is on fire!" someone yelled as they ran past.

Civilians rushed past us, shouting and carrying the wounded. One man was carried out on a stretcher, his brains spilling out on the feet of those bearing him. Tom managed to get us connected to the internet and we were up live. We knew we couldn't push forward any closer inside the square—the gunfire was too intense. I reported in real time, walking and talking to the camera surrounded by wounded people. I pointed out that we were hearing some return fire above our heads. I tried to stay as calm and focused as I could, speaking clearly and loudly over the bullets and the noise of the crowd. The control room thanked us and dismissed us without any additional questions. Tom and I looked at each other and then at Russ, who shook his head. A producer in Doha called to say we would not be going live on air from that spot again. Al Jazeera wouldn't publicize armed protesters, no matter how horrific the massacre against them was, I thought.

As we stood there, appalled by the violence and indecisive about where to go next, another wave of panic swept through the crowd. "They are coming!" someone screamed in Arabic. "The soldiers are coming this way!" We were standing at a junction. One street led to the black smoke and chaos of the square, from where everyone had been running, limping, and carrying the dead, and now people were running from the opposite direction, too, claiming the soldiers were coming from there. One way out remained, up the hill from which we had come. Russ looked at me and said, quite calmly, "Run." I turned and ran up the hill as fast as I had ever in my life. The sounds of gunfire lessened as I fled. Despite the fact I smoked, I was still fast. When I finally stopped in the laneway to the right, I realized Russ and Tom were far behind and waited for them to catch up.

"What the fuck, Jane?!" Russ joked, bent over, hands on knees, trying to catch his breath as Tom labored up the hill toward us, carrying his heavy camera over one shoulder. Between gasps, they roared with laughter. In the midst of everything, we all suddenly experienced a moment of hilarity. "That's it," Russ said after he stopped laughing. "From now on, we call you the Jackal."

We gathered ourselves and decided to make our way back to the hotel on foot, walking through the crowds of people all headed in the same direction.

People were piling the dead and injured into vehicles and rushing them to the hospitals and morgues. A middle-aged man stood next to a parked car, his arms bent above him, hands clasping the top of his head. He was wailing, expressing such pain that people around him stood in silence. He was standing next to the open back door of the car, staring inside. On the back seat was a young man in his early twenties. He had been shot in the head and chest and was clearly dead. Blood was running over the seat onto the car floor. "My son! My son!!" the man screamed into the air around him. We stood there in silence, our heads down, this man's pain loud in our ears. Russ put his arm around the man's shoulder and held him while he sobbed.

A familiar dread rushed through me. I stood there and felt my body react while my mind went blank. I felt suddenly and unmistakably dissociated from the scene around me, as if I were watching it from a remove. I didn't know at the time, but this was how my mind was trying to protect itself. My phone rang and pulled me back down to the street. It was a producer back at the bureau. The bodies are being taken to mosques in the area, he said. We should head to the biggest one near us and get ready to go back on the air.

We slipped off our boots and entered a nearby mosque. I felt a twinge of panic for a moment at being separated from my shoes. I always need to be ready to flee, and being shoeless renders me vulnerable. Inside the mosque, neat rows of white shrouds covered the floor. It took me a moment to realize they were wrapped tightly around dead bodies. Slivers of plush crimson carpet showed between them. I looked up in disbelief. Ornate brass chandeliers hung from the ceiling, giving off a warm glow, away from the cruel white heat and light of Cairo in August. The whir of fans used to keep the bodies from decomposing replaced the roar in the streets. Fathers and mothers wept as they shuffled between the long white bundles on the floor. They crept along, faces crumpled in pain, as they searched for missing sons. Others sat on the floor, forearms resting on their knees, staring blankly ahead, in shock.

I picked my way around the bodies on the floor and tried not to step on a shroud, a sheet-covered foot, a face pushing out from behind the fabric. My heart thumped hard in my chest. I felt a kind of paralyzing numbness. I focused, filming and talking with Tom in hushed, serious tones. The air smelled of fresh blood, like a butcher shop in the morning. A floral scent of air freshener floated by, too, sprayed periodically overhead by wandering, wide-eyed men.

Volunteers placed black bags of ice on top of the bodies. Bloody water spread across the shrouds and leaked into the carpet and my socks as the ice melted. It was August 14, 2013, and we had just witnessed the Rabaa Square massacre.

I arrived in Cairo a few weeks after the military coup. It had Al Jazeera English's full attention. Salah Negm, the news director back in Doha, was Egyptian, and this was the story of his lifetime, the biggest since the 2011 revolution in Egypt, and perhaps even since the 1973 war between Egypt and Israel.

Another development might have played a role: the state of Qatar, Al Jazeera's owner, now had a new emir. Whereas the previous emir. had been hands off with Al Jazeera, his replacement seemed to take a more aggressive approach to foreign affairs. He supported Muslim Brotherhood movements across the region, which angered Qatar's neighboring rivals Saudi Arabia and the UAE. The Muslim Brotherhood's reputation for upholding armed uprisings against dictators put royal families in Riyadh and Abu Dhabi on high alert. But to Qatar, the movement was a potential tool for greater leverage in the Arab world. And it was clear at the network's Arabic channel that a pro–Muslim Brotherhood rhetoric was now more marked on air. At Al Jazeera English now, too, fears were growing over tinkering with the coverage. Many of us who worked at Al Jazeera were massively proud of its legacy of unbiased, serious, and humanistic journalism. We now sensed a shift.

When we returned to the hotel that evening, we walked straight to the lobby bar. I collapsed in a chair, all dried sweat and clammy tobacco-stained hands. I smoked and drank and watched myself talk and watched the others talk while I waited for the storm to pass, worked to come back to myself. I couldn't shake the feeling that what I had witnessed was something I could not do justice to as a reporter. What was my role here? Was I helping at all?

I slipped back to my hotel room, finally shedding the tears I had been holding in. My phone rang. It was Ben. I knew his network was flying him in now that the killings had become massive news. I flung the phone across the room with such force I fell to the floor. As I reached down to loosen my bootlaces, the tears fell from my chin. I tugged my boots off, and the smell of the dead wafted up from my socks. They were still wet with melted ice and the blood of lifeless men. This time the smell was of bodies in the heat. Sobbing now, I peeled the socks off my clammy feet and hurled them into a trash can under the writing desk. I ripped open the minibar and pulled out some small bottles, gulping red wine down frantically between loud, painful sobs, burning my throat and eyes, all tears and wine and overwhelming grief.

Human Rights Watch estimated the death toll that day was at least 1,000 people. The Muslim Brotherhood said over 2,500 were killed. We stayed on, reporting for several days, as the bravest of the protesters continued to take to the streets in pop-up protests across Cairo and various Egyptian cities. In Alexandria city I ran from police and pro-government thugs and had a young boy confront my team with a machete. I broadcast live on the phone, describing everything around me.

The military imposed a 7:00 p.m. curfew. Anyone approaching one of the countless army checkpoints across Cairo after that time risked being shot in their car. All foreign media was under suspicion and potentially subject to attacks. But Al Jazeera was the most loathed, seen as a voice of revolution and Muslim Brotherhood's main mouthpiece. Being found working for them was dangerous. Anyone being asked for ID by the military risked being outed as Al Jazeera staff and threatened. The management started handing out stab vests for us to wear. Mine was so clearly visible under my shirt it gave everyone a much-needed laugh when I put it on in the office.

Al Jazeera headquarters had grown frustrated with the lack of reporters on the streets, given the violent crackdown. The bureau chief asked me to cover a pop-up protest place in a suburb of Cairo. As we discussed the particulars, it was being broadcast live on Al Jazeera Mubasher, Al Jazeera's live news channel.

I was worried I would not be able to find it and get back before the curfew ended. The military had said they would shoot anyone found driving the streets after curfew. After what I had witnessed, I believed them, but the bureau chief pressed us to go. As the afternoon slid into the evening, Russ, Tom, and I drove around and around the suburban Cairo neighborhoods the footage had been aired from. We kept an anxious eye on the time. The driver asked passersby if there was a protest. They told us it was long since over. I called the bureau chief and told him we would return before the curfew. "Don't worry," he said. "They moved it to eight p.m. Keep looking." When I finally gave up and returned to the office I discovered they had not changed the curfew at all.

13

The Scarlet Woman Award

I WALKED INTO THE GANDAMACK lobby, too weary for words. Nawaz offered me a sympathetic smile and welcomed me back.

After Cairo, I had flown back to Dubai, to the empty apartment and the life I had tried and failed to build with Ben. After a number of painful and tear-filled conversations, we ended it. Guilt consumed me. I had never been good at accepting failure. "I'm so sorry," I found myself saying. I looked him in the eye and told him I didn't want to be in a relationship anymore, that I needed to chart my own course. Ben was sorry for adjusting so badly, and I was sorry for being unwilling to stay home, and we were both sorry because we couldn't make it work, despite being so sure we could. Sorry, sorry, sorry.

I drifted off to sleep on my bed in the Gandamack, into a dream of running through Cairo, gunfire in the air and blood on the ground. Someone shouted—was it Ben?—that I should look up. Then my phone pinged. It was a message from Major Nasrallah. "Is madam back? Free tonight?" he asked.

Sitting under the glow of the hanging lightbulbs in the hotel garden, we clutched bottles of beer and chatted for hours. Major Nasrallah had arrived in a suit—the first time I had seen him out of military fatigues—and right on time. *Is this a date?* I thought. We talked about Afghanistan, his life growing up under Taliban rule, his love of being a soldier, and his experiences in the United States and the UK at military academies. I enjoyed how he smiled and became animated, how he asked me questions about myself and the bureau, my work. We talked about breakups, his former marriage, his divorce, his son.

He leaned back in his chair, exuding a massive, impish confidence that filled every room he entered. He was everything I was not. I felt myself slide with relief out of the uncomfortable emotions I walked around with normally—fear and exhaustion and self-recrimination. I was slipping out of myself and into someone new, a woman who could allow herself to be desired, loved even.

I looked into his hazel-brown eyes and was aware how much I wanted this. I would never let myself have it, though, would I? I had always been so straitlaced about men. A virgin until I was twenty. An awkward girl with thick glasses, the frumpy girl, the nerdy one, the shy sister. The stories I had done on Nasrallah's unit had been wrapped up weeks ago, and we were no longer working with the special forces at all. Besides, reporters in Kabul were hopping into bed with soldiers, diplomats, and aid officials all the time. Why was I so afraid?

We looked at each other with intense, unspoken desire. I felt like a woman, no matter how much I tried to be one of the guys. This time I felt it amid something much more fundamental inside me, something that was almost always there. I felt my own loneliness, my desire to be seen and felt, held. Loneliness and lust. I let myself fall so hard in love with this stranger it was like I was lost. I loved the feeling of being desired just as much as I loved the loss of control. Now, for the third time in my life, I giggled as I headed up a staircase to my bedroom, a man's willing, strong hand in mine. His hair felt like silk between my fingers.

When the banging on my bedroom door woke me, he was already up and pulling his shirt on, still buttoning it as he opened the door. A red-faced Afghan waiter, embarrassed to find a man—and an Afghan, to boot—in my room, spoke to him in Dari. As I rushed around, my head spinning, hopping on one foot to get my shoes on, Farzad told me they wanted him to move his car. His car was parked in a restricted area outside the hotel in front of the Afghan intelligence headquarters. They had called to complain. He dashed off to move it. *Jesus Christ,*

I thought, standing in the suddenly deafening silence. *They will have run his number plates. And they know who he is and that he stayed the night.*

Later that day, I was sitting in the garden distracting myself with the news when Qais called. He wanted to come over and talk to me. He sounded serious. When he arrived, he offered an awkward half hug. I sat silently while he lit a cigarette.

"What you did last night was very stupid, my dear," he began. My heart sank. "This asshole is now going around telling everyone he spent the night here with you, bragging about it to the entire unit and commanders."

I argued, despite my growing embarrassment and fear, that I was allowed a love life, I was allowed a life here. That it was not unusual for journalists and diplomats, soldiers, and aid workers to meet and date here, that I was being held to an unfair standard, that it was only because Farzad was Afghan that anyone was clutching their pearls.

"Exactly," snapped Qais. "He is Afghan, and that makes it different. He's married, he has a family." I suddenly felt cold. This betrayal hurt like hell. My heart literally ached at it. The more I insisted to Qais that that was not true, that we had talked about it, that Farzad had told me he was divorced, the more I could hear how naive I sounded. Whatever young woman I had let myself be the night before spoke foolishly. Hot tears rose to my eyes and fell down my cheeks. My breath quickened. How could I have been so stupid?

The afternoon sun suddenly felt like it might consume me. The presidential palace was already angry with me about the reports from our embed, Qais continued. They had already disciplined Farzad, and this gave them more ammunition. They could come and question me if they wanted to. They could accuse me of being a prostitute, formally complain to the bureau, cancel my visa, throw me out of the country. I did not question any of Qais's catastrophic predictions. I just sat there, smoking frantically, wiping tears from my eyes and occasionally attempting to defend myself.

"Janie, of course he's married, don't be stupid," he jeered. "I didn't realize you actually liked him this much."

A flash of hurt darted across his face and in his voice. He stubbed his final cigarette out and promised to do his best to keep this from becoming a scandal.

The next day I arrived in the bureau having barely slept. Mahmoud, Abdullah, and Nadir all leaned in toward their screens when I walked in, but nothing in my colleagues' judgment could compare to my own self-flagellation. When Qais arrived, he looked hungover and exhausted. As we sat on the terrace with tea as had become our morning ritual, he told me about the night before.

He had gone out to meet up with friends and connections working with NDS, the National Directorate of Security, as the Afghan intelligence forces were called. He had brought a crate of vodka with him, to sweeten a request to read my "file," he explained. The only thing they had was a few benign chats over Facebook and a few text messages about my travels. It seemed they didn't plan to dig any deeper. Qais had worked hard to counter Major Nasrallah's narrative among the Afghan military commanders that he had slept with me. He insisted it was not true.

The truth was, it had never been true. Despite the breathless need and desire I felt as I kissed Farzad and ran my fingers through that soft hair, despite his gentle imploring, his entreating, wandering hands, I couldn't let myself go further. I couldn't let myself have even that one moment of abandon. The real truth was, in that moment, when it came to such intimacy, I was far from the woman I presented— fearless and wild and passionate and irreverent. I was not that woman. After we chatted and drank and kissed in my room, he fell asleep next to me in my bed, with only his shirt missing. I watched the dark hair on his chest rise and fall, and he, unlike me, slept like a rock, unmoved and unbothered by fear of anything in this world. His pistol was on the table near the bed. He had placed it there when we crashed into the room. It was still there, I realized, as I sat with Qais, mortified.

I went into the edit suite and called Lesley in Australia. I told her Ben and I had ended it, and I was having a difficult time. I had been feeling entirely unmoored ever since Cairo, maybe since before, maybe always, I don't know. My legs weakened, and I sat down on the floor and cried. I desperately wanted nothing more than to throw myself into my sister's arms. Suddenly a sentence fell out of my mouth. "Lesley, am I a bad person?" I heard myself say. It shocked me to hear this voice. It had been quietly berating me my whole life, my original sin, now made manifest.

Qais's efforts to contain the scandal worked, and I threw myself wholeheartedly into my work. I wanted to understand how civilian life was changing in Kabul as the international forces prepared to depart. Afghan women were in a precarious position. Perhaps my gender would help me more than it would hurt me this time. It had in the past.

I stepped inside a beauty parlor in Kabul's Shar-e Naw neighborhood. It took a few moments for my eyes to adjust. The bright sun and familiar whiffs of sewage and generator fumes gave way to an aura of nail polish, hair spray, and copious perfume. I stood for a moment by a swirling fan next to the door, shaking my blouse loose from the summer sweat on my back. A dozen women looked up and smiled at me, and I smiled back. They chuckled, maybe at the sudden diversion of a Western woman crashing into their world, maybe at my disheveled appearance.

The salon was a long narrow room with a small glass front onto the street. The windows at the front were covered by large stuck-on images of glamorous women, offering privacy to those inside. Several women sat in front of mirrors, while others stood over them, busily placing rollers, painting lips, and running blow-dryers. To the right, a bench along the wall held those waiting for their turn. Curvy women squeezed into T-shirts and jeans shuffled between them.

A young female translator introduced us to the owner, Soraya. A few of the women were looking at my combat boots. They wore high heels and were dressed in an assortment of bright pink, red, green, and pastel chiffon, floral shawls, and decorative dresses. Everything about them spoke of feminine effort. I was wearing a khaki-green shirt and a pair of jeans. My mascara and lipstick paled in comparison to their striking makeup.

Qais had arranged for me to visit and film there without Mahmoud. No men were allowed in the salon. It was the first time I'd seen a group of Afghan women alone together, uncovered. This salon was a female sanctum, a private place of trust. And although it was no boardroom, it manifested female empowerment. Soraya was, after all, a business owner and manager. Her staff were all female breadwinners supporting their families. In her fifties, she wore a green short-sleeved shirt, black slacks, and a pair of impossibly high heels. She eased herself into a chair by an old TV set at the back of the salon and told me about running this business under cover during Taliban control in the 1990s. Their laws may have banned it, but the tradition of women getting their hair and makeup done for weddings endured, despite the threats. The day the Taliban arrived in Kabul in 1996, unkempt, bearded fighters in fatigues careened through the streets in pickup trucks. They came to her beauty parlor.

"I had to do the makeup for five brides that day," she remembered, pointing to the street outside. "The Taliban came with guns and smashed the windows. They told me to close the shop." She secretly defied them and carried on running the salon from her home. "I used to go out in a burka and I would secretly buy makeup," she said proudly.

The women sitting against the wall leaned toward us and listened, nodding. All the women in the salon were enrapt. "Are you married?" Soraya asked, smiling at me. The women leaned in a little closer. "Yeah, I'm married," I responded with a sly smile, fiddling with my camera. "Married to my job." The women all laughed when the translator explained what I had said.

Women and girls had the most to lose if the Taliban gained ground. Since the U.S. invasion, girls had had greater access to education and women had been able to build careers. Covering the change would mean getting into rooms like this and clutching a camera myself.

At the table next to Soraya, a girl around ten years old sat staring into the mirror in front of her, her legs swinging below the salon chair as a stylist pinned her hair up. I looked at her and wondered what kind of life she would be living by the time she was my age. The war was just a few feet from us, held back by only a storefront. Absolutely everything was at stake for her.

The Taliban were on the march, their attacks growing bolder, buoyed by the retreat of U.S. and Allied troops into their bases. The group were assassinating government figures, ambushing Afghan army units, and launching complex attacks on guesthouses and restaurants in Kabul, using suicide bombers and gunmen. I reported live often. The more I did it, the more comfortable I became. My hands still trembled each time, so I learned to hold a small notebook to hide from viewers the slight shake in my fingers. I would stub out a cigarette, look straight into the camera lens, and breathe as low in my belly as I could, so as not to appear out of breath.

Still, I continued to be socially awkward. I was intimidated by the lively community of *Washington Post, New York Times,* and BBC reporters in Kabul. On the few occasions I went to parties thrown at other media organization's bureaus, I felt out of place. Western journalists felt like a high school clique. Almost no Afghan journalists were ever invited to those events back then. I felt like I had to choose one group to be friends with. I picked my Afghan colleagues. When they were at home with their families, I spent my evenings in my hotel room, studying Dari, smoking cigarettes, and reading books. I had created a safe cocoon. My Afghanistan life.

I asked Qais to recommend a Dari tutor who could help me learn basic conversation. Qais and I wanted to tell stories beyond the fighting and killing, to show real Afghans living their lives in some really tough circumstances. If I was fluent with the local dialect of Persian, it would help us get closer. Throughout that winter and the following spring, we traveled across the country, talking to people from every walk of life—civilians, soldiers, government officials. We talked to laborers waiting for work by the side of the road and injured police officers waiting in vain for compensation money from their corrupt

commanding officers. We interviewed pop singers and visited the local TOLO TV station, attended political rallies filled with men on
horseback, and filmed soccer matches and fashion shows. I wanted to
see and hear it all, and the team took pride in our being one of the
network's most productive bureaus. The sense of purpose for me was
thrilling.

When I turned twenty-nine that September, the guys all came to
the Gandamack with party hats, several cakes, and gifts for me. They
laughed as I pulled on a traditional ornate dress they had bought for
me, one often worn by brides for weddings, over my clothes. I felt
more deeply connected to my life than ever before.

That fall, Qais, Mahmoud, and I set off north in our small car. We
climbed higher, and the world fell away in a blinding, cool white.
Snow lay soft and rounded over each mountaintop, reaching across
rivers and dips between the steep-sided humps of the Hindu Kush
mountains, a silvery blanket reaching out to the blue sky. We crossed
over the Salang Pass and through the Salang Tunnel, built by the Soviets in the sixties, which connects Kabul with the northern provinces
and cuts through the most forbidding part of the mountains.

We were on our way to Baghlan Province, at the very north near
the Tajikistan border. In Baghlan, mineral wealth was being heralded
as a potential source of income for Afghanistan as the United States
and its allies left and foreign aid dwindled. Afghanistan's ability to
stand on its own feet financially was a question no one seemed to
have a reasonable answer to, despite the billions of dollars spent on
developing the country's infrastructure since 2001.

Winding my window down, I leaned my head out, felt the cold
on my face, and breathed in the clean mountain air. All my life I had
wanted to see the Hindu Kush, and here I was, skidding over them
in a car with my Afghan colleagues, a foreign correspondent. When I
was a little girl, studying maps and atlases in my bedroom, these very
ridges had been tiny jagged triangles under my small muddy fingers.
We had set off from Kabul before dawn, stopping for breakfast at a
small roadside restaurant as soon as early light started to reveal the

countryside around us. We sat outside on carpets, munching lamb kebabs and fresh naan bread and sipping cups of steaming green tea, as the sun rose over the hills ahead of us.

We arrived at Baghlan's provincial capital town Puli Khumri later that day, at the headquarters of a now near-defunct cement factory where we would spend the night. Because there were no hotels in town, Qais had asked the governor to open the complex for us to stay at. This, too, had been built by the Soviets in the 1960s, and driving up the crumbling cement driveway toward the factory's accommodations and offices was like moving through a time warp. Neat little houses like Russian dachas sat around a common square, where the factory managers had lived, while laborers had bunked in a dormitory-like building at the top of the square. The entire complex was like a living museum of Soviet factory life.

The governor had ordered the complex to be preserved in hopes that it could one day, with some investment, be up and fully running again. Afghanistan had to believe in its future. To do so, many had no choice but to look to the past, to better times when economies were less dysfunctional, when investment in the country showed a belief in its long-term prospects. Afghans hardly remembered the Soviet invasion and occupation fondly, but when that time was compared to the current period of violence and corruption, many saw something there that they wanted to get back to.

The next morning, I tiptoed across the broken tiles of the factory bathroom and gasped as I stepped under the freezing water trickling from the one working showerhead. There had been no functional boiler for decades, and an icy breeze blew in through the broken windowpane and around my shivering limbs. Yes, I may get hypothermia, but damn it, I would have decent hair today. I laughed at myself as I scrubbed shampoo into my hair frantically, as fast as I could, reciting through chattering teeth, "I love my job, I love my job, I love my job."

I looked out the smashed window at the snowy countryside and thought about a lunch I'd had with a former network producer in Manhattan a few weeks before. "It needs to be bigger," he had said across the table in a restaurant overlooking Columbus Circle. "Much bigger!" As he imparted this career advice, he raised his hands above his head to further emphasize the point he was making. I watched and listened, thoughtful, earnest, and deeply naive.

I had gone to New York in search of an agent. Everyone I had asked, which largely included Ben and the internet, said that if you wanted to get a job in American TV, you had to get an agent. I had tried to connect with the heads of network news organizations, making painfully awkward calls from my room in Kabul. Each time I was met with a cold response from assistants and receptionists, and the occasional laconic promise to "pass along the message" to whatever executive producer, vice president of news, or talent executive I was trying to reach. These people did not talk to talent, I learned. They talked to agents. So I had reached out to agents and asked for meetings. I sent them my clips from Syria to Jerusalem, Yemen, and Somalia. As thrilled as I was to work with Qais and Mahmoud, my doubts about Al Jazeera's direction lingered. I was determined to make it into an American network.

It had worked. After stumbling around Manhattan in high heels and a dress I had deemed network worthy, I had shaken hands with an agent from Bienstock, the biggest and oldest agency representing TV news talent in America. I had taken a week of my downtime from Afghanistan to fly to New York, nervously riding in taxis from my hotel to agency offices because I could not walk in heels. I had walked down the bustling streets of Manhattan, staring up at the glass towers above me with just as much wonder as I had done as a teenager ten years before. It still made my heart beat faster.

Returning to the life I loved in Kabul, I exhaled, feeling as if I'd been holding my breath the whole trip. The stress and tension of being on display in New York City, desperate to fit a mold of perfection in looks, demeanor, and confidence, fell away. I worried I didn't fit in the glamorous world of network news, so closed off to a hillbilly girl like me. The audacity of even wanting it felt like a secret, exciting taboo. I wanted to belong there, but trying to be the person I thought they wanted me to be exhausted me. In Afghanistan I felt like myself. I felt like I was home.

As I climbed down into a fifty-year-old coal mine in a remote area of Baghlan province, my perfectly blown-out New York City hair was now covered in thick black soot. At the bottom, men raised huge pickaxes over their shoulders and heaved them into the coalface with a grunt and dull thump, forcing chunks of dusty black rock to fall at their feet. The small mines had not been maintained at all since the 1960s. The men worked in medieval conditions, facing extreme dangers. "This could all fall in at any time!" explained the supervisor with great enthusiasm. He pointed up to the wooden beams that had been placed there to keep the mountain above our heads from crashing down. My heart beat fast as I tried to conquer my claustrophobia.

I asked one man who was leaning on the handle of a pickaxe to catch his breath if he feared the dangers of this work. Qais stood next to me, hard hat on, translating, as the man looked at me with angry eyes. "As soon as we enter, we pray," he said. "We are not sure if we can make it back. Ten times I have seen people get blocked in here and it took very hard work for us to rescue them. Three people died in front of my eyes. They went under this mountain." Properly managed, these mines should provide a decent living for communities like his. The failure to end the war and to build a functioning economy had damned him to this hazardous, exhausting, and pitifully underpaid work.

Unintentionally, the war efforts by America and its allies deepened corruption in Afghanistan. They handed out massive multimillion-dollar developmental contracts, transport contracts, and military supply contracts, which the Afghan government passed on to their cronies. All the while, ordinary citizens like the coal miners here eked out just enough of a living to buy some food for their families.

When we agreed we had enough footage and interviews, we walked back up the black tunnel to the surface. The workers there laughed at our blackened faces as we emerged, especially me, the foreign woman with coal dust filling my nostrils and my ears and smeared all over my face. I fell to my knees under a nearby faucet and turned the tap, sending cold water down my neck and black coal dust into the earth. The team cackled at me, so keen to wash before my live reports. "Big hair! I love my job!" I shouted as they laughed, watching, arms folded.

The following spring, as soon as the snow melt permitted passage over the mountains, we headed north once more, this time to the region surrounding Kunduz city. This was Taliban country, and one of Afghanistan's most precarious in terms of government control. I wore traditional dress as we raced down roads cutting through green fields filled with cows in countryside that felt like rural Ireland. The snow had melted here, and a low gray sky fell over the area. I pulled my scarf over my face at checkpoints, aware that Taliban informers were common within the local police and army, and kidnappings on these roads were a serious threat. Qais was on constant lookout for danger, staring out windows and telling me to hurry when getting in and out of the car.

Soon I was standing in a small classroom listening to a chorus of little girls reciting the Quran in tandem at the top of their high-pitched voices. The girls sat on the floor at long, low tables, each with an ornate holy book open in front of them, shouting and rocking back and forth. They were no older than six or seven years old, and black cloaks covered their bodies. This was a fundamentalist madrassa, or religious Islamic school.

In the Arab world, *madrassa* is simply the word for school, and can include religious scholarship as well as any kind of academic pursuit. In Afghanistan, the word held a more sinister meaning. Many associated it with the extremist madrassas in Pakistan that trained Taliban fighters and groomed and brainwashed young male suicide bombers. But this school was for girls, and that was why we wanted to see it. Several men with long beards and big black turbans had greeted us at the gates, enthusiastic to talk to Qais about how the Taliban support schools for girls, but only religious ones.

The school represented one part of a multisided argument over what would happen to women and girls in the future Afghanistan, if and when the war should end. Would women lose their hard-fought and extremely spotty rights? Shouldn't schools like this technically be allowed, in a democracy? We wanted to hear their answers. I watched the little girls rocking back and forth and drilling the Quran into their memories and knew they were not going to be allowed by these men to study anything else.

As I entered another classroom, I encountered one of the most bizarre scenes I've ever run into in all my years of reporting. Girls in their midteens sat at tables in a seemingly normal classroom setting, fully covered in their black cloaks save for a slit across their eyes. But at the head of the classroom was a large wooden box, about ten feet tall and three feet across. It looked like a coffin standing upright. In the front of it was a slot, like an old-fashioned mailbox. A muffled sound came through the slot, a man's voice. The teacher was sitting in the box communicating with the girls, who would then respond to the box. Occasionally one of the students would get up from her desk and approach the box, sliding a book into the slot or receiving one. The girls would never see their teacher, and he would never see them. The teachers showed us their innovation proudly. It not only preserved the girls' dignity, but it reflected the men's charitable nature in allowing the girls to learn from them. When I played dumb and asked why they didn't simply hire female teachers, there was a collective smirk amongst the men.

About a year after our visit to the school, the Taliban captured Kunduz city. It was an event that shook the Afghan government, and the U.S.'s plans to leave, to the core. The group withstood a ferocious offensive by Afghan security forces for more than two weeks. In the final battle to retake the city, a U.S. war plane dropped a bomb on a Doctors Without Borders hospital, killing twelve staff members and ten patients, including three children. The Taliban had never taken a major city before, let alone held it for months. Afghanistan's own special forces units, alongside American Special Forces, proved essential to retaking the city, but the reality was undeniably clear, now that their mettle had been tested: the Afghan military could not hold the line alone.

In the months before the Taliban took Kunduz, their attacks on Kabul grew more frequent and more brutal. One night in my room in Kabul as I read next to my Afghan bukhari oil stove top heater, I was almost rocked from my chair by the force of an explosion. The bang felt closer than anything I had experienced before. As I moved around my room methodically, carefully trying to stay calm and remember the things I would need to put in my backpack, Taliban fighters were rushing into La Taverna du Liban restaurant in the main diplomatic area of Kabul and going table to table, executing diners, just a few streets away from the bureau. The huge explosion had been a suicide bomber rushing at the fortified steel doors to blow them off, letting several gunmen enter and open fire on diners and staff inside.

Twenty-one people were killed as the Taliban gunmen went from table to table. Qais and I had planned to eat dinner there the next day. The owner, Kamal Hamade, was a Lebanese businessman who was known to the clientele of mostly Western aid workers, diplomats, and wealthier Afghans for his charisma and generosity. The ultimate host, he would enforce a strict policy of standing over customers to make sure they ate the free chocolate cake he handed out with every meal. He would serve special tea, which included boxed wine poured into a teapot, with a sly smile underneath his gray mustache. Kamal ran from the restaurant to the kitchen to grab a gun and returned to face the attackers. He was killed.

I dashed to the restaurant where the attack was ongoing and shivered in the headlights of the Afghan security forces' Toyota Hilux trucks, next to a dozen Afghan journalists, recording pieces to camera, helpless as the sound of gunfire and explosions rang out. The special forces' footage of the crime scene showed people lying facedown on the floor under their tables. The gunmen had shot them where they hid. I imagined the absolute horror and fear of their last moments, completely trapped and helpless. I also remembered something Farzad had once said to me: "If the Taliban get into the Gandamack, just hide under your bed and call me," he said. "When the special forces come in, they will kill everyone."

The reality was, the Gandamack was ripe for attack, too. It was largely defenseless, and we all knew it. They had only a few gunmen on the door and the same metal gates as were on Kamal's restaurant. Each day fewer organizations and employers would allow their foreign staff to go to the hotel for dinner or drinks. Even Al Jazeera management, rarely ever concerned about the safety of their field staff, became uneasy about my accommodation. They moved me to the Serena Hotel, Kabul's larger, swankier international hotel with high walls, private security, and metal detectors. The heightened security was simply an illusion.

14

Under Attack

EACH SPRING, AFGHANS CELEBRATE NOWRUZ, the Persian New Year. In 2014, the Taliban marred the usual celebrations in Kabul by assassinating a provincial governor, only their latest in a series of attacks that March. I stayed late at the Al Jazeera bureau to report live.

When I returned to the Serena Hotel after nine p.m., the downstairs restaurant was rowdy and full of revelers intent on marking the holiday in spite of the heightening conflict. I kicked off my shoes to place tired feet into slippers and ordered room service.

As I hung up the room phone, I heard a sharp bang coming from down the hallway, near the elevators. I twitched, my body's paranoia now inbuilt. *Someone must have slammed a door,* I thought. I leaned my ear against the door of my room, ready for another bang. It came. Bang, bang, bang—three gunshots, followed by shouts in a man's voice. The Taliban were inside the hotel.

I grabbed my shoes by the bed and slipped them on before going back to the door and looking through the peephole. *Single shots, probably from handguns,* I thought. *Not automatic fire.* Now it was quiet, and I could hear the beating of my heart. Adrenaline raced through my body. My cell phone rang. The sound was deafening. I rushed to silence the ringing.

No gunmen were visible on the other side of my door, but there was no way to try to make it out of the hotel through the main entrance. It was too late. The only possible exit was along the hallway, down the staircase at the end of the hall, and out through the lobby and courtyard. That was where the gunshots had come from. I heard people's doors opening and some murmurs in other rooms. I opened mine and leaned my head out. A hulking British security consultant was rushing down the hallway. "Get back in your room!" he ordered, making eye contact with me. "We are under attack."

I ran to charge my phone in the wall socket under the window, knowing what I needed above all else was my shoes on and a working cell. I crouched under the window and called Qais. His phone was out of the coverage area. I called Abdullah, the number two producer in the bureau. No answer. I looked out the window and into the main entrance courtyard below and saw all the security guards run toward the hotel doors and then suddenly retreat back to the main gate and parking area, taking cover behind the armored SUVs. I tried Qais again, and this time he answered. "Qais, the hotel is under attack, the Serena is under attack," I whispered urgently. "There are gunmen in the hallway."

I could hear that he was in a room full of men, talking and laughing. As it happened, he was at a party with the Afghan special forces. Qais was calm and clear. I must quietly push whatever furniture I could against the door and prepare to jump out the window if they try to break the door down. He would ask the security forces what was going on and call me back.

"The Afghan special forces are five minutes away," Qais said when he called me back a few minutes later.

"What do you know about who is inside, Qais?" I whispered.

"They don't know. They think they have handguns, so it's probably just a dispute that got out of control," he said. "Just stay in your room." He was going to call the interior minister to find out more.

Twitter came alive with updates, many incorrect: "Explosions have been heard." "This is not an attack, just a row between diners in the restaurant."

Bang, bang, bang! More gunshots pulled me from my phone. I could hear shouting now, but the firing sounded farther away. It was definitely downstairs, I told myself. I hoped.

I dialed Qais again. "This is *not* a row between two people! This is an ATTACK!" I said as quietly as my growing panic would allow. "You tell the interior minister this is an ATTACK!" I was anxious for the special forces to arrive. The attackers would likely come door to door, I thought.

It was time to move the furniture, as silently as possible. I reached for the wooden writing desk in the far corner of the room, wrapping my arms around it to lift its weight off the tiled floor completely. I carried it over to the door and set it down with a sudden loud thump. I froze for a full five seconds, listening through the door for movement in the hallway. My heart seemed to have taken up residence between my ears.

Soon the sofa, desk chair, and coffee table were piled up against the door also. I scurried back to below the window and peered out. I was on the second floor, and the window could only be opened about ten inches. I would not be able to squeeze out. The double-glazed glass would be tough to smash.

Suddenly the courtyard swarmed with special forces soldiers. Some were running with boxes of machine-gun ammunition. They broke off into two groups, lining up on either side of the hotel doorway. I knew the drill, having been on raids with this very unit. On a signal, they raced through the doorway, and I heard their loud shouting in Dari. Now machine-gun bursts tore through the hotel.

I desperately needed to pee. But the bathroom was next to the doorway, and I worried an attacker could hear me. After several minutes of internal debate, I made a dash for the bathroom. *I really don't want to die on the toilet,* I thought as I attempted the great farce every woman who has ever shared a bathroom is familiar with—the silent pee.

An hour later, I heard someone shouting my name in the hallway. Qais had told me to be ready for this. To open the door for no one until I heard my name shouted. The shouting grew closer. I pulled the furniture back from the door just enough to squeeze past it and wedge the door open. There stood Farzad's former deputy, now commander of the special forces unit. He was clad head to toe in his full combat gear and flanked by two other soldiers. He told me in halting English to walk, not run, and stay by his side. They marched me down the stairs to the reception area, by this point buzzing with special forces soldiers. The sound of sporadic gunfire from down the hallway in the restaurant ricocheted off the marble walls and floors. As I walked fast toward the main door with my escorts, so close to freedom, one soldier pointed at me and laughed. "Hey, Farzad's girl!!" he shouted over the din of the bullets and yelling soldiers. "For fuck's sake!" I shouted over the roar, into the air around me.

I ran across the courtyard where I had seen the security guards from my window take cover and burst into the small one-room building that housed the security camera and baggage scanners leading to the exit. There were still isolated automatic rips of gunfire inside the hotel, but no more firing of handguns. The Afghan special forces were winding down their work. As I ran through the room to the final exit door, a man with a trimmed white beard looked up at me. He had been studying the security camera footage and mumbling stern orders into a handheld radio. We caught each other's eye for a moment as I ran out. I immediately recognized him as the interior minister, and he had chosen to position himself just meters away from the attack. I gave him a nod before I ducked out the door, hoping he saw in my face how impressed I was.

As I rushed out through the final steel door and thick surrounding wall of the Serena, a crowd of people were waiting, their faces fixed tight with fear, curiosity, and shock. Journalists, police, and civilians stood helpless in a large group, waiting for news of their loved ones. Qais ran toward me and guided me to the car, where Mahmoud and Nadir were already waiting. "I'm so glad you are okay, Jane!" Mahmoud shouted, wide-eyed. Nadir nodded at me with a relieved smile. Ever our leader, Qais climbed in the front passenger seat and ordered the driver to get us to the bureau fast. He lit a cigarette and handed it back to me. I realized I was shaking.

We reported live from the rooftop of the bureau throughout the night, until I was driven to a safe house run by a British security company to sleep for a few hours. Our hosts explained that if we were to come under attack, we would run into the tiny kitchen and lock the steel door behind us. "See?" said the guesthouse manager in a thick London accent, rapping the steel door with a closed fist. "It's very safe!" I looked around at the scattered teacups and coffee jars and examined his face for signs he was joking. For years after this, I would walk around hotels to find the exit routes in the building and would check the windows to see how wide they could be opened and whether they were too high for me to jump down to escape.

The next day, I marched into the bureau, running on reserves of adrenaline, cigarettes, and cups of instant coffee. The guys were already there, Mahmoud, Nadir, Abdullah, and Qais, all looking shaken and shocked. Devastating details of the attack had begun to trickle through, including rumors that the Agence France-Press correspondent Sardar Ahmad was missing. No one could get hold of him. As the guys talked to one another in Dari and made calls, their faces stony and eyes watery, the news came through. Sardar had been shot dead in the Serena restaurant where he had taken his family to dinner for Nowruz. We sat in utter incomprehension as we learned his entire family had been shot at the dinner table, including his three young children. Only his two-year-old son survived, despite appalling bullet wounds.

In total, nine people were killed in the restaurant. Four Taliban attackers had gone table to table and executed diners. Even by the standards of Taliban attacks on civilian targets like this, the close-range shooting of small children was an atrocious, shocking act that few could ever hope to explain.

The guys were painfully professional, setting up the live shot position with quiet, saddened souls. We all spoke gently to each other that morning. I had not met Sardar, but the guys had known him well. The murder of Sardar and his family members was more than just a tragedy for their community of friends and Afghan journalists. It was the worst possible reminder that in Afghanistan you don't have to be a reporter on patrol with troops to get killed. Just eating in a restaurant, taking your family out to dinner, put them at risk. For ordinary Afghans, the very air they breathed seemed dangerous. Every second came with a perilous risk of loss; the blessing of a family could be undone at any moment. As the Islamic phrase offered to those in mourning goes, *It is from God we come and to God we return.* This was uttered repeatedly in Kabul that day.

The executive producer in charge of my region called later that day. She wanted me to fly back to Doha that afternoon to discuss with management the best way to handle my accommodations going forward. I was confused. The presidential elections were in just a few weeks. I needed to be here to work. As I walked out the bureau doors to head to the airport, I shouted back over my shoulder to Qais, "I'll be back soon!"

When I got to the Al Jazeera headquarters in Doha, I felt a wave of exhaustion that ran deeper than the lack of sleep or even the after-effects of fear—fear for my life, fear of failure, fear I was not doing a good enough job. I felt tired in my heart and soul. At twenty-nine, I still didn't understand it beyond something I must push past.

I entered the huge newsroom and found two male colleagues, senior producers, were waiting near the central desks where the sitting executive producer works. They looked at me with sympathetic nods. "Sorry they pulled you, Jane. What a bummer," said one of them. "I know it's totally unfair, but I kind of understand," added the other. I felt a growing panic. An executive producer opened the glass door to his office and waved me in.

"So tell me what happened, Jane," he said after settling down into his chair behind his desk. He hadn't shaken my hand or asked me how I was. He stared down into his BlackBerry phone as he spoke. I gave him a frank description of the incident at the Serena. He did not once look up from his phone. Given his clear lack of interest in my answer to his question, I gave him the short version and ended it abruptly. I presumed he did not want any tidbits about my thoughts of jumping out the window, the movements of the special forces through the building, or my final exit.

He carefully placed the phone on the table in front of him on the desk, folded his arms tightly across his chest, and leaned back in his seat. This was the first time he looked at me. His face was a mix of deep thought and irritation. "Jane, after much consideration, we have decided to replace you in Afghanistan for the time being with Bernard," he began.

I was not being sent back to Kabul. I began to unravel, sitting in my chair, stumbling through my own arguments. "I am no more at risk there than a man is." I tried to maintain a calm voice. I wish I had shouted at him and employed cutting humor, but it took whatever reserves of energy I had left not to cry. I would not cry in front of this man. He didn't understand that Afghanistan wasn't just an assignment to me, interchangeable with any other. I had found something there I couldn't give up. I had a home and friends and a purpose. I had to get back there.

"I am devastated by this decision," I pleaded. "I have reported for ten months there bravely and professionally."

"There is no need to get upset, Jane," he spat disdainfully. He was lecturing me now and leaning over the desk. "And stop interrupting me."

Now I yelled. "You sent me to Syria with ten thousand dollars and a handicam!! I covered Yemen, Somalia—much more dangerous places for women!"

It was a lost cause. He was obtuse and defensive and shut me down entirely. "I don't owe you an explanation," he said. I walked out of his office feeling utterly broken but desperate not to show it, timing the agonizing seven or so seconds it would take for me to walk past all the senior and executive producers in the newsroom and behind glass office walls and outside to the parking lot, where it was somewhat more dignified to cry. Salah Negm, Al Jazeera English's director, came to talk to me.

"I don't want a woman covering that story," he declared. "For now." He had removed the small pipe from his mouth to speak and looked at me with a withering gaze. His short gray beard framed a frown. As he saw my shocked face, he turned, walked up the steps of the Al Jazeera headquarters before I could reply, and shouted over his shoulder, "And don't be all feminist about it!" before disappearing through the sliding doors.

I was left standing there, in the heat of a Qatar spring, staring at my own reflection in the glass. I lit a cigarette and stared out at the dusty carpark. I sniffed back tears, but inside, I was hardening into a silent, familiar rage.

"You have to suck it up. You have to put your big-girl pants on," a Canadian lawyer friend from Kabul told me later that night when I called her from my Doha hotel room, desperate for advice. "There's nothing you can do—it's Qatar. Get over it, but never forget the guys who did it. Remember those fuckers' names."

15

Growing Basil in Beirut

IN THE BEGINNING, ALL MY plants died. In line with my usual approach to failure, I spent a short period of time chastising myself and then tried again. Gardening may be seen by most as a way to relax, and certainly that was my plan, but by the summer of 2014 I wasn't quite there yet. At the small flower market set up in a parking lot of the Armenian Bourj Hammoud neighborhood of Beirut, I walked up and down the rows of potted roses, daisies, geraniums, and lavender with the same intensity I had brought to the last ten years of my life.

The Mediterranean sun did what it has done for thousands of years, gently turning the faces of the city's windowsill flowers toward its rays and coaxing them into beautiful bloom. This was lost on me as a put-upon cabdriver helped me load an entire garden's worth of plants into his small car. Two olive trees stuck out the window as we drove back to my apartment building in Gemmayze.

As I heaved the potted plants and trees and bags of compost up several flights to my third-floor walk-up home, I should have realized that the pattern of my life was becoming clear—a tendency to make everything hard bloody work. Even when I had time off, I managed to come up with backbreaking labor for myself. I was also not yet ready to see that. But Beirut would teach me.

I spent days planting hanging baskets and pots of flowers that would decorate the small balconies surrounding the apartment, each adorned with curved plaster, antique tiles, and emerald-green wooden shutters.

The apartment was beautiful and simple, with sunshine pouring in everywhere, dappling the tall-ceilinged rooms with light. It was everything the glass towers of Dubai were not: lived-in, full of character, and in desperate need of renovation. I was in love.

Ben had moved to Lebanon after our breakup. The war in neighboring Syria was raging and many journalists were moving to Beirut from cities like Istanbul, Cairo, and Kabul, pulled by the story of Syria and propelled by increasingly autocratic regimes and dangerous environments elsewhere. We had gingerly reconciled before I left Afghanistan and had agreed to make a fresh start in Beirut. I still didn't believe that I could face the world alone. I loved him and he loved me. I continued to tell myself that was enough, sinking back into this familiar reassurance and love.

I poked and prodded my plants: daisies by the living room balcony doors; the grapevine hanging lazily over the balcony off the tiny kitchen; the spindly young olive trees. I doubled up on fertilizer, wielding the watering can like a weapon. My plants yellowed, crumpled under my impatient desire to make things happen rather than let them.

A few weeks into my quest to develop a green thumb, I stuck the watering can underneath the faucet and turned the handle. Nothing came out. I ran next door to knock on my neighbor Christina's door.

"Christina!" I yelled as she answered the door. "There is no water!"

"Yes, dear." She smiled beatifically back at me. "There is no water."

Christina was a godsend. Lebanese, divorced, and in her mid-fifties, she spent much of her time arranging for cleaners and trash collectors and negotiating with the building owner. Gossiping, too. Christina was the ultimate mother. It was impossible to knock on her door without an invitation to come in, and as soon as you did, you were holding a glass of strong Turkish coffee and munching on whatever she had been cooking. When she knew Ben was away on assignment, she would often bring me fried fish, figs from the market, and chocolates, knocking on my front door and marching into the apartment to set the latest plate of delicious food she had decided I must eat on the dining table.

Christina was a proud, committed Maronite Christian, and her warmth and hospitality, which was paired with an intense suspicion of Muslims, reminded me very much of Northern Ireland. She was delighted to find us moving into the apartment across from hers at a time when Syrian refugees were moving to Lebanon to escape the war. Middle-class Syrians were renting apartments in our neighborhood, causing much grumbling among the locals, who argued the refugees pushed the prices up. In truth this discontent betrayed a deeper prejudice against Syrians generally, regardless of their religion.

I was baffled by Christina's lack of concern over our dry faucets. "Well, I mean, should we call the plumber?" I eventually offered.

"No, dear, there isn't any problem." She laughed. "It will come back on again."

"Oh, thank god, I was so worried. Okay, great. How long do you think it will be off?"

"We never really know. Probably few days, maybe a week."

With that, I was learning the difference between visiting a country and living in it, one reason why journalists must have at some point lived in the regions they report on. Beirut has a devastating water shortage due in part to old water pipes, left to rust out while corrupt officials pocket public funds intended to mend them. The same officials take kickbacks from men who truck in mysteriously sourced water. People paid these water haulers to fill the tanks on their roofs. Syrian laborers would eventually show up in old jeans and vests, haul a pipe onto the roof of the building, and fill water tanks for individual apartment tenants. Syrians did a lot of the work around here, as it turned out. When they were hauling water, fixing problems with electricity, delivering food, and clearing garbage, they were apparently most welcome.

Hours later, determined to shower after a sweaty day of murdering my plants and unpacking boxes, I poured a several-gallon drum of water purchased from the local store over my head and tried to wash my hair. My laughter drifted out the open windows and doors and mixed with the scents of tobacco from the waterpipes outside.

I was freelancing full time for Al Jazeera English, but I had eased back from taking assignments since I had been pulled from Kabul. As I chatted with others at the network who were unhappy with the slope toward pro–Muslim Brotherhood coverage, many talked fearfully about the state of the media industry in general. By 2014, the war in Syria had become too dangerous for networks to send reporters in, and the Arab Spring had fallen into a complicated stalemate of revolution and counterrevolution, so coverage in the Middle East had fallen away. Al Jazeera's coverage may not be perfect, we worried out loud when we were together, but at least they are covering the region.

One assignment I took kept me doubting. Three Israeli teenagers had gone missing in the occupied West Bank, believed kidnapped from their car. They were hitchhiking their way home late at night, as is common in settler communities in the West Bank, when they were picked up by Hamas members, who shot all three dead. Tensions were higher than ever in the area, with skirmishes between communities of Jewish settlers and local Palestinians rising ever since the war in Gaza in 2008, but the disappearance of three youngsters, one nineteen and two only sixteen years old, shocked and outraged Israeli society. Al Jazeera wanted me to get to Jerusalem and then on to Ramallah, the de facto capital of the West Bank, as soon as possible. I spent several weeks reporting from the occupied West Bank, where Israeli security forces raided homes and neighborhoods and searched endlessly for the three boys.

As I broadcast live from the West Bank town of Ramallah, a request came through from Doha that I was to call them settlers and stop referring to them as teenagers. The implication was that I was using overly sympathetic language. I refused. I told the executive producer that the fact that two of the victims were children mattered, and that I would not scrub that from my reports or my live updates. They conceded, unhappily. I was proud to do work at Al Jazeera that highlighted Palestinian suffering. It was one of the few English-language broadcasters that fully cast light on human rights abuses perpetrated in the West Bank and Gaza. But facts were facts, and reporting on suffering no matter where it was felt was and is sacrosanct to me as a reporter.

The killings in the West Bank precipitated a devastating war in Gaza that summer, which killed 2,251 Palestinians, according to a UN report, more than half of them civilians.

For the first time in my reporting career, I hung back from a conflict. I needed time away, and not simply from the network. The events of the past year and my tumultuous love life had left me feeling unmoored. I knew whatever grit had defined my life so far was running low.

I made an effort to take care of myself. I turned thirty, quit smoking, and took up running. I joked that this was a natural indication of my fledgling maturity. In reality, it was a bow toward a newfound sense of self. An act of kindness toward myself, the green shoots of self-love.

Six months after my broadcasts from Ramallah, I went for a run on Beirut's corniche. I labored along next to the sea, the sun setting beyond a beautiful old lighthouse.

I had that morning drafted an email on my laptop and had pledged not to send it until I had gone for a run and come back, settled in my mind. It thanked everyone at Al Jazeera for over three incredible years of reporting but let them know I was resigning. I was at peace with this decision. I knew I needed to move on and was still learning to trust my sense of what was best for me, even if I couldn't see the path ahead. No one else was offering me work, and I had no idea what I would do. But I had saved most of my money from my years at Al Jazeera and knew I could survive on that for now. What I really wanted, what I really needed, was rest. And Beirut was the right place to do that.

I loved the sense of community in Beirut, the closeness of everything. On the balcony off a small, neat living room, I could sit drinking coffee and see across the neighborhood to the local hotel, a renovated apartment building like mine turned into a trendy boutique hotel, its small front terrace filled with European backpackers. Directly across the alleyway lived Paul, an elderly man with no teeth whom I could not understand when he spoke. After the civil war ended in 1990, it was made illegal to evict the elderly when they could not pay their rent. For thousands like Paul, however, that wasn't enough to put their lives back together. He lived in half of an old Ottoman-era house. His half was virtually uninhabitable: the windows were broken; Paul had no electricity, so at night he was dependent on candlelight. The other half of the house had been renovated by Lebanese owners. During the day, Paul sat on his front step and peeled vegetables into a bucket, like the ghost of an unhealed past. Each day I waved at him as I walked by. He waved back and smiled.

In the apartment below mine lived two Syrian musicians in exile, much to Christina's indignation. Tremulous, mournful notes of traditional Syrian music formed the muffled soundtrack of my afternoons. We all lived in such close quarters, mixing the sounds and smells of cooking and tobacco and music and chatter. In Beirut, when I was alone, I didn't feel lonely.

There is a natural loveliness to the city, despite its scars and the dysfunction and chaos of its newest construction. Beauty comes so easily to Beirut, effortless and enviable, like a woman who is naturally elegant, whatever she is doing.

As I allowed myself to slow down to a Mediterranean pace, I was able to see the beauty of Beirut more clearly. Mornings began just before dawn with birdsong, then the sound of metal clanking as the coffee shops opened their shutters. The local fruit and vegetable sellers came by in small open-top trucks or vans, selling whatever was in season from farmers outside the city. My neighbors lowered baskets from their apartment windows, with some notes of Lebanese money inside, as elderly ladies with aprons leaned over their balconies to hear about what tomatoes, radishes, cherries, and figs were available. During the summer months, ladies of leisure bronzed themselves by the ocean.

As light faded from the antique plaster of Ottoman and French buildings, bats scooped up bugs in fast, silent circles between the trees and streetlamps. Sunsets over the Mediterranean provided a stunning nightly show. Old men and women sat on benches along the corniche as though in the audience at a theater. Boys of all ages, skinny kids from working-class high-rises nearby, leaped screaming with laughter from the rock formations into the water, jumping in and climbing back out as long as the light permitted.

Bars begin to emit dance music as bottles of local wine are put on ice. The smell of sewage from the ocean, the odd whiff coming from the broken pipes when the wind changes, is ignored. That's how life is lived here. And the sprawling jasmine hedges, falling like green and white lace across old stone walls and over balconies, fan sweet scent through the streets. In the bougie neighborhoods of Achrafieh and Downtown Beirut, SUVs and sports cars begin gathering outside bars, restaurants, and apartment buildings where parties are getting under way. No one knows how to enjoy life, often against the odds, quite like the Lebanese.

Sitting on my balcony one night, sipping a cold beer and watching the bats circling over the rhododendrons, I let myself feel the weight I had carried with me all my life, that I had run from, humming under the surface. It was a feeling of worthlessness, a deep-seated shame. In that moment I was at the same time a recognized, celebrated thirty-year-old international TV correspondent and a little girl hiding under the stairs from her parents and incapable of loving herself. I knew well how to escape this feeling—head out on a plane, to a place with no cell service, a place where I didn't really belong—but this time I would not. I would sit there and feel it. And it didn't kill me. Those months felt like a cease-fire. A fragile peace emerged. Even my plants began to survive.

I avoided the news as best I could. I knew that watching TV news would make me want to be out on the road, covering these stories. As I was slowly learning to feel comfortable with myself, ISIS were sweeping across the region.

The group shocked the world as it seized territory from Syria through Iraq, the Iraqi army fleeing in terror having watched the group's propaganda videos of mass executions. ISIS were attacking civilians in Paris, London, and New York, inspiring young, disillusioned men and women to travel to their Caliphate and destabilizing the region unlike at any time since the U.S.-led invasion of Iraq in 2003. They reached across Syria and right to the Lebanese border, their presence less than two hours away from my peaceful apartment.

As I approached the one-year anniversary of my life in Beirut, I knew it was time for me to get back to work. "But to where?" I wondered out loud one night to Ben. "For whom?"

"Why don't you try PBS?" he replied.

Part III

16

No Foreign Accents

AT THE OPPOSITE END OF the Middle East from my new home in Beirut, civil war was erupting in Yemen. In September 2014, the Houthis had joined calls for interim president Abd Rabbu Mansour Hadi to resign and swept down from their northern strongholds into Sana'a. In a deeply cynical, Machiavellian bid to secure a comeback, Ali Abdullah Saleh had ordered elements of the Yemeni military still loyal to him to let the Houthis in.

The Saudis viewed the Houthis just as Hadi had when I saw him in a refugee camp five years before: an Iranian proxy. For the Saudis, caught up in a regional proxy war with Iran already, a new, dangerous front had opened. Iranian-aligned forces were at their very border. In March 2015 they launched air strikes and a partial air, sea, and naval blockade on Houthi-controlled territory of Yemen. I knew I needed to be there.

Weeks before I left, I had pitched stories to *PBS NewsHour's* foreign editor. Perhaps I could report for them from Beirut, I had suggested. I followed up and finally got a call. The editor declined. "We just can't have any more foreign accents on air. We need Americans."

This time I pushed back, as politely as I could. I deserved better than this. I continued to pitch and reached out to the show's new executive producer, whom Ben had known at her previous network. I decided to do what I had always had to do to get in anywhere: get access that no other journalist could.

Throughout my Beirut break, I had been watching Yemen descend into a deeper and deeper crisis. I felt guilty about not returning to cover the news there. As the Houthis had swept into the capital and the country edged deeper into the civil war Fuad and Mohammed and all the others had feared, they reached out to ask if I was coming back. Sitting on the beach, sipping a cold Lebanese beer, or pruning plants on my balcony, I sometimes felt like I had abandoned a story few others covered. I picked up the phone to ask about getting access. Mohammed, as usual, pulled off the impossible. PBS was intrigued.

When I reached the airport's check-in desk for the flight to Sana'a, journalists for CBS News and the UK network Sky News were also waiting to check in. Mohammed had other clients now. I thought of the faded photos of tourists in his office and was relieved for him that he was able to make a living for his family. This was the first time since the Detroit bombing on Christmas Day in 2009, carried out by a Yemeni-educated member of Al Qaeda, that I had heard of news networks from the United States flying into Yemen.

Under the Obama administration, the U.S. was providing logistical, intelligence, and weapons support to the Saudi-led coalition that was bombing the Houthi rebels in Yemen. When the Saudis launched air strikes, Americans were helping in every way. In the background was incredible tension over the Iran nuclear deal, which Saudi Arabia (and to a certain extent their partners in Yemen, the UAE), America's traditional ally in the region and the sworn enemy of Iran, viewed as a betrayal. Support for the war in Yemen was a counterweight to Iran's expansions and a way to assure Saudi Arabia that America had not abandoned them entirely. But Saudi goodwill toward the Obama presidency had faded and never fully recovered. The Western world was paying attention now.

For this trip, Ben joined me as my cameraman and producer. It would be the first time we had ever worked together and his first time ever being in Yemen. I wanted him to see the place that meant so much to me, and he wanted to get more experience working for other networks, having gone freelance when he moved to the Middle East. I felt a heavy responsibility in this situation. Ben had never traveled to a conflict zone like this without a security team, as was common for the networks. He had never worked in the pared-down, bare-bones freelance manner I had, operating on local knowledge and the good graces and connections of your contacts.

A sense of chaos met us even before we landed. Yemenia Airways was able to run only chartered flights now, from Jordan, arranged by the United Nations. Permission to be placed on the manifest was difficult to get, particularly for journalists. The Saudi government had blockaded Yemen, and no direct flights were permitted. Our plane was forced to land in a small airport near the border with Yemen, where mustached Saudi intelligence officials walked up and down the aisles in crisp white thobes, headdresses, and aviator glasses, while nervous Yemenis held their children and fanned themselves in the exhausting heat. We waited for hours as they unloaded all the luggage for inspection.

In the meantime, a ferocious sandstorm engulfed the plane. After much discussion between the Saudis and the Yemenia pilots, it was decided that we must take off. None of the Yemenis on board had a right to enter Saudi Arabia, and the Saudis didn't want the plane waiting on their runway any longer. Regardless of the conditions in the air, the aircraft needed to leave.

The plane pitched violently to one side, then the other. A woman screamed. The man in the seat in front of me leaned forward and gently chanted, "Allahu Akbar, Allahu Akbar, Allahu Akbar." God is great. Every time the plane dropped or was dragged sideways by the wind, my hands gripped the armrests and I closed my eyes, breathing as slowly as I could, terrified. Opening my eyes, I looked out the window next to me at a thick orange-brown wall. Even the plane's wing was not visible through the dust storm as we approached Sana'a.

When we finally thumped onto the runway, I hardly recognized the airport. The plane shared the tarmac with pieces of a smaller aircraft that had been blown up not far from the terminal building. Mohammed Saif was waiting for us. As the summer heat wafted in through the broken windows, and parts of the ceiling hung down, there he was, wearing his usual impeccable suit and tie, smiling with arms outstretched.

As I looked at the battered city, I remembered my driver Fuad's uneasy, stony face throughout the revolution. The Arab Spring, those heady days of revolutionary hope and fervor, had yielded to power plays by strongmen, those who would choose war over capitulation. As had happened in Libya, Syria, and Egypt, Yemen's young thinkers and dreamers were being swept aside by those with guns. At that point I had no idea how much war was to come.

Sana'a was a maze of armed men, the Houthis and their allies among Saleh's troops alone in control. Most of the actual Houthi fighters wore long wraparound skirts, filthy vests or threadbare collared shirts, and sandals, with headscarves wrapped untidy around their heads and AK-47s slung over a shoulder.

As soon as Ben and I landed, word came that a Saudi air strike had hit the Old City, destroying one of the ancient houses in the UNESCO World Heritage Site. We rushed there to film. In the center of the Old City—Sana'a Qadima, as it was called in Arabic—a crowd had gathered around a gaping hole in the row of ancient redbrick buildings, half a dozen stories high. Hundreds of years of stone and brick and wood lay in a heap of dust, and the same materials poked out in jagged wounds from the buildings on either side. They would likely have to be torn down also. As I stared, shocked, at the site of the air strike, I remembered the first time I had run my hands over the walls of these structures, seven years before, yet a lifetime ago. I had felt awe.

As we got closer and talked to rescuers, local people digging with shovels and their bare hands, we learned that five people had been killed, and another, still alive, had been pulled out of the ancient wreckage. The locals were angry and keen to talk to us. Here was Saudi Arabia, the Middle East's richest country, bombing the poorest country in the region and killing people in their homes. "They don't have any history of their own, so they destroy ours," one woman shouted in disgust.

A few days later, I stood on a rooftop with the head of the Sana'a historical preservation society, the whole city before us. He looked around him, his voice straining with frustration. I was coming to recognize that look in his face, when people watch their whole life's work—for him the preservation of generations of history—disappear and know there is nothing they can do about it. I saw it again and again in the faces of archaeologists in Syria, businessmen in Iraq, women's rights activists in Afghanistan. The sudden and heartbreaking reversal of progress that war brings.

Saudi Arabia and the UAE don't fight ground wars. Flushing rebels out of the capital of Sana'a with air strikes, individual groups of them hiding in laneways and buildings, was like using a hammer to rid a house of termites. Still, the Saudi planes tried. We drove between the sites of air strikes, deep craters in the road outside destroyed buildings as multiple bombs dropped around targets. Crowds of stunned Yemenis stood around each new hole, occasionally squinting up at the sky with anxious faces.

After much campaigning from us and the other journalists, the Houthis' media contacts finally relented and granted our cohort of Western journalists interviews with a senior leader, Mohammed Ali al-Houthi. After we drove to him in a frighteningly exposed convoy of military vehicles, he met us in the bombed-out presidential palace as fighter jets flew overhead. The Houthis would not tell us the location ahead of time for fear of air strikes. The building and grounds already bore the scars of recent hits.

We were each offered fifteen minutes with al-Houthi, and I volunteered to go last. Experience had taught me that conversations could be longer and more casual at the end of a long chain of interviews. When it was my turn to go in, he smiled at me like a cat—a very fat one. Mohammed Ali al-Houthi looked as though he'd gained a vast quantity of weight since putting on his gray suit. He bulged out of it so violently it appeared certain to rip apart at the slightest movement. He had a trim, dark beard and breathed loudly. When not speaking, he stared at parts of me with a grinning, grunting lasciviousness. I found him profoundly repulsive.

The Houthi movement was formed in the 1990s as a revivalist faction of the Zaidi branch of Islam, practiced by around a third of Yemenis and seen as more closely aligned with Shiism than Sunni Islam. They focus tightly on an anti-Western and anti-Semitic viewpoint of the Middle East and wider world. Their slogan, which at this point was posted all over Sana'a, was as follows: "God is great, death to America, death to Israel, curse the Jews."

It was conjectured that the Iranians provided aid and weapons to the Houthis. I pressed al-Houthi about this. "We don't have any links whatsoever with Iran, and Iran doesn't have any influence on us," he said with a smile. "We are completely independent and separate."

In reality, there was some truth to this. Despite the breathless coverage by some news outlets comparing the Houthis to Hezbollah, the group were in fact an indigenous Yemeni group. It was clear they had political ties with Hezbollah and Iran, and weapons shipments coming from Iran had been discovered, but the relationship was more complex than that, and the Yemenis were not going to take direction from any Ayatollah. In the years that followed however, the Houthis' relationship with the Iranians appeared to become a self-fulfilling prophecy as Iran's Revolutionary Guards and Hezbollah grew closer.

When I emerged from the frustrating interview with al-Houthi, the other reporters and crews were waiting in the hallway, arguing with the guards. The Western reporters looked alarmed. "You are invited to lunch!" Mohammed Saif, who had come along to make sure everything went smoothly, declared with a nervous smile when I gave him a perplexed shrug. There was a guard standing across the doorway with an AK-47.

"That's nice, Mohammed, but we really should get out of here," I replied. "I mean, we are so exposed, there could be an air strike." There was uproar from the reporters in exasperated agreement. Apparently, I was late to this discussion. We were being barred from leaving. The invitation to lunch was less invitation, more hostage-taking.

Mohammed leaned over and whispered in my ear. "Please, Jane, make the others calm down and stay," he pleaded. "It will be a huge insult to Mohammed Ali al-Houthi if you don't have lunch with him. And he really, really insists." A bead of sweat emerged on his temple. This might be the last meal we ever have, but we were staying. I cheerfully declared how hungry I was and tried to rally the troops and downplay the dangers.

In a room that seemed surprisingly intact, we were served plates piled high with rice and roasted chicken, vegetables stewed in tomato sauce, and other delicious Yemeni dishes as well as heaps of fresh bread. Al-Houthi sat at the top of the table, grunting and laughing and making comments to the women in the group while shoveling food into his mouth, a significant portion of which ended up on his own rounded front and lap. There were around twelve of us in total. *This would be a dreadful reason to die,* I thought as I filled up with warm spiced rice.

Sweating young rebels stood around in the doorway and at various points of the room. Skinny and wide-eyed, they looked with longing at the platters heaped high with food. I noticed the presidential seal of Yemen on the porcelain plates we were eating off of. We were using the official state china. I looked around the room and watched al-Houthi and his deputies, so uncouth they would make any Yemeni family blush, these men who had swooped down from the mountains, scooping fistfuls of food from the palace plates. There seemed a metaphor in there somewhere for the state of Yemen at that moment. We survived the lunch, waved goodbye, thanked them for their hospitality, and finally were permitted to leave.

Throughout the trip I considered how to shape my story for PBS. Up until this point in my career I had always worked on short two- or three-minute TV pieces—packages, as we called them in the business. Longer-form reporting, which was what the situation in Yemen called for, was different. Such reports require a narrative arc, strong characters, and context—the kind of background information a story of this length could offer. Other than *60 Minutes,* PBS was the only game in town doing that, and I felt like I had a golden ticket to do it well. I would certainly try. What meant the most to me was including

Yemeni voices from the streets. Whether ordinary Yeminis were examining a crater produced by a recent air strike or shopping in the Old City, theirs were the perspectives that mattered, more than those of any politician.

When filming around town, I also took great pride and happiness in the fact that Ben was finally experiencing the city I had been talking about from the time we had met, six years earlier. When I ducked into a store to buy a headscarf for him, a man pointed to "my husband" and asked if the scarf was for him, an American man traveling here in Yemen. Within seconds a white plastic chair had been fetched and placed down in the middle of the narrow street of shops. Ben was held in place while a small crowd gathered around us and this older gentleman, who wrapped the scarf around Ben's head, showed him how it was done. The people around us laughed and smiled and shouted, "Welcome to Yemen!" Ben did not remove the headscarf for the remainder of the trip, he was so delighted.

Despite these precious moments, the reality of the situation was that ISIS were finding opportunity in Yemen's chaos. The Houthis had clear control of the capital, Sana'a, and had managed to push Al Qaeda cells from the city. In a strange irony, this meant that for the first time in years, I felt safe walking the streets of Sana'a, eating in restaurants, waiting in traffic. During the past few years, in the midst of all the political disorder, Al Qaeda had attempted to snatch Westerners from cars, shops, and sidewalks. Now one group controlled the city, and it seemed at first to have a clear grip. I was wrong.

The day before we were scheduled to fly out of Sana'a airport and on to Jordan, a series of car bombs detonated near Houthi headquarters and two mosques where Shia worshippers were attending prayers. Several dozen were killed and more injured. ISIS were quick to claim responsibility. The group had never pulled off such a brazen string of attacks right at the center of Houthi control before. Everyone was shocked. The Houthi grip on the city suddenly felt fragile.

As we drove back to the hotel for the night, I was reminded of how isolated it felt to be in a city controlled by rebels aligned against much of the wider world. There were no embassies, no United Nations representatives present, and the Saudi blockade meant the only real way out was the airport. We were stuck. If ISIS had wanted to get into the Sheba Hotel in Sana'a and make a media splash by killing foreign journalists, they absolutely could. I started to feel guilty for bringing Ben. He had never been in a situation like this before. For me, it was relatively normal. I smiled and maintained a stoic exterior as we headed to bed for the night. But I didn't sleep for a moment.

I rested my flak jacket against the side of the bed and placed my boots next to it. I left my contact lenses in. An ISIS attack on the city seemed imminent, and I wanted to be ready.

Even a year after the Serena attack, I couldn't sleep in hotel rooms. I would get up in the middle of the night and wander the grounds, on some sort of subconscious perimeter patrol. I sat bolt upright in our bed in Sana'a that night and felt fearful and alone, even with Ben sleeping right beside me. I willed the morning to come, for the plane to take me away from here, yet felt guilty for leaving once again.

Suddenly, the dark space around me was filled with the sound of the muezzin, the call to prayer. The imam's pleading voice, imploring worshippers to come to God, filled the room and slowly soothed me, like water washing over me. He sang the call to prayer with such emotion that I was moved. I had felt suspended in time—with the darkness holding me in place. The muezzin reminded me I was not alone. I was with millions of other people, sleeping or awake, in that city, all of us hoping for the morning to come peacefully. I prayed to see the dawn light, to get home safely, for Yemen and everyone here with me to be okay. For peace in this country and in my heart.

When the piece aired, PBS loved it. They aired it in full, an eight-minute segment on Yemen that night on the *NewsHour*. I stayed up until two a.m. in our apartment in Beirut waiting for it to air. They seemed willing to make an exception about my accent for now.

In the months that followed, I reported for the *NewsHour* from Beirut and elsewhere in the region. They had no budget for a staff salary for a foreign correspondent, I was told, so this would be as good as it would get, but I was thrilled. No one else on American TV was doing such extensive in-depth coverage of global affairs at the time, and I wanted in on it. I knew it couldn't last forever. I could survive in Beirut for now on my savings and the small amount I made in public broadcasting, but sooner or later I would have to find a proper job, I told myself, at one of the networks.

That winter the phone rang. NBC were looking for a new foreign correspondent in their London bureau and they wanted me there for an interview. *This is it,* I thought. *Finally.*

17

Auditioning

THE STUDIO WAS A SIMPLE desk at the end of the small London newsroom. They had a stool and a camera and lights all set up. I had only ever filmed live standing in the field on rooftops or sidewalks in places like Afghanistan, Yemen, and Gaza. I perched on the stool, unsure of where to put my spiky high heels. Producers and cameramen slumped over their keyboards in the studio, unmoved by the auditions happening a few feet away. Stage fright gripped me, stripped me of my armor. The controlled environment of lights and air conditioning and well-heeled producers was not my comfort zone.

I was to give a briefing into the camera in front of me about a terror attack in the Indonesian capital of Jakarta that week. I had read everything I could find on the event that morning after a predawn jet-lag-fueled run around the still-sleeping streets of West London. Even Buckingham Palace had not a soul outside but the guards.

Deep down, I knew my work was unlike anything any of these executives had ever seen from a thirty-year-old reporter. I had covered everything from the Arab Spring to the Syrian civil war, Al Qaeda franchises, and the rise of ISIS. I spoke Arabic, and I could film and produce and edit my own stories. I had spent years polishing my skills as a live reporter in the field during breaking news. I was brave. I knew I could do the job and had proven it time and time again. For some reason, that confidence I projected in the field, all my moxie and grit, was suddenly so fragile in these offices.

I fretted over my hair, was gripped with absurd indecision about what to wear as I got ready in my hotel room, checked my makeup in a handheld mirror innumerable times. I just didn't trust people to like me. The young woman who once smuggled herself into Syria with $10,000 and a camera, who ran through the streets of Mogadishu filming battles against Al Qaeda–aligned fighters and worked under-cover documenting the bloody Yemeni revolution—and all of this by herself—felt more self-doubt and insecurity in those network offices in London and New York than anywhere on the planet.

At the producer's cue, I looked into the camera and began to speak. "Wait, wait, one minute!" interjected the NBC News' senior vice pres-ident of talent just before the words came out. She had been waiting in the corner of the room, just to my two o'clock vision. She marched over and gently pulled a lock of hair off my shoulder. "There," she smiled, standing back and looking at me across the desk. "Now remem-ber, Jane, an American accent." I looked back at the camera. "Five, four, three, two, one—go!"

I wanted the job so badly I could barely breathe.

I looked into the camera and spoke in an accent that wasn't mine about the Indonesia attacks, as well as the updates on world news that day, my heart thumping in my chest, and hoping my face didn't betray my nerves. Occasionally, the executive would stop me and ask me to start again when a word I had pronounced was a little too British. All they wanted was sixty seconds of my talking into the camera for the president of NBC News to scan, flicking between me and an unknown number of other candidates. He would not be looking at my résumé, my language skills, or my field experience—only this audition tape.

The executive in the room had flown in from New York to over-see the tryouts, alongside the bureau chief. She was kind to me and seemed to want me to have a shot. As we sat in an office off the newsroom after my audition, she explained that the president of NBC had requested only Americans, "but you are quite transatlantic, so I thought we would try it."

My accent was becoming a complex part of me, a potential liability, yet a malleable projection. Every time I came close to getting the job I wanted, I was always compelled to change something about myself, and my accent was usually the easiest option. Sitting cross-legged on hotel beds around the world, I would read *The New York Times* aloud, with as American an accent as I could muster. Practicing.

NBC had also asked me to prepare for a TV breaking news script-writing test. This was a part of me I did *not* need to change. I had been studying good scriptwriting my whole career, watching and transcribing the best reports on the news so I could study how other correspondents (or their producers) shaped stories, wove quotes in, and wrote to whatever limited video images were available. I had sat with script editors at Al Jazeera absorbing the best lessons on writing, and Ben had also coached me on scriptwriting. Before my trip to London, I had taken print stories and shot lists from the agencies, the Associated Press, and Reuters, and given myself one hour to write a good script. I practiced for hours each day. I was ready.

When I pressed send on the script after my designated time, I leaned back in my chair and exhaled. As the bureau chief showed me out, he shook my hand and said, "Your script was perfect." I beamed the whole way to Heathrow. A few weeks later I got the news that I didn't get the job.

The talent executive agreed to chat with me on the phone. "You don't want this job, Jane," she said. "It's mostly studio work and stand-ing in front of live shots. It's not the kind of enterprise reporting you do." It seemed I was somewhat overqualified for the few jobs that were available. The truth was, she was right. I didn't want to be reporting from behind a desk or on a hotel rooftop. But I desperately needed a job. I couldn't afford to keep reporting independently from the field. I had to be practical. Besides, however dull the work, jobs like these were a foot in the door at a network. If I could get this job, it might lead me back into the field, eventually, this time with real staff credentials. Like tenure in academia, such a job would secure my place in this work long term.

While I was contending with these career considerations, plans for the upcoming battle against ISIS were developing. The much-anticipated battle for Mosul city was imminent. I flew to Iraq. I stood on the ramparts of an ancient monastery, looking out over the plains of Nineveh, north of Mosul, the city where almost two years earlier, ISIS leader Abu Bakr al-Baghdadi had ascended the stairs to a pulpit and declared himself head of the Caliphate. For centuries, the Christians of northern Iraq had been fleeing to these defensive positions, stone cut and carved out of caves in the hillside, for safety. Down below were Christian villages, silent and grown up with weeds. Most had fled. I was filming a story on the Christian militias fighting ISIS, as well as visiting the front line with Iraqi government forces as they launched simple mortar attacks on ISIS positions in the countryside well north of Mosul city.

ISIS were now the most ambitious terror group in the world. They'd taken territory across the Arab world and lashed out across the West with attacks on the *Charlie Hebdo* magazine headquarters and the Bataclan Theatre in Paris. Western intelligence agencies were on high alert, monitoring their own citizens traveling from London, Paris, and Brussels into Syria's chaos on the promise of a God-given paradise, and then returning to those cities to enact showy, indiscriminate violence against the public. A huge American-led military bombing campaign had been hitting ISIS with air strikes for two years, at a cost of over $8 billion. Named Operation Inherent Resolve, it was the result of a coalition between the military arms of American, European, and Middle Eastern nations. The air strikes were softening the positions of the ISIS militant strongholds, but we all knew a major ground offensive would be needed to rout such a deeply dug-in terror group. America would probably send special forces, but after the disastrous Iraq war, the Obama administration was still determined to draw down the U.S. presence in the Middle East, so the task was always going to fall to the Iraqi forces themselves, and eventually to Syrian fighters recruited, trained, and armed by the United States.

A massive war was coming. ISIS knew this, too.

18

Thumbing Humvees in Hell

AN IRAQI SOLDIER CARRYING A tiny boy in his arms rushed into the clinic, followed by his father, a wide-eyed man in his forties wearing a leather jacket and jeans. The father's face was silent with distress. The soldier placed the man's five-year-old son, Karam, on a gurney in the front-line hospital carved out of an abandoned cement bungalow. The man leaned over his son, murmuring comforting words and caressing the boy's head with his hand, utterly powerless to help his son. "Ba-ba, ba-ba!" wailed the boy, tears running down his cheeks.

A young bearded American man with a stethoscope hanging around his neck leaned over Karam. Wearing camouflage fatigues and white surgical gloves, he occasionally barked orders at the three Iraqi soldiers around him. Another American in a flak jacket and combat clothing stood next to him, handing him bandages and tape. They all kept a close watch on the American with the stethoscope as he replaced the bandages on Karam's leg as quickly and gently as he could, the boy squirming and burying his face in his father's chest.

Karam's right thigh had a huge metal brace sticking out. Standing to the side, trying to stay out of the way, I asked his father what happened. "Hawan," he said, looking up at me and gesturing with his hand an arc and landing. Mortar. Two weeks ago, his house had been hit and Karam's leg shattered. Within ISIS-controlled Mosul, where they lived, hospitals were still able to function, and the doctors had operated on his leg. Now the wound was infected. The boy had a fever and was in terrible pain.

Karam's father had carried him on foot across the front lines to escape ISIS territory and make it to this clinic. Here, on the edge of the city, was the only operating triage center, treating civilians and soldiers. Whoever could limp, be carried, or finagle a ride in a military Humvee was welcome. The Iraqi military had banned all civilian vehicles from driving in Mosul, in reaction to the onslaught of ISIS suicide bombers in cars attacking their front lines. For the hundreds of thousands of trapped civilians, that dramatically reduced their chances of surviving an injury. Even ambulances, if anyone could find a rare one, were stopped and held at checkpoints for long stretches of precious time.

The American treating Karam inside was Pete Reed, a twenty-seven-year-old former Marine from New Jersey. He came outside and leaned against the wall next to me, lighting a cigarette and exhaling a cloud of smoke. He and Derek Coleman, another young American from California who was also twenty-seven, had arrived months before as idealistic young volunteers with the Iraqi Kurdish forces who had begun the battle against ISIS, north of here on the Nineveh Plains.

An Iraqi military Humvee, battered from battle, came careening down the street toward the clinic, throwing up yellow dust everywhere, and slid to a halt by the metal front gate. A young soldier carrying a large pink blanket jumped out of the back seat. At first, all I could make out was some long, dark hair falling from inside it. When I approached him, I could see that inside the blanket was a little girl, around six or seven years old. There was blood dripping down her hair. She had been shot in the head. Her eyes were closed, but remarkably, she was moaning. She continued to moan as she was rushed into the clinic and placed on a bed, Pete and Derek worked with furious, focused energy. An Iraqi soldier held a bag of saline solution above her head.

The girl's moans made me feel as though my heart was on fire. Pete struggled to wrap her wounds in bandages. "Hold her fucking head!" he yelled. Oxygen was being hand-pumped into her little mouth.

She was no longer moaning. Blood began to seep from her fore-head through the bandage and dripped onto the gurney. As the group worked on her, I stepped outside to give them room.

The girl's aunt was standing outside, screaming and holding her head. She came to me with her arms outstretched and collapsed at my feet, weeping. The family had been fleeing ISIS-controlled areas when the group opened fire and shot the girl in the back of the head. I had heard stories like this in recent days. To ISIS fighters, these people were abandoning the Caliphate. Killing them would frighten others from leaving. Pete tried his best to stop the bleeding and called for an ambulance to come and collect the girl. She needed surgery im-mediately. Her bleeding largely contained, and bag of saline solution attached to her tiny arm, she was rushed into another vehicle that disappeared in a cloud of dust, headed through checkpoints toward a hospital far beyond the front.

Pete stepped outside the small triage center and stood in the soft-ening late-afternoon sunlight, lit a cigarette, and let out another one of those full-body sighs.

"You can see only so many dead kids a day so many days in a row before you are going to be changed," he said. "I have seen a couple hundred.

"They are shooting people with white flags. They are shooting kids. Last week, we had two kids in a row who had been shot in the neck or the head by an ISIS sniper because they were fleeing Mosul, not acci-dental grazing fire or anything like that, proper sniper shots, head and neck and face. They're purposely trying to kill these people."

Pete got a phone call with the news that the little girl had died on the way to the hospital. Despite all the children who had their lives stolen by the war, he and Derek saved an untold number of lives by giving soldier and civilian alike a fighting chance to survive their wounds long enough to get to a hospital. They helped young soldiers, barely men, know their lives were worth something more than can-non fodder. They risked their lives to provide fleeing civilians some hope they can find help. I had spent only one day with them, and the impact they'd had on others in front of my eyes was more than many of us will ever make in a lifetime.

As I worked on my script in the hotel room a couple of hours' drive away in Erbil city, I, too, sighed and sunk into my seat. Doing this story justice—telling it well, making people listen—was something I wanted more than ever. This would be my small contribution, paling in comparison to what people like Pete and Derek were doing, but I needed an act of service. I was drawn by the desire to contribute in some way, but also pushed by fearful doubts over whether I was helping.

Several months before I met Pete and Derek, I walked into a refugee camp not far from Fallujah city. Families who had recently fled the fighting there made it to this government-sanctioned camp and had little support from the UN or wider charities. An older man with a white beard came to me and indicated I should follow him. I walked behind him in the blistering heat as he winded his way down the trash-strewn pathway between the tents. Then he disappeared into one. When he came out, he held a baby in his arms, clearly ill, barely conscious. He reached for paperwork, doctors' notes and prescriptions, and asked me to give him medication.

"He thinks you are a doctor," my fixer explained. The man looked at me, and as he realized I could not help him, his eyes filled with confusion, then hopelessness. When I looked in his face, I felt a sharp stab of shame.

Those moments are the worst I ever faced as a war reporter—not the rough conditions and not the danger, but the feeling that I was not helping. I still don't know the real solution to that, but I was coming to learn that doing the work well was a start. I had a huge platform now—American Public Broadcasting, and longer magazine-length TV pieces on the nightly national news. I was determined to use it to get beyond the "bang bang." It was the one service I could offer.

Our story on the volunteer clinic at the front received an overwhelming response from viewers. Other networks covered their work also, and eventually more volunteers and NGOs arrived in the city to help with medevac efforts. They would be badly needed. As Iraqi forces pushed ISIS back, they followed, deeper and deeper into the city, being drawn by the group into a hellscape of fighting and death.

The United States was barreling into its own tumult. I woke one night in my hotel room in Iraq, having gone to sleep long before presidential elections were called. Checking my phone's screen, I learned that Trump had won. In the final days of his administration, Obama loosened the rules of engagement, thereby allowing a lower criterion for air strikes on buildings in Mosul. Trump, not to be outdone, increased air strikes, making good on his campaign promise to "Bomb the shit out of them."

ISIS had drawn the battle lines from the start in Mosul. Now as the final push across the river and into western Mosul began, they retreated into the Old City, where narrow alleyways blocked the Iraqi army's Humvees and any military vehicles, and death stalked each and every soldier as he entered on foot and was attacked from every doorway and window possible. The civilians still trapped in the Old City, many of them not allowed by ISIS to flee, were used as human shields, some locked in houses as fighters launched attacks from their rooftops.

Iraqi troops on the ground often tried to help civilians flee, getting word on the radio that some were attempting to sneak across broken bridges or swim the waters. Down by the river, one special forces unit got word that there were two men crossing the river, clinging to the underside of the bridge. We waited with the troops, some crouched against a wall and others behind Humvees as they shouted instructions to the young men. They came over the bridge in their underwear, carrying their clothes under their arms, jogging, looking half exhilarated, half petrified. The soldiers told them to take off their clothes to prove they had no explosives. When they reached us, the soldiers hugged them. Panting with adrenaline and from the exertion, they pulled on their jeans and T-shirts by the sidewalk, free men. Thousands of civilians still trapped in ISIS-held areas would not live to know the feeling.

I returned to Mosul several times throughout the campaign, each time the battles pushed deeper into the city, led by Iraqi special forces. On one assignment I got up before dawn and left the Kurdish capital, heading west to Mosul on the highway through multiple checkpoints before getting to the outskirts of the city. At the final checkpoint, before entering Mosul and what was the start of the militarized zone, we pulled over, got out of the car, and put our flak jackets on, pulling out iPhone maps to double-check the route. Mosul was the most accessible war zone on the planet—the Iraqis insisted on accreditation and then let us go wherever we wanted. The problem was that the front line would snake through streets and neighborhoods in a seemingly random pattern, changing daily. The Iraqi forces were not thoroughly clearing houses, and ISIS fighters were often hiding in neighborhoods, popping up behind forces and sniping at them.

As we drove into the city, I watched the road out the windscreen for correct routes to the front line, via the Iraqis' command center, with gritted teeth and shallow breaths. A wrong turn could bring us straight into an ISIS ambush or find us taking cross fire. Armored vehicles were being rented for several thousand dollars a day by the big networks. So ours was soft-skin. At times we would see up ahead the wreckage of a suicide car bomb or other rubble from destroyed buildings, dragged across the road. Those piles of tangled, rusting debris marked the end of Iraqi army control. Bouncing down the narrow, potholed streets that felt like a maze, I watched out the front and back windows for car bombers, amazed at how much of the city had been retaken since I had last been there.

The command center was an abandoned villa in a built-up neighborhood of alleyways between cement houses surrounded by whitewashed walls. Jumping out of the car, we ran inside the building with my cameraman Alessandro. We heard the sound of stray gunfire from the nearby front rush over our heads. On the roof of the building, commanders sat on abandoned sofas or paced up and down, talking to their troops on radios and mapping positions on digital tablets. I marched over to them with a chipper smile and asked for access to the front. *Worth a shot,* I thought. Explaining in Arabic to several stern-faced officers with thick mustaches that I was with public broadcasting in America, I smiled and asked for a ride in a Humvee. Somehow it worked, and they nodded, gave me a name to drop to the next passing Humvee headed in that direction, and wished me good luck.

Outside, a single armored vehicle roared down the road and I waved it down. The driver inside, a young, wide-eyed, and nervous-looking soldier, was alone save for a gunner in position above him. Fine, he said, and gestured to me to get in the back. The Iraqi Reuters TV cameraman had been waiting, too, and, as soon as he saw I had persuaded the driver to take us, came running over to climb in as well. "Can we share?" he asked. "I have a medic with me." Standing next to him was a massive bearded New Zealander with a weather-worn face and a wide grin. Okay, I said, figuring having a combat medic with us would be worth the squeeze. Being by far the smallest, I crouched below the gunner, cross-legged, ducking to avoid getting slapped in the face with swinging ammunition belts.

The driver looked in the rearview mirror and saw an enormous Kiwi, an Iraqi reporter, an Italian cameraman, and a tiny Irishwoman. He shook his head and returned to driving as fast as he could over the bumpy, war-churned road, leaning anxiously over the steering wheel and looking out for ISIS cars. In that moment, I thought about Tim Page. He had said there would never be access like there had been in Vietnam, where he was "thumbing choppers." This was close enough.

At the front we were able to move around and talk with officers in charge with remarkable ease. The combat they were experiencing was a terrifying new type of warfare that ISIS had pioneered and prepared for. They combined traditional military tactics on the battlefield, like ground assaults, with insurgent tactics like car bombs and suicide bombers. This was more than these soldiers had ever faced.

I met Major Ziad Al Ghobary in an abandoned house occupied by Iraqi special forces troops. He was keen to show us around. In his forties, he wore no body armor, clad instead in combats and a fleece. In his trouser side pocket was a small iPad-like device he used to map the coordinates of ISIS positions. Clipped to the other pocket was a radio he used to call in U.S. air strikes when they needed them. And they needed them a lot. ISIS were sending explosive-laden car bombs into the positions of his troops, Al Ghobary told us, to distract and unnerve them before then sending wave after wave of troops on foot. Even after they managed to clear streets, ISIS booby-trapped houses as they retreated, leaving trip wires attached to door handles and IEDs in children's toys, on faucets, and underneath rubble.

As we filmed Major Al Ghobary talking to his men, the rattle of gunfire coming from the roof filled the room. We raced up the staircase to find three young soldiers firing frantically into the street in front. ISIS were attempting to attack our position and were closing in. Major Al Ghobary crouched below the wall and I crawled over to the fighters as they took turns to duck or stand up and fire toward the ISIS troops. "Watch your head!" he yelled at the soldiers in Arabic. Two of them were wearing baseball caps instead of helmets. A car bomb had been spotted moving into position. The soldiers held them off.

The previous day a major battle had taken place in an open-air food market. Major Al Ghobary took us there on foot to see the destruction, shouting over his shoulder as he marched ahead that we should not touch anything in case it was booby-trapped. The rusty metal frames of abandoned market stalls remained in rows, some collapsed in heaps of blue tarpaulin and boards, others leaning there. On the ground lay the bodies of several ISIS fighters. One in light khaki combat clothing lay on his back, arms outstretched. His neck was almost entirely severed, leaving his head hanging to the side, a mop of thick, wild curly hair catching dust from the street. A soldier stopped to snap a picture of him on his phone, looking up at me and smiling.

As we walked through the market, lumps of what looked like meat lay about, scorched in places and red and raw in others. Flies buzzed around a khaki-green ammunition belt, smeared in blood and flesh, that had landed on one of the stall tables. I had never seen the remains of suicide bombers before. I had by this stage become fairly hardened to the sight of dead soldiers, but not to this. I've never eaten a rare steak since. For a long time, I avoided the butcher's counter at the grocery store.

The final checkpoint out of the city did not allow movement after dark, and we had spent so long filming that day we missed our window to get out. The soldiers had commandeered an abandoned house already and set up a simple cooking stove in the garden. I slept there next to the Iraqi fighters, my cameraman, and our fixer Arshed. They had built a small campfire in the garden, too. Arshed disappeared for half an hour and returned with a victorious smile, hot food, and a bottle of Johnnie Walker whisky. I sipped the golden liquid and felt it burn my throat and warm my belly. I had been numb since the marketplace and was anxious to feel something. We were shown to a small room filled with wooden bed frames with no mattresses and fleece blankets as the night's chill set in. The soldiers bantered and laughed and shared stories and pictures on their phones. They could not have been more gentlemanly to me, the lone female in their midst. I fell asleep to the sound of their laughter and conversation, grateful for the safety.

When I finally returned to Erbil and the comfort and modernity of my hotel room, I slipped into a hot bath and lay still amid the steam and soapsuds. Perhaps I thought I could sweat the images of Mosul out of me. I sipped a glass of red wine and waited for emotion to come. It didn't. I needed more time.

Ben had flown in and was coordinating network news coverage of the offensive from the Rotana hotel in Erbil. We met other journalists at a hotel bar to share notes. As we walked in, a tall, scruffy-looking man waved across the room at me. He had wild hair and a deep tan. It was the Kiwi medic.

"I got shot!" he shouted across the busy room, half laughing and half shouting in disbelief.

"What?" I replied, confused.

He was holding a beer in one hand, and with the other he pulled up his trouser leg and hoisted his foot onto the barstool next to him, revealing a massive bandage around his calf. "Those fuckers shot me!" he said in his thick New Zealander accent, before letting out a roar of laughter and returning to chat to the barman. It was a nasty flesh wound inflicted most likely by an ISIS supporter firing an old gun from their backyard, later that day after we had gotten separated.

As winter 2016 turned to 2017, the Iraqi military pushed ISIS west to the Tigris River and eventually across it. The city split in two, between everything to the west of the river, including the Old City, controlled by ISIS, and the east, parts of which were trying to recover and rebuild. Civilians returned to the eastern parts of the city. Small markets and restaurants popped up. Fighting and gunfire across the river was often drowned out by the sound of generators.

The number of bombs that fell on Mosul's Old City as the spring of 2017 turned to summer set records. Some 1,250 air strikes were carried out throughout the ten-month-long campaign, with 29,000 munitions. Most of them fell on the Old City as Iraqi ground troops faltered. The Baghdad government was impatient to declare victory. So they pushed forward exhausted elite units that were taking an unsustainable 40 percent casualty rate. Air strikes were called in to finish the job.

A year and a half later, I stumbled over the rubble, astonished and silent, and watched a woman stack cinder blocks high enough to sleep under. Her children stood nearby and watched. Thousands of bodies still lay under the rubble, a thought that haunted me as though anguished souls were watching me. I had never seen destruction like it. Mosul's Old City was reduced to rubble, and the rubble was then pounded to dust. The very few local people we could find who had returned—made possible with bulldozers creating a pathway to their destroyed homes—told us all their neighbors were dead.

The commander of Operation Inherent Resolve, Lieutenant General Stephen J. Townsend, later described the destruction of Mosul's Old City as akin to that of Stalingrad during World War II. An estimated 10,000 civilians died in the campaign to retake the city, more than the number of ISIS fighters killed. The final months of the campaign, when the battle for the Old City intensified, were the most brutal.

I wasn't there. I watched it on TV and my colleagues' social media accounts. The day victory was declared in Mosul, I was shooting a cooking demonstration of fried chicken in a trendy London restaurant for CBS.

19

A Relapse

AS I FLICKED BETWEEN CHANNELS, coverage of Trump's first foreign trip as president was wall-to-wall. White House correspondents trailing the president were now live on air discussing Saudi Arabia's counterterrorism stance, efforts to modernize, and historic friendship with the United States. Riyadh was hosting the Washington, D.C., reporters, not the legion of foreign correspondents who had been covering the Middle East for years.

Trump descended from Air Force One next to Melania, and there was a flyover of U.S.-made, Saudi-bought fighter jets, leaving a trail of red, white, and blue smoke streaks in the sky. None of the TV reporters mentioned the use of the jets in Yemen. Coverage continued to an elaborate public signing of a more than $100 billion deal for more American military supplies. They would soon ship out to Yemen.

Just as Yemen was not mentioned, neither were Saudi ties to Islamic radicalization in the region and beyond, or the repression of groups like Shias and women's rights activists. There were smirks about the glowing orb Trump and the Saudi royals clutched, and snark about the gold necklace he was gifted and traditional Khaleeji sword dance he and Secretary of State Rex Tillerson took part in. Commentary on his meeting with Egyptian dictator General Abdel Fattah el-Sisi made no mention of the coup, the Cairo massacre, or ongoing human rights atrocities.

The Saudi charm offensive was not only working on Trump; their efforts to spin the press with tales of a new Saudi Arabia were a triumph. I threw a cushion at the TV in anger and winced in pain. My nose hurt badly. My whole face did.

I slowly stood up from the sofa, crept into the Manhattan apartment's classic white-tiled bathroom, looked in the mirror, and flinched. I was in the early stages of two black eyes. There was angry swelling all throughout my cheeks. My upper lip was so swollen it protruded down and outward. The tip of my nose was now a bloodied, inflamed nub pushing out from under a white bandage. I picked up a tube of antibiotic cream and dabbed the ointment inside my nostril with a Q-tip. It hurt so badly tears gathered in the corners of my puffy eyes. I was too afraid to take the opioid painkillers the surgeon had prescribed.

That I found myself in May 2017 recovering from a nose job in an Airbnb apartment on the Upper West Side was not something I failed to view without humor, despite the pain. How far I had come from the Al Jazeera reporter with no makeup in just a few years was due in part to my own growing cynicism concerning the industry as much as to my insecurity. I was grateful for the naiveté of my younger self, who thought I would be judged on my experience and skill alone. Without her, I never would have kept on, undeterred. But the more I worked in the business and the longer I watched myself being passed over for jobs I desperately wanted (and needed), the more a grittier realism set in. Maybe what was really holding me back was something simpler than my sense of not being polished enough, I thought. Maybe it was staring me in the face.

I had reached out to CBS's London bureau chief, Andy Clarke, about summer stand-in work for the network's affiliate news service, Newspath. The full-time correspondent was on leave and they were looking for a temporary replacement. Andy seemed confused at my application. "Why would you want this gig, Jane? You have the best job in TV news!" he asked, astonished, when I sat down with him in his office soon after. "This is a far cry from war zones and serious news." He was right. This job would take me from a national news show, covering the biggest stories in the world for a serious news network, to reporting on British royals and quirky European tales like the rise of American food trends in the United Kingdom.

Everyone thought I had the best job in journalism. They forgot I didn't have a job at all. PBS kept me on as a freelancer, and what I was earning on my assignments could not sustain me. If my career was to survive, I had to figure out a way to another network. Newspath might, just might, put me on the radar of the CBS executives long enough for them to hire me in the bureau as a foreign correspondent. London was the main hub for their foreign news teams. I was willing to try. "Well, war reporting is my passion, but I have bills to pay," I replied to Andy. He shrugged and turned back to his computer.

As I was about to walk out of his office he shouted over my shoulder, "Why do you speak with an American accent? Where is that from?" I shrugged and murmured a half response about living with an American boyfriend.

People who got into TV news during its previous heyday struggle to understand the hustle of my generation. I wasn't angry, I had seen this confusion from those who had been on the inside before. No one got a job even as a desk assistant now without a master's from an Ivy League school, and likely family connections on top.

"Meet our new intern!" One of the producers at the CBS bureau beamed as she walked him around the office to introduce him, a young, affable-looking, floppy-haired recent graduate. "He's a family friend!" No one seemed in the slightest dazed by this. Family friend had a great chance of getting hired as a desk assistant at the end of his summer internship.

I didn't get angry. Andy agreed to hire me for the summer; I had the on-camera work he was looking for. However modest this step was, it felt like forward momentum. But first I would fly to New York to take care of my face.

Ben, in an act of extraordinary tenderness, met me there to take care of me for five days post-surgery. Once I had explained to him my plan to look after myself, which was entirely on brand for me, he overruled my decision and arrived in time for the surgery. He shopped for mac and cheese and tubs of ice cream, stocked the freezer with ice for the swelling, and held my hand throughout. I was grateful for the help. Help was not something I found easy to accept.

As my nose began to heal and I braved a few walks in Central Park with my baseball cap low over my face, I began to get ready for the London assignment. I hadn't told anyone I was in New York or what I was doing there. I didn't know how to explain it, even to myself. I kept thinking about that little square box around my head in the video I had recorded for NBC executives and agonizing over what they had found unacceptable. The more qualified and experienced I became, the more personally I internalized the rejection.

A friend had once told me long ago, by means of kindly advice, that if a woman has not become a household name in TV news by the time she is thirty-five years old, she isn't going to become one. I knew in my rational mind that this statement was absurd, but it still haunted me. I was turning thirty-three that September. I booked the surgery with the last of my savings. *When I present myself to CBS in a few weeks,* I thought to myself as I looked in the mirror that morning after the operation, *I will be perfect.* Even my large round nose will be fixed.

London felt like a foreign country to me. Many friends had moved there over the years, from Dubai and Beirut, yet I knew I didn't belong. On the outskirts of the city in a bland hotel, I looked out at low cobalt skies and fought the feeling that this was not home.

Each morning when I arrived at the bureau, I was to select the headline stories from around the world and write up a script to add to the teleprompter. Then I would head to a desk at the top of the newsroom and read the headlines into the camera for the affiliate stations across the United States to use should they wish to. Heading out to report features from around London, I covered stories the local stations were interested in. The July Fourth celebrations piece we decided to offer was a visit to Benjamin Franklin's former home in London. Perhaps he felt as at home and comfortable there at the seat of the British crown as I currently did with this new job.

Between these trips out around London, I rushed back to my desk and checked the news from Iraq online. I knew the end of the battle for Mosul was close, and politicians and generals were itching to make an announcement. News crews from around the world were there, or at least close to the fighting, as the worst blow against ISIS's control over territory was about to be completed, but at a terrible cost to civilian life.

One morning, I woke extra early as usual to do my hair. I climbed into high heels, looked at my new face in the mirror, and felt exhausted—a painful fatigue from pretending and trying and forcing myself into shapes and identities I just was not. The voice of the BBC's Orla Guerin blasted from the TV as she reported from Mosul's Old City with her usual marriage of humanistic civilian observations and the brave front-line experiences of the soldiers. I sat cross-legged on the bed, my hair still in curlers, and watched. I desperately wanted to be there. *What am I doing here?* I thought.

I got a call from the cameraman I worked with in Mosul, Alessandro. He was there, on assignment for another outlet, filming with the Iraqi troops as they fought street by street to inch their way forward, through a hail of bullets and bombs. I sat at my desk in the CBS office as he described the hell there. He was shouting through the phone, likely due to his hearing suffering from being close to intense gunfire, but also to the shock of it all. There was horror in his voice. I walked over to the glass door and pulled it shut.

He described the troops running out of drinking water and refusing to move forward, near mutiny, until more was sent. The fighters were collapsing of heatstroke in the blistering Iraqi sun. The team had gotten trapped inside buildings, surrounded by ISIS, and had to run behind exhausted soldiers, fighting their way out with the last of their ammunition. Civilians were trapped in basements, more than anyone could even know. I told him to take good care of himself. We both knew I didn't just mean physically.

After he hung up, I looked out the window at the leafy London suburb and felt searing guilt that I was not there. My years in the field had prepared me well for a story like that. I knew I had the skills to do it well, and that PBS was not sending another correspondent into the last days of this battle. I struggled to answer my own question of why I was not there.

On the day that victory was declared in Mosul, the network was filming a cooking segment on how classic American food was becoming hip in London. I smiled and feigned interest in this new development while a celebrity chef, launching a restaurant in the trendy Shoreditch neighborhood, did a quick demo of fried chicken. Handing a drumstick to me at the very end, I went to take a bite. "Don't eat that!" he yelled. "It's not cooked through, it's only for show."

A more uniquely British story followed: Prince William and Catherine's son, Prince George, was about to start his first day at school. South of the River Thames, in the now-gentrified Battersea area of London, I stood with the press pack on the pavement as parents and nannies took their littlest ones by the hand to be greeted by the school headmistress at the door. There was much suspense over whether Kate would be there in person or not, owing to her current severe morning sickness from her second pregnancy. In the end, William came with little George. I filmed my stand-up and headed back. My feet were very sore. I was cross with myself. I knew that I was wasting my time.

As I flew home to Beirut at the end of the summer, my body ached in a way it never did when I returned from war. I knew I would have to find another way to approach my work. Sure, I needed to make a living, but was this about that entirely? Or was this rush to the networks about an inner need for validation? The thing that truly spoke to me, that I adored most about my work, was talking to civilians and finding the humanity in troubled places. That was what this epic journey from the farm in South Armagh had been about. It was about helping connect people. I had done none of that in London. Not since I had been in the Mazda showroom in Dubai had I felt this strongly I was on the wrong path.

I vowed never to do this to myself again. *I'm done trying to impress the casting agents of the networks,* I told myself. *I cannot keep begging for acceptance from an industry that wants someone different from me.* I needed to get back to my work.

20

Women of War

I SAT LISTENING TO THE young woman. "I never thought I would be happy again. When something so terrible happens to you when you are just a girl, just seventeen, it's very hard to forget it." When she talked about what had happened three years earlier, her face became blank, her eyes looking away—at the floor, the wall, anywhere but at me. She crouched over as she spoke, sitting cross-legged on a cushion on the cement floor, making herself smaller.

I had seen similar symptoms of trauma in several other former female victims of ISIS. When their fighters swept into her village in Western Iraq, they killed her father and kidnapped her, her eight siblings, and her mother. She was taken across the border to Raqqa, the capital of the so-called Caliphate, and held as a sex slave to fighters for a year before she escaped.

She wore a large navy blue shirt and baggy pants. Her dark brown hair swept across her forehead under a loose blue headscarf. We called her Zahida in the interview and filmed from various angles to keep her from being identifiable. Her attackers were still on the loose. Zahida was raped repeatedly, as were thousands of Yazidi women when they were rounded up by ISIS in an astoundingly medieval act of genocidal cruelty and mass slavery. Outside, several children rode their small bicycles in circles in the yellow dust. Only a handful of families had returned to this village since the genocide.

On August 3, 2014, ISIS militants poured into the Sinjar district of

Nineveh province in northern Iraq, the ancestral home to the Yazidi people, unleashing two weeks of unspeakable violence. The Yazidis are an ancient people from Iraq, estimated to number around 500,000 in 2014, who worship God in the form of an image of a peacock, colorful and symbolic of all life. Christian and Islamic practices are woven into their traditions, and tiny white temples with small spires can be seen scattered across the hilly dry landscape of Sinjar.

ISIS fighters went on a rampage of killing when they reached villages like Zahida's in the Hardan area of Sinjar. Men were buried alive and gunned down when they refused to convert to Islam. Women and children were driven away in trucks to ISIS-controlled areas, where they were sold in slave markets. Kurdish forces had left the area, leaving the Yazidis unprotected. Some 50,000 fled to a nearby mountain and collapsed from heat exhaustion and starvation until Iraqi government helicopters sent a small amount of help. For days, the world watched as ISIS surrounded and massacred this ancient, peaceful minority in rural Iraq.

After my summer in London, I had returned home to Beirut and made a plan for coverage that I cared about. The Yazidi genocide had made headlines in 2014, but so little had been said since. In late 2017, I wanted to go there and talk to the women who had been freed, to find out if their community could ever heal, and if the women themselves could. This was a crime against women unlike the world had seen since the days of the Taliban rule in Afghanistan, and we could not let it fall away, replaced by new, fresher headlines.

I followed my instinct. I was not interested in chasing "exclusives" anymore. I needed to tell stories that mattered to me.

Zahida's mother sat on the cement floor of her simple home next to her. She had been freed only three days prior. Zahida and her mother reached for each other as we talked, placing fingers on knees or a hand on a wrist.

Women like Zahida's mother were taken by ISIS and sold as house slaves, forced to cook and clean for the high-ranking families. The family was transported to a sorting center the militants had prepared before raiding villages. Once there, Zahida and her sisters were taken away first, leaving their mother with her younger children. Eventually, they, too, were separated.

Zahida's mother was bought by a wealthy Saudi family living in Raqqa city, she explained. Raqqa, the Caliphate's capital, was across the border in Syria. She wept silently as she remembered the cruelty of the mistress she was enslaved by. When Zahida's mother told her captor she dreamed of returning home to Sinjar one day, the woman had sneered back, saying she would die in her house as her slave. Zahida took her mother's hand in her own. When the young female interpreter with me, Adiba, also from the Yazidi community, relayed this sentence, I felt my throat close over and my eyes become wet.

Zahida's mother didn't die in that woman's house. As the offensive against ISIS moved west from Mosul, across the Iraqi border and into Syria, air strikes and attacks on Raqqa city were spooking some of the foreign fighters and their families. Many began to secretly plan to flee and head home, selling assets they couldn't take with them, including their slaves. The family sold Zahida's mother for $13,000. Wealthy Yazidis from around the world had quietly pooled funds to buy the freedom of thousands of women and girls. It was a bitter pill to swallow, giving money to such monsters, but one that saved many lives.

While she was waiting, working, and dreaming of coming home, her daughter Zahida had escaped already, a year after they were all taken, and was living alone in one of the many refugee camps tens of thousands of Yazidis had fled to in northwestern Iraq. While she was waiting there, life finally gifted her some kindness. One by one, her sisters were ransomed and arrived at the camp. Then she met a young Yazidi man there and fell in love. Just a month before we sat on the floor of her extended family's home to interview her, she had her wedding. "I have experienced both great sadness and great happiness in my life," she said, with remarkable acumen. Her mother came home to find all her daughters had made it out alive, and one was a new bride. Her sons were never found.

The whole Yazidi community felt the choking betrayal. The rage that lived on inside the women who were enslaved and raped flashed for a second in these interviews. But their stories betray a deeper, more shocking treachery. The ISIS fighters that came for them weren't some sort of foreign strangers from lands far away. Some were their neighbors, men from nearby Arab villages. The one time Zahida truly looked me in the eye was when she told me that the boy who came to claim her was someone she knew. "My father had invited him in for meals with us," she said, her mother nodding and staring at the floor. Something as simple as a crush by a boy from a nearby village had devolved into an unspeakable crime.

As we said our goodbyes, Adiba hugged Zahida tightly and held on to her for some time. After the interview they talked together on the front porch of the house as I waited in the dry, dusty street outside by the car, surrounded by the empty houses, those universal symbols of genocide. It felt hard to breathe. I was impatient to go, feeling a profound physical and emotional unease. I told myself it was the heat, but the grief in the air there was strangling. I had draped an arm around Zahida's mother and fought tears back before heading outside to kick at a patch of weeds and wait for Alessandro the cameraman and Adiba to join me.

As we drove away, bouncing down the dirt track from the village to the main road, we passed an area covered with mounds of disturbed earth, baked hard and overgrown with dry grass. About a dozen meters long and half that wide, the patch of earth was surrounded by flimsy metal rods and a plastic fence. A mass grave. The men from Zahida's village were not coming home. They were already there.

Adiba was looking out the window with a lengthy, pensive stare. Various connections of mine had recommended Adiba Qasim as a good point person, guide, fixer, and interpreter for journalists covering the Yazidi genocide. She was only in her early twenties but had a quiet force about her that communicated a knowledge far beyond her years. Her big brown eyes were sad. She wore blue jeans and a baggy T-shirt, her shoulder-length hair uncovered.

"What did you guys talk about?" I finally asked her, farther down the road. Still looking out the window, she answered, "I asked her if she had seen any of my cousins when she was in captivity."

Adiba had, I was about to learn, lost over seventy members of her extended family, all vanishing into ISIS's clutches. We stopped the car by the side of the desolate road, surrounded by dry grass and rocks. I stood in the hot breeze and listened.

"She told me that she saw two of them. And the last time *I* saw them they were, like, twelve years old," said Adiba. "She told me that they had been bought and sold. They were slaves." That was a year ago. There had been no word of them since.

Her face hardened, save for a small crease between her eyes that appeared for a few seconds. Her emotions were buried somewhere much too deep inside to break free. Alessandro and I later discussed asking Adiba how she might feel about being in the story, agreeing she should become a major part of our reporting. She agreed.

Before visiting Zahida's village we had been taken to a house by the side of the road—a lonely single-story home with a small garden. Inside, we found a young woman sitting on the floor of her bare living room, her back against the wall, staring into space. She wore a long floral dress and scarf around her neck and looked as if she could have been in her late twenties. She had recently been freed from ISIS captivity. Her husband had joined those off fighting as volunteers against the group, leaving her here in this empty house with only her own torturous memories.

We asked Adiba if she would like to talk to us, and she said she would like to talk with the camera off. The truth was, she didn't want to be interviewed, but she also didn't want to be alone. Adiba took her hand and we sat quietly next to her for a while. She sat underneath a ceiling fan on the cement floor of her simple cinder block home and appeared trance-like. I have never in my life before or since seen a soul as alone in this world. For years I had mournful dreams of driving away from her house, leaving her there.

By late 2017, some reporters, impatient and hungry for a gripping story, dug deep for the shocking and salacious details of rape, asking women and girls to recount exactly what had happened, point by point. This level of granular detail may make for compelling reading, but it meant those women were forced to relive the devastating moments in their lives all over again. It is the essence of re-traumatizing a person, and the human rights equivalent of reporting on only the explosions and the gunfire, not the civilians. Adiba's sympathetic presence around the women we talked to reminded me to do better than that.

I wanted to approach my work with the same empathy and compassion that she did.

I asked Adiba if she would like to take us to her village. She hadn't gone back in years, since she, too, had fled to the nearby Kurdish capital with her parents and siblings. She shrugged yes, feigning a sort of casual agreement, but it was clear to me from her eyes that this trip came with untold emotional weight. Once on the ground and pulling filming gear from the trunk of our car, she looked around in silence, and I wondered whether she had preferred not to come here alone. Arriving with a news crew, as part of a team of journalists, she could peer at her old life from a somewhat safer distance.

As we walked down the street in her village, Kahana Sor, a small collection of cement homes divided by weed-choked roads, some children's voices could be heard from nearby homes. One shop was open, selling groceries like bread and boxes of biscuits and small bottles of cheap whiskey. Adiba walked me down the very street she grew up on and told me what had happened.

The village had been inundated with rumors that ISIS fighters were sweeping through the area and ransacking entire villages, kidnapping whole communities. This notion seemed almost too absurd to believe, too unthinkable. Her father called men in some neighboring Arab villages, she said, her voice betraying the bitterness she felt. They told her father not to believe it, to stay put and not worry.

Eventually, they made the decision to leave, packing Adiba and her siblings into the car and driving away. Fifteen minutes later ISIS fighters careened down the street, the one we were now standing on, and went house to house. Her aunts and uncles and their children were taken. Most of the men were murdered and many of the young women are still in captivity. We stood outside the large brown metal gate of her childhood home, long since abandoned. I said very little. Adiba spoke when she felt ready to.

"I lost everything. This house is full of memories of mine, beautiful things, but not anymore," she said, staring at the outer wall. I asked if she wanted to go in. "No," she replied, her face hardening.

"There is something in our hearts, and we will never get healing for it, never," she said angrily. "And it will never be forgotten."

"You can't forgive?" I asked.

"It's difficult to forgive. It's not easy."

When I watched the footage Alessandro had filmed, I realized he had captured on-camera the moment Adiba's little cousins came running out of the house to greet her. They squealed joyfully as Adiba laughed and cheered. When one little girl leapt up into her arms, the microphone attached to Adiba's shirt caught the ruffling noise generated by their hug.

I played this section over and over again. I was finally able to cry, releasing the sorrow I had stuffed down while I was out reporting. Here was the reason why I did this work. Women like Adiba were teaching me, in a subtle way, how to find a place for myself in journalism, engrossed in real stories with real people.

I didn't know how I was going to navigate the industry or build a career doing this, but this was the work I needed to do. This was the only kind of journalist I wanted to be.

21

A Bitter Return

WHEN THE MAN RUSHED INTO the children's ward, I thought he was carrying a small bundle of clothes. He stepped forward quietly, a simple scarf wrapped around his head and his face tightened in anxiety. He didn't seem to notice the Westerner and the camera crew in the room. The bundle of cloth in his arms had two small white feet hanging out the side, on the end of limp sticklike legs.

When he gently placed the bundle on the hospital bed, her tiny body, a limp little skeleton, rolled out from under the multicolored blanket she was wrapped in. A pair of nurses in white medical coats worn over black robes and full-face veils and headscarves pulled the girl's shirt up under her chin and placed a stethoscope on her emaciated chest. I stared at her ribs, which seemed to want to escape her body entirely, pushing up and out through tight olive skin in sharp anatomical detail.

The girl's eyelids were nearly shut, with long thick black lashes framing eyes that had rolled back in their deep sockets. She was close to death. Her cheekbones, like her ribs, seemed to push away from her body itself. Mohammed the cameraman filmed in silence. Nizar from the Ministry of Information and I stood still, somber as though at a funeral. Watching a person die in a hospital produces its own kind of fear. I become hyperaware of the sound of my breathing, the blood rushing through my body, as I try to be as quiet as a human can be. Time is measured in fractions of seconds. I was afraid that this child wouldn't live and that I was intruding. That I was in a room I didn't have a right to be in.

The young man sat on the end of the bed staring down at the little girl with intense fear, mumbling answers to questions the nurses occasionally asked over their shoulders as they attached an intravenous line to her tiny hand, pulling her waiflike arm away from her side. I asked him with a whisper and a gentle hand gesture toward Mohammed if we might film. I placed my hand over my heart, looked into his big brown eyes, and offered to leave. The nurse, impatient with all the niceties and formality, barked at him that I was a foreign journalist and wanted to film. "Is that okay?" He nodded, eyes downcast, and said, "*Mafi mushkila.*" No problem. He was her brother, Najib, and her name was Maimona. She was eleven. He began to tell me what happened. I noticed he was skeletal himself, with several woolen sweaters layered under his shirt, despite the intense summer heat. Maimona had diarrhea, her brother explained. In reality, diarrhea was only a symptom of the severe malnutrition that was actually killing her.

Maimona, like every child in this miserable building, was a victim of the Saudi-led, U.S.-aided civil war in Yemen. She was abandoned by the international community, and in the end, betrayed by her own body. There were children and babies in metal-framed beds all throughout the room. These were the ones whose parents could afford the taxi or bus money to get into the town and make it to the hospital. There were countless more out there, I knew, in the mountain villages, dying silent, unrecorded deaths. I looked around that room and felt a pure, intense rage.

An air, sea, and land blockade of the rebel-held northern part of the country, enforced by Saudi Arabia and its partners like the UAE, had tanked the economy. Most Yemenis lived in these areas; most could no longer afford to buy enough food. The Saudi-backed Yemeni government led by the exiled president, Abd Rabbu Mansour Hadi, had moved the central bank from Sana'a to Aden, a city in the south. Government employees in rebel-controlled areas could no longer collect their salaries. Because the government was the biggest employer in the country, that meant over 1 million people, most with upward of a dozen dependents, were going unpaid. Maimona's father had been a schoolteacher—a fairly middle-class job—but he hadn't been paid in a year. The family had no food at home. The blockade also made it harder to get food into rebel-held areas, pushing the prices of staples beyond the reach of millions.

By the time I made it into Yemen, 8.5 million Yemenis were in what the United Nations described as "pre-famine conditions," with no way of feeding themselves properly. The UN also predicted that without an improvement of the situation on the ground, another 10 million would join them, making over 18 million people victims of famine by the end of 2018. That is *half* the population of Yemen—all innocent victims of war far greater in number than those brutalized by bombs and bullets.

The hospital was perched high in the peaks of northeastern Yemen, in the town of Hajjah, among the same mountains that had captivated me as an Arabic student a decade earlier. Gray and cobalt mountaintops spread out around us, fading into the mist and clouds. The hospital did care for wounded fighters and civilians from the front line, but mostly it treated malnourished children and those suffering from diseases the war had revived. Sandy-colored tents had been erected in the courtyard for holding suspected cholera patients before they could be transferred into cholera wards.

After our day of filming at the hospital, I sat on the wide windowsill of my hotel room and dangled my legs out over the edge, as I had done ten years before in Kawkaban. This place had once hosted tourists, weaving their way in white Toyota Corollas or Land Cruisers to hike and bird-watch and visit the ancient citadel nearby. I leaned against the window frame and watched dusk fall and distant bulbs light up against the fading outlines of mountains and walls. The gentle hum of generators emerged in the night.

I was the only foreign journalist in the entire blockaded, rebel-held north of the country. I absolutely couldn't fuck this up.

Ahmed Baider, a Yemeni journalist I knew, had arranged from his base in Cairo for me to be smuggled into rebel-held areas. It took many months. All the details of the trip—everything from the route I'd take to the minutiae of what I would wear—had been discussed on encrypted messages between him in Cairo and me at my home in Beirut. Getting into Yemen was even harder now. The Saudi blockade had included journalists, especially international reporters. All Yemenia flights to Sana'a had been stopped, and the Saudis would not allow the United Nations and other NGO flights arriving into Sana'a to carry reporters. They checked the manifests of each and every plane. Journalists had tried and failed to get in on small UN flights from the nearby African nation of Djibouti and been pulled off the plane at the last minute, as Saudi officials would not give permission for it to fly into Yemeni air space with a journalist. Other reporters had made it to southern Yemen on flights and even fishing boats from Djibouti, but no one had managed to get up the road and cross the front lines to rebel-held areas like the capital Sana'a.

No one at PBS knew I was there. I hadn't told anyone I was going because I just didn't know if I could pull it off. But I had to try.

The road was dotted with dozens of checkpoints controlled by the internationally recognized government. Beyond that were the front line and no-man's-land, with a heavy Al Qaeda presence just to the east, and beyond that, Houthi rebel checkpoints. Mohammed Saif had been finessing permissions with the Houthis for me for months, going from official to official to make sure they would give me the necessary paperwork and permissions to enter. They were keen for the world to see what was happening there because it suited their own goals to end the blockade. The Houthis were no friends of a free press. They disappeared Yemeni journalists into a network of shadowy prisons. I had been given guarantees of safe passage, aware that no such thing really exists.

As I got word that my driver north to rebel territory was ready, I left my hotel in Aden as swiftly as I could. It was still bombed out from the 2015 fighting when the Houthis had swept south and tried unsuccessfully to take the city. I had spent three days waiting for this signal to leave, anxiously looking through the broken window of my once-bourgeois seaside hotel room.

My driver smiled and nodded at me. I was traveling with another family, it turned out, so I would look like I belonged to it. Women were almost never addressed directly by soldiers, but the men in the car might be asked for my papers. In that case, there was little to be done. I had arranged to text Ben on my local cell every half an hour. If there was no cell service, I would text every hour. If he didn't hear anything for two hours, he should call Ahmed Baider in Cairo.

For much of the twelve-hour-long journey, bouncing around in the back of the SUV, I felt my heart beat hard in my chest. Sweat gathered across my face, trapped underneath the black face veil. The dark poly-ester was tied tight around my forehead with a strip of fabric. The veil, headscarf, and long abaya were my disguise, my armor. At checkpoints, I looked down at my feet through the hazy black mesh and counted my breaths. I held my phone tightly in my hand. If it looked like I was be-ing busted, I would have time perhaps for one last call to give away my location. I feared most being disappeared into some unnamed prison and used as a pawn by one side or another in this complex war.

This risk was one I never once hesitated to take. No story had mat-tered more to me. This was a personal, painful journey into what was left of a place I had once loved. I was fueled by Yemeni coffee and rage at the crimes committed here with such casual brutality. On my last night before leaving Beirut, I had gone to dinner with my Lebanese journalist friend Leena. I nervously sipped local wine and briefed her on the plan. She rested her hand on mine and said with confident sternness: "Just be careful and trust your instincts, Janie. This will work only if your fixer is good to his word."

The danger to Ahmed was greater than to me, especially if we were caught. So I traveled with his trusted contacts: kind strangers moving me from one place to another, by now a familiar shuffle. When we reached the front-line area, there was no active fighting. The driver had made calls to people up ahead to make sure the road was safe. We all fell silent in the car as it sped up.

There were no other cars on the road. A few burned-out military vehicles littered the rocky landscape on both sides. I steeled myself until we reached the next checkpoint, a few miles down, this time manned by young, scruffy men in mismatched uniforms. The driver wound the window down and showed them some paperwork, and they nodded us onward. At a roadside gas station and restaurant, we pulled over and I recognized Fuad's little SUV before I saw him, standing next to it in his usual thobe, suit jacket, and headscarf. He smiled at me and held out a hand. I had never been happier to see someone in my life.

Local cameraman Mohammed, Fuad, and I headed north toward a Yemeni camp where Oxfam was distributing cash and food to those most desperate. We approached the Saudi border, where temperatures hovered at 100 degrees. It was Ramadan, the Islamic Holy Month, and everyone on the team observed the fast, even going without water from sunrise to sunset. I didn't want to be a jerk by drinking water in front of them, but the farther north we drove toward the Saudi border, the harder that became.

The camp was a godforsaken huddle of several hundred makeshift tents and shelters fashioned out of tree branches. This far north, the mountains had given way to plains, and a hot wind swept dust for miles. The thump of artillery and air strikes could be heard coming from up the road.

An elderly woman approached, wanting to talk to us. She wore a black abaya and no face covering. A wide-brimmed straw hat, traditional in those areas, kept the worst of the sun off her face. A thin black line was tattooed from the center of her bottom lip down to her chin, traditional face markings now seen only on the older women from the villages.

She told me she had been displaced before, in the Mazraq refugee camp. I recognized the name immediately. This was the camp to the east of here where I had traveled nine years before, in my first ever TV piece. In 2015 Saudi jets bombed the camp, killing at least forty-five people. One of them was her grandson. She left with the rest of her family and walked for days to get to this spot. For three wretched years they had been surviving here. Now they faced even graver danger.

As we drove away and headed south, news came through about an air strike just the day before at a cholera treatment facility not far away. The brand-new building was due to open in days and was filled with lifesaving equipment. As Fuad pulled up outside the facility, a dazed security guard with a bandage on his arm and face wandered out to greet us. Behind him was a scene of complete destruction. A huge warehouse-like structure had been destroyed entirely, clearly hit dead-on by an air strike. Boxes of medical equipment were scattered among the rubble.

Mohammed and I stumbled as we picked our way through the debris, over shiny sheets of tin that had been the roof of this precious new building. I had not eaten or drunk water all day, and my shirt was soaked through with sweat. I was severely dehydrated and was having trouble putting words together. We had to do over a dozen takes to get a stand-up in front of the destroyed clinic. I walked back to the car, tripping over my toes. My vision was beginning to fade to black. With shaking hands, I grabbed a bottle of water from the trunk, crouched in the dirt behind the wheel, and drank with desperation. Documenting this scene was absolutely imperative. I had to do it right. No one could ham-handedly deny that human rights abuses were rampant in Yemen if we got evidence of them on film. This is the job. And it's infinitely more crucial when you are the only one there to do it.

After being largely eradicated, cholera had returned to Yemen with the war. The collapse of the state, which led to a lack of access to clean running water, had caused it to spread like wildfire. Yemen was now the epicenter for the world's worst outbreak, and the Saudi coalition had been given the coordinates of all medical facilities across Houthi territory.

We investigated the use of U.S.-made weapons in the civil war next. I was led to a storage facility just outside Sana'a, located on a flat valley floor among the mountains. Once a training ground for

Yemeni special forces under the Saleh administration, it also held the
rusting remnants of decades of war. The weapons were neatly spread
out before us: some former Soviet military equipment, some from in-
determinate sources, rusting there, the dry grass growing up between
them. A terrible legacy of foreign weapons sales to a poor Arab nation
at war with itself and now with the wider world.

Inching as close as I could and almost holding my breath, I filmed
and took photographs of one piece of ordnance that was light blue-
gray in color. It was badly scratched on one side where it had fallen but
failed to detonate, apparently in the city center. It was a 2,000-pound
Mark 84. I needed to get close enough to use my phone to photograph the serial number and writing on the side. The phone will
carry biodata to prove where and when the picture was taken. Later, a
weapons expert traced the bomb back to a factory in Garland, Texas.
There was also a fin of an American-made Mark 82 bomb, used to
guide the munitions to their target. I would find American bomb tail
fins in various places across Yemen.

Walking in the Old City again, I sat with men in a tea shop and
asked who wanted to talk about the war. People were apoplectic. An
elderly gentleman who said he was a former college professor agreed
to speak with me.

"The missiles that kill us, American made. The planes that kill
us, American made. The tanks, Abrams tanks, American made," he
said, ticking these things off with his fingers. "You say, 'Where is
America?' America is the whole thing."

Mohammed the cameraman had given me our footage of the last
few days on a hard drive so I could watch and log it in my hotel room
in Sana'a. Sitting in my room overlooking the city, I watched the images of Maimona again and again. We had gone back before leaving
the area to see how she was doing and found her sitting up and leaning on her elbow. She even flashed me the briefest, tiniest smile when
I touched her hand. Her eyes looked into mine, their emptiness gone.
The family still had no food. Maimona was the anomaly. I picked up
the phone and called Mohammed Saif to ask him to dial the number

we had for her brother just one more time. It was disconnected. I was never able to find her again.

I decided to break a promise I made to myself. For the first time since my previous summer of British royals and cookery demonstrations, I was going to call a U.S. network that could potentially reach ten times as many viewers as PBS. *60 Minutes* was the most watched news show on American TV, and its famous pedigree for foreign reporting went back generations. Surely that would make lawmakers and the Pentagon, maybe even the White House, pay attention. It's not my job to change policy, but the most fundamental principle behind what I do as a reporter is to inform. Change doesn't happen without awareness. The Saudi censorship of the war in Yemen was working. I was desperate to change that.

Pacing up and down my hotel room in Sana'a, I called Kate O'Brian, a former senior executive at Al Jazeera America and ABC, to discuss it. A mentor and friend, Kate was one of the tiny handful of industry people who knew I was there. I had caused her no small amount of stress, as she checked in regularly and fretted about my safety. Her support meant the world. She reached out to the president of CBS News, who put me in touch with someone in the London bureau. I sent him some of the footage and notes on what I had filmed, including images of Maimona and the evidence of destroyed medical facilities.

"Yeah, but that's just one girl," he said over the phone, unimpressed. "We need more than that. Where's the fighting? Where's the 'bang bang'?"

I sat down on the end of the bed, stunned. The media fetishizes a Hollywood version of war, not the slow, quiet, cruel reality of it. "Bang bang" is how people in the TV news business often refer to gunfire and fighting, captured on-camera. It's an essential part of what we do, but largely the crudest, most attention grabbing, and least informative. It might be thrilling to film and exciting to watch, but it's not, in its essence, journalism. If we are not careful, the risks of war become an odious form of nightly entertainment.

I called Morgan Till, the foreign editor at PBS. "Wow!" he said when I told him where I was. "Okay, yes, we want this. Let me pull a budget together." We would air it in a three-part series, and I would fly to D.C. to discuss the situation in Yemen on set with the anchor Judy Woodruff. PBS had just enough budget to cover the costs of the trip.

I also called an editor at *The New Yorker*. I had written for them in tandem with my PBS reporting from Somalia earlier that year. Before joining *The New Yorker* as an editor, David Rohde was a former foreign correspondent for *The New York Times* and a Pulitzer Prize–winning war reporter. He had been kidnapped by the Taliban and held in Pakistan for months before escaping. Few editors were as attuned and sensitive to the dangers of reporting in the field.

"Make sure you put my cell phone number down as your emergency contact" was the first thing he said when I told him I was in Sana'a. "Do you need me to send you some money?" was the second. "It doesn't matter if you write for us or not. What do you need?" No one had ever said any of those things to me before, certainly no media person.

Getting from Sana'a to Washington, D.C., with my hard drives of footage was a daunting task in the near future. In my disguise, I would have to return the same way I came in and make it out through Aden airport without the authorities there detaining me or confiscating my footage. Mohammed the cameraman and I made several copies of the footage and agreed he would send it to Morgan at PBS if anything were to happen to me or my hard drives on the way out.

I prepared for another goodbye with Mohammed Saif and Fuad. We drank tea in his garden for the umpteenth time, my bags packed and in the back of the car in the driveway. Yet this time felt different. There seemed a kind of finality in the air. Surely I would be back to Yemen again, but covering this humanitarian crisis, getting to this spot to tell the story, had felt like a culmination of an era of my life. Ten years felt like it had somehow all led to this spot. Something I couldn't quite explain yet was finished.

We embraced and I drove away, sitting behind Fuad, stern-faced and driving with an AK-47 poised by his side. I looked out the window at Sana'a rushing past and realized I had spent the previous few weeks completely free of all career concerns. It seemed so clear to me that the purpose of my work was to do exactly what I was doing at that very moment. And if I had to give up this work or if my career never really panned out, it would still have been worth every second of it. *What a privilege all this has been,* I thought as we bounced along. How trivial and petty many of my concerns around my job were. This moment and the thousands of others on the road over the last ten years were the reward. I was filled by a sense of clarity that comes with knowing beyond any doubt that you are exactly where you are meant to be. I felt infused by purpose, that great elusive source of a good life.

As for the dangers ahead, I was afraid, but I wasn't going to let my fears stop me. I felt entirely at peace with what I was doing, more so than any time before. I thought about how the Saudi government and military had kept journalists from covering the cruelty and crimes of this war. I thought about how the Assad regime also, albeit with far more brutal techniques, got inside the heads of journalists in an attempt to scare us away. *Fuck those people,* I thought. If I'd learned one thing in my life, it was that you cannot, must not, let bullies intimidate you. Never let others use your own fear as a weapon against you.

A couple of days later, bleary-eyed and dazed, I walked into the *NewsHour* studios in D.C. with my footage. I was wearing heels and a skirt suit I had bought in a nearby Macy's after getting off my flight from Jordan. Astonishingly, I had made it out without anyone stopping me at Aden airport in Yemen. When immigration asked where I had traveled to, I told them Aden city, and they simply stamped my passport and waved me through. I was jubilant.

Our stories aired as a three-part series and did grab the world's attention. Politicians calling for international intervention to prevent a famine shared the pieces online. The world's worst humanitarian disaster, entirely man-made and aided by the U.S.'s direct policies, was for the briefest of moments under a spotlight. Still, it felt like no one cared. The Saudi embassy declined to talk to us. I knew other journalists wanted to go to Yemen, but getting the story to the front page and in the evening news lead was the real challenge. Millions were at risk of starving. Other reporters reached out to ask about logistics. Because a correspondent from one main news organization had gone in and emerged unscathed, I knew there was perhaps just enough leeway to argue that it was safe enough to send others. I handed out the contact information of all the team members to trusted colleagues at *The New York Times,* the BBC, and other European outlets. I spent hours on the phone walking them through how it could be done. Media coverage needs momentum. This story needed an extra push.

A few weeks after I returned home to Beirut I was sitting on my balcony when news came through from Yemen. The Saudis had dropped a bomb on a bus full of little boys on a school trip. Forty of them died, all between the ages of six and eleven. Dozens more who survived were cruelly, agonizingly mangled. As I sat on my balcony that day and allowed myself to think about the children of Yemen, brutalized from all directions, the rage inside me burned anew.

Fuad texted me photographs a few days later, of what locals were claiming were fragments from the bomb found near the bus. It was the tail fin of a Mark 82 bomb, the same ones I had seen in Sana'a.

A couple of months later I was in Colorado giving a speech at a documentary festival when my phone began to ping with news reports about a journalist who had gone missing in Istanbul. His name was Jamal Khashoggi. He had gone into the Saudi embassy and seemingly disappeared.

22

"I Will Be Your Leg"

THE SMALL CAR COULDN'T MAKE it over the final mountaintop. It roared underneath us, wheels spinning in the gravel of the foothill. The driver, Adil, cursed and took his foot off the gas to let the car roll back, then floored the accelerator. It was futile. I gripped the sides of the seat in front of me, sweating into the clothes underneath my black abaya. The niqab trapped my panicky breaths against my face. It was well after dark. We were on the dividing line between territory controlled by the Yemeni government and the lands of the rebel-held north, clinging to the side of a mountain.

Adil activated a small handheld radio and spoke to the driver of the SUV up ahead, which was carrying a crew of reporters from another network, the only other vehicle in our small convoy. Since the murder of Jamal Khashoggi by Saudi agents, and my reporting earlier that summer, more journalists had poured into Yemen, making it across to rebel-held areas. Khashoggi's grim ending had been ordered by Saudi crown prince and defense minister Mohammed Bin Salman, according to the CIA. Media interest in MBS the man, and his brutal war in Yemen, increased.

"Hey, guys, wait, wait! Let Jane come and get in your car, our car can't make it!" Adil yelled into the radio. On the other end, someone could be heard saying in English, "No, don't stop, just keep going."

"Motherfuckers! Stop and come back for Jane!" Adil screamed into the small device. "What the fuck!" No answer this time.

"They left you here," he said, thumping the steering wheel with a fist and turning to me, his face lit up by the blue light of his cell phone. There was little to no cell service. I looked out the window into the dark and wondered how many fighters were out there, and if they had heard this commotion.

I had hired Adil to get me from the government-controlled south to Houthi territory. Fuad and my usual team would pick me up on the other side and take me to Sana'a, and Adil was to drive back south again. Unlike on my previous trip, when we could use a pockmarked but otherwise intact main road, now the only route was dirt tracks over the mountains. The fighting had intensified in these parts, and anyone moving across the front had to take their chances on dry riverbeds and secret trails.

Days before, at my departure gate in Cairo, I was told by an apologetic Yemenia Airways staff member that I was no longer on the flight manifest to Aden. The Saudis had flagged my return. I seethed with anger. I flew to the capital of Jordan, Amman, instead—the only other airport from which Yemenia Airways was flying—and somehow managed to slip through. I was enraged by the Saudi-led efforts to block journalists from the war, in part because they were so successful. They'd effectively closed an entire conflict off from the world, for fear that its crimes and brutality would be exposed. These rules were made to be broken.

Adil, myself, and the other team had spent a grueling day on the road, and now we were stranded in the dark on a mountain, on the front line, miles from the small town where we were to meet our ride to Sana'a. I tried hard to quell the rising dread. Adil was impatient, angry even. We couldn't turn back because the areas we had come through were too dangerous at night. We were trapped. Adil made a few more attempts to yell into the radio, but the network's team were gone.

For one anxiety-provoking moment, another vehicle, a pickup, came up behind us and then passed us. It was so dark we didn't see it until it was upon us. The headlights on the vehicle were turned off to prevent it from being seen by fighters on the ground or in the sky. The cargo back of the pickup was filled with men with guns. Houthis? Government soldiers? Regular Yemeni civilians? It was impossible to tell. My heart pounded as I stared down at my feet, desperate not to be seen. A woman on the move across these parts in the middle of the night would only draw suspicion. The men with guns passed without incident.

One bar of cell coverage appeared on Adil's phone. Adil called Fuad, who tried to come up with a solution. Fuad decided to send a local driver over the mountain to get me, someone who knew the mountain paths. I would have to walk over the mountaintop myself to meet him.

Petrified the next figure to emerge out of the darkness would be a soldier, I climbed out of the car and into the darkness. The gravel crunched underfoot. I hoisted my rucksack onto my back and dragged the bag holding my flak jacket and helmet behind me. Stumbling now over the loose rock and breathing heavily, I caught the earth in front of me with my hands, grabbing stones in the darkness.

I kept thinking, *I'm so alone! I'm so alone!* I tripped on the bottom of my abaya and fell, my right knee landing hard on a rock. Scrambling to my feet, I could feel the blood sliding down my leg. I began to weep, quietly, with fast, panicked gasps. The air around me felt like an unbearable weight. I stopped for a moment and looked up at the sky full of stars above me—a beauty and vastness beyond description. I climbed on.

When I made it to the small town, there was still a trickle of late-night traffic and one small cinder-block restaurant remained open. Fuad stood on the sidewalk, his face full of apologies. "It's not your fault," I told him, and stormed into the restaurant. There, around a plastic table, sat the network team, eating a meal. They froze, staring at me and then at each other. "Oh, um, hi!" the cameraman offered. "Where have you been?" The others looked down at the table.

It was December 2018, six months since my last trip to Yemen. I was there to cover the growing humanitarian crisis, now the world's worst, and the uptick in fighting. Troops loyal to the internationally recognized Yemeni government, supported by the Saudi-led coalition forces, were on the offensive. They were hoping for a major strategic victory in Hodeidah. This western port city formed the front line of this bloody war. Many of the country's food supplies passed through the port at Hodeidah. The Houthis were also accused of running weapons and munitions through it. Government forces surrounded the city from the south and east. Yemen braced for the coming battle.

The UN's World Food Programme planned to increase their provisions to starving Yemenis, from 8 million to 12 million of them, in the coming months. Most of that food came through Hodeidah port. Aid officials admitted to me that in reality 20 million Yemenis needed some form of food support—out of a total population of around 30 million—but the UN couldn't help that many. Nowhere else on earth were so many people in danger of starving.

The day I made it to Sana'a, the U.S. Senate voted to end U.S. military support for the war in Yemen. The uproar over the murder of Saudi journalist Jamal Khashoggi in the Saudi embassy in Istanbul had cast a light on the U.S.'s ugly allegiance with the Kingdom. In a bipartisan alliance, the Senate utilized the War Powers Resolution to limit the president's ability to declare war without congressional approval. It was the first time the 1973 act had ever been applied. Trump vowed to veto it.

Days later I drove into Hodeidah with Fuad and Abd Rabu the cameraman, down the coastal road from the north. The orange sun was dropping over the Red Sea to our right, and we weaved around defensive sandbanks placed by the city's entrance. This was the only road still open to enter and leave the city; all the others were controlled by government forces. Forklifts were moving shipping containers across the road, to slow any potential advances from the Yemeni army. In other places, trenches were being dug in anticipation of the coming offensive. I had fought with my Houthi contacts for days to get to Hodeidah. They were more paranoid and defensive about access to this city than I had ever seen them be. They assumed that every journalist was spying for the Saudis.

As we drove toward the city center, a long white wall hand-painted with elaborate anti-American murals flashed alongside us. One mural had an image of Donald Trump milking a cow with the Saudi king's head on it, into buckets labeled with dollar signs. In another, the head of the Statue of Liberty, including her crown, had been replaced with a skull covered in the U.S. flag. Emblazoned above all the images were the words *USA Kills Yemeni People* written in English and Arabic. The clear message was that God was on the Houthis' side. No one, as usual, was on the side of the millions of civilians who were trapped between these combatants.

At the main government hospital across town, a defensive bank of earth had been erected across the street by the front entrance. Once we were inside, the heat and noise of the crowds were overwhelming. Yemen's healthcare system was collapsing under the pressure of the economic crisis caused by the war. The clinics and hospitals that were still open were inundated with those injured in the fighting, suffering from resurgent diseases like cholera and diphtheria, or ravaged by hunger. Desperate, anxious people were rushing from one place to another, waving pieces of paper in the air. Others, exhausted, slumped against the wall. Everyone was trying to find a doctor. The pediatric clinic had starving babies and toddlers in almost all its beds.

Upstairs, I tiptoed into a silent ward and internally gasped when I saw Ofah Hadi. Bandages were wrapped around what was left of her thin legs. Her left leg was missing below the knee and her right leg was pulled together with a metal brace. She really wanted to talk to me, she told the staff. An air strike had hit their apartment, she said, killing six other family members. A nursing student, she realized quickly when she woke up in the ICU how serious her injuries were.

"My right leg moved but my left leg didn't. I knew the moment I tried to move my leg," she said, pausing to gather her composure. "When the doctor told me to try to move my toes, I tried to hold myself together." Tears gathered around the edges of her long dark eyelashes.

"Later my father came to check on me," she continued. "And he told me, 'I will be your leg.'"

In my hotel room that night, I looked out the cracked window at the city, which was mostly dark except for those with generators. The internet had been cut off in all Hodeidah, so I sat on the old bed next to a creaking fan and read my notes. The walls, the port, the people, their names, ages—all in a day's work covering this brutal war. When I finally tried to go to sleep, the sound of the fan was joined by the thump of air strikes. Only the occasional air strike was loud enough and close enough to wake me before I fell back into feverish, restless sleep.

In April 2019, four months after my trip to Yemen, Trump vetoed the approved bill that would have halted U.S. support for the war in Yemen. He informed Congress that the $8 billion in arms sales to Saudi Arabia and its partners in the war in Yemen, the UAE and Jordan, would go ahead.

In November 2021, the UN released a report saying that by the end of that year at least 377,0000 Yemenis would have died in the war, over half as the result of hunger and disease. Some 70 percent of those who perished were under five years old. As of this writing, the war in Yemen and the humanitarian catastrophe it spurred continues. Also as of this writing, no one has ever declared a famine.

23

Ceremonies

I'M A PERSON WHO SOLVES things, usually by myself. Part of me had viewed my career in journalism as a problem to solve—secure the access, nudge toward to the front of the press conference, change my accent, insist that the Houthis make an exception for me. After Yemen, I felt like I'd finally cracked it.

When I heard my reporting from the humanitarian crisis there in 2018 had won a George Polk Award, I laughed in disbelief. I traveled to New York to accept the prize. Over wine and a formal luncheon at the swanky Roosevelt Hotel in midtown Manhattan, I gathered with journalism giants and was photographed, my work applauded and celebrated. It was a milestone that every young person knocking on every door in the industry hopes to reach one day: the epithet *award-winning*. Not just a journalist—an award-winning journalist. One who has been anointed thus by the industry. I had also recently been short-listed for a Peabody Award, the highest honor in broadcasting. And more awards and accolades were to come.

It was thrilling. On its own, viewed through the narrow lens of me and me alone, it was the ultimate mark of success. This was the validation I had once craved so much. I was no longer an outsider.

The truth was, the more successful I became, the less successful I felt. I struggled to accept the limitations of reporting on a crisis like Yemen. I'd made sure the world knew what was going on, only to find that nothing changed as a result of this knowledge. That quiet, dangerous little question whispered to me when I was alone: What is the point of exposing war crimes and the appalling price of war if it is never going to stop it? Does my work make a difference? I still don't fully know the answer, but I do know that maybe having an impact is something we cannot and should not look for. Maybe it's our Western mindset, our individualism, that wants to witness and feel the influence we have on the world, to see results. Maybe it's our ego. In all honesty, the only question I can answer is, Did I do my part?

I also thought I had solved my relationship with Ben. A few months after my final trip to Yemen, Ben and I married. After years of telling him I didn't ever want to get married, I suggested it. I was trying to save our relationship. In the past few years, we'd been more and more at odds with each other as I grew beyond the young woman he'd first met on the steps of the Gandamack. I thought maybe I could find a way to make the relationship work. The truth is, a part of me also wanted to believe I could be normal, like other people. Could I change my life, come in from the road, and settle down, after all my railing against the quiet life? Marrying Ben seemed the best way to inch toward a solution for us and for my life.

We got legally married in Belfast city hall on a frigid February afternoon. My parents, my sister Laura, brother Andrew, and some other family members joined us for the awkward ceremony. As I stood for photographs next to my parents on the lawn of a coastal hotel, I smiled uncomfortably for the camera while shivering in the cocktail dress I had bought the day before in Belfast. The shop assistant had looked at me with wide eyes, speechless, when I explained I needed a dress to get married in the next day. I was solving another problem, quickly. But deep down I knew our wedding was merely an attempt to steer us toward a future in which we still made each other happy. Months later it was brutally clear our marriage would not work.

Since our wedding, I had been on the road constantly, speaking about my work in Yemen. When I found out I was headed to Israel and Palestine on assignment, I suggested Ben come with me. He could film and produce, and we would get to spend some time together while we were working. It had been over a year since I had covered the protest march in Gaza in which dozens were killed and thousands injured. I wanted to return and film the injured, to see how their families were coping. Before long, the tension between Ben and me was undeniable. We visited a hospital where amputees were being measured for prosthetic legs. I called Ben over to film an interview with a patient that I'd carefully chosen for our story. Ben exploded in anger. "How dare you direct me!" he spat, utterly apoplectic. As we stormed out, I blinked into the sunlight of the hospital's yard, in shock, trembling.

I had taken the lead on the shoot, and he was appalled. I no longer needed his direction, his help navigating the industry, his advice to wait a little while before entering a bomb site. In this moment, in war-torn Gaza, I was the leader. I had become everything he did not want me to be.

Later that evening, I realized we could not deny it anymore. "We should never have gotten married," I said, weeping. The sun was setting over the Mediterranean in its usual splendor as I fell to pieces, sitting in a plastic chair on the terrace of Gaza's Roots Hotel.

Yet, as we'd done so many times before, we stumbled on. I traveled on assignment, lingering on location after each one before returning to Beirut, both of us pretending those words had never been said.

News of further industry awards for my reporting in Yemen made it easy for me to disregard our inability to fix our relationship. Come October, I was back in New York to accept an Emmy. My heart was full as I stood onstage at Lincoln Center, flanked by Ahmed Baider and Morgan Till, my editor at PBS. It was thrilling to stand under the lights again, to accept an award that proved I belonged in this business, and to speak out about the importance of unflinching reporting on war crimes.

Ben seemed excited for me that night. We attended PBS's after party on top of the Empire Hotel, snapped pictures, and chatted with my colleagues. His feelings, however, were complicated. The next morning, as I bounced around our hotel room, he was brooding. "I don't want to spend the rest of my life following you around awards ceremonies," he said. "Everything is about your career."

His words weren't meant to attack me, but they stopped me in my tracks. Ben wasn't jealous of my success. Instead he was exhausted by the thing my career had become, like a third person in our relationship. He wanted a different, simpler life. And, I knew in that moment, a different, simpler wife.

And yet to get divorced after just a few months would have constituted a humiliating failure. Make it to the end of the first year, they say. *Surely we just have to keep trying,* I thought.

Follow the main road in the west Beirut commercial district, Hamra, downhill toward the shoreline. The late-twentieth-century cement apartment buildings and shops and the occasional crumbling grand Ottoman-era building begin to thin out, the sea air drifting up the hill from the Mediterranean. At a point where street cats sleep under trees and old men sit on plastic garden chairs smoking cigarettes and watching time pass by, you will find the Abu Shadi manousheh bakery. Few would dispute Abu Shadi's reign among the very best of Beirut's bakeries.

A humble one-room concrete structure, the place has a counter underneath a simple brown-and-cream-striped awning open to the street. That's how it is done in Beirut. The best places remain exactly the same, for decades. Only time and the sun fade the colors and age the faces of the men, waiting and chatting quietly, arms folded. You must get there on time. By noon, all the best local manousheh spots are sold out and shut.

Manousheh is the traditional Lebanese flatbread eaten for breakfast or an early lunch. One dollar buys the simplest flatbread, with za'atar as a topping, a mix of dried thyme and other spices, dried sumac, and sesame seeds. Other options include cheese. Spiced ground meat is a favorite of mine. Abu Shadi's specialty is manousheh made with locally grown spinach and melted cheese. He offers half a lemon to squeeze on top of it. The dough is hot and crispy on the edges, thin and soft in the middle. In the center, the softened spinach, now citrusy, combines with salty white cheese.

So of course, it was Abu Shadi's where I needed to eat before I said goodbye to Beirut, my friend Nabih Bulos insisted. I was leaving Beirut to move to New York. For the first six months I was going to teach a course on war reporting at Princeton University. After that, I would figure it out. I knew my time living in the Middle East had to end. I had done everything I felt I could, based in the field. The sense of closure I had felt leaving Mohammed and Fuad in Yemen had followed me to Beirut, too. It was time for something new.

I twisted the wedding band on my finger as I sat with Nabih. Ben had already left Beirut, incensed by life under COVID-19 lockdown. After being on hold with the U.S. embassy for days and buying a charter flight seat, he was able to get to New York first. I would stay and pack up the apartment and loose ends. He had never taken to life there as I had, less forgiving of the dysfunction and quirks of the city.

I had spent months going through paperwork for the hallowed O-1 visa. Finally, I was, according to the U.S. government, an "alien of extraordinary ability" and would be permitted to live and work in the United States. Ben was starting a new job with his network as a producer in New York. I was elated, but the reality of leaving Beirut was now sinking in as the "last times" stacked up.

The last time for a manousheh. My last Sunday farmers' market with local wines and cheeses and jars of honey, and one more handblown glass vase I just don't need. One last dinner party at my landlady Nayla's apartment. One more time to drink wine with Leena Saidi, the famed British Lebanese TV producer and mother to us all, on her terrace in West Beirut. The foreign press club would forever be gathering on her terrace for parties and dinners long after I was gone.

As I waved goodbye to Nabih and my taxi pulled away from Abu Shadi's, Beirut rushed by in its glittering, summery beauty. My heart felt huge and tender as I watched it go. The streets that had offered me a home, arms wide open. The city I had described as living in a bad relationship, where you swear you can't take any more—not one more power outage, not one more garbage collection strike or water cut. Then someone decides to host a live jazz festival in the street or projects old 1960s Lebanese movies onto the building next to yours for the Syrian refugee children to watch. Maybe a near stranger invites you to their kitchen table to taste their cooking or brings you cherries from their farm, placing a hand on your face and calling you *habibti,* my darling. And there you are—back, hooked, in love. Not going anywhere. For six years I had learned how to live from Beirut and with the people there.

Silent tears slipped down my face as the taxi bounced over potholes home. The taxi driver looked into the rearview mirror and gave me a nod. I wiped my face and nodded back. *I'm okay.*

Flying out, with my Western passports and a new life in New York City, felt like a betrayal. These kinds of goodbyes had for years felt guilt-ridden, but with Lebanon I was also still constantly filled with immense gratitude toward a city that gave me so much I could never repay.

Around six weeks later I was unpacking boxes in my new apartment in Hell's Kitchen, overlooking the Hudson River, when videos appeared on Twitter of some sort of bombing in Beirut. I sat my laptop on the kitchen counter, clicked on one such video, and gasped. It was my street. Buildings were smashed, rubble and glass strewn across the road, trees snapped. *It must have been a car bomb,* I thought. Then more videos, but from different streets far away from each other. Was this a coordinated series of attacks? By now the team of Polish movers were leaning over my laptop with me, all of us joining in a chorus of "Oh my god!" all at once. I began to call everyone and anyone there, my hands trembling as I fumbled with my phone.

What had happened in Beirut was not a series of car bombs. In Beirut's port, nearly 3,000 tons of fertilizer, ammonium nitrate, had been unsafely stored in an old warehouse, and it appeared a fire broke out in a nearby shed. The resulting explosion was one of the largest non-nuclear explosions in history, felt in Israel, Palestine, Turkey, and Syria. Over two hundred people were killed, a miraculously low number owing to the fact that COVID lockdowns had kept most people off the streets and out of nearby office buildings.

Added to the casualties were the city's ancient homes and old palaces from the Ottoman era and many traditional French buildings. I clicked through picture after picture of beloved neighborhood spots, now rubble or beyond repair. By the end of the day all my friends were accounted for as alive, but more than half were injured, some seriously.

It was an incredible coincidence that I had left just before the explosion. My old apartment was smashed; the streets I loved—my favorite Armenian restaurant; the café where I was smoking a waterpipe the night I found out I won the Polk Award; the corner store, outside of which old men sat outside on plastic chairs all day—were rubble or damaged beyond repair. I didn't know as yet if any of the staff in these places were injured or dead. I was grateful I had not been there, and yet the guilt I had felt the day I left now waxed stronger. My grief about the tragedies that had befallen the remarkable places I have called home, from Sana'a to Beirut, was paired with a quiet guilt that I was able to fly out, move on, start again. I had searched for home my whole life. As I began my new life in New York, the old one seemed more deeply sunk in the past. I could never really go back.

Part IV

24

The Deal of the Century

BY LATE 2019, THE WORLD had stopped watching Afghanistan, but the war was raging worse than ever. I landed back into Kabul for the first time since I left the morning after the Serena Hotel attack five and a half years before, staring out the airplane window as the city came into view. The streets felt the same. Woodsmoke and dry dust filled the air; traffic jams and blast walls and fruit stalls vied for space with crowds of shoppers. There were fewer burkas in the street. I marveled at the young women in jeans and shirts, sitting together in cafés with no men. As I looked around, it seemed everyone was very young—like I had been when I had first come here as a cub reporter, full of fear and utterly artless hope.

After months of negotiating with the Taliban's press office and one trip that was canceled hours before my escort was due to meet me, I would finally make it into Taliban-controlled territory. I wore a burka to get through Afghan government intelligence checkpoints and brought two trusted Afghan cameramen. The road south from Kabul, the famously dangerous highway from Kabul to Kandahar, was ripped apart by IEDs, air strikes, and car bombs. Afghan security forces, driving at high speed and in convoys of armored Humvees, still attempted to make it up and down the stretch of pockmarked road. But where the tarmac ended on either side of the highway, Taliban territory began, and they were a constant target.

We had arrived at a small farmhouse compound of mud walls and various buildings, with the odd chicken pecking about and children peering out of windows. I climbed out of the car to greet the local elder who was hosting us as we waited for the Taliban commanders to arrive, and suddenly all hell broke loose. The sound of fighting erupted from across the fields, coming from the direction of the main road we had just left. This was why the Taliban commander I was due to meet with was late. Heavy weaponry fire could be heard from nearby, likely the .50-caliber guns on the turrets of the government Humvees. The farmhouse was surrounded by orchards filled with fruit trees. It felt as though every leaf—indeed, even the very earth beneath us—trembled as the battles raged.

My producer Naseer ran inside the house, and I ducked behind the car as bullets zipped around and over us. The farmer ducked into his front door, protected by nothing but mud walls. Shortly afterward, we were ordered to move, heading to a field that seemed dangerously open to the fighting. I was not able to bring my flak jacket, in case the car was searched at government checkpoints on our way to Taliban-controlled areas. We even got temporary SIM cards and threw them out the window when we returned, in case we were caught by the government.

As we stood next to the car, in a field where our Taliban escorts on two motorcycles had led us, the rumble of fighting nearby continued. Then suddenly a convoy of cars and more motorcycles emerged over the hill. Out stepped the commander, a tall, stony-faced man in a huge black turban and a camouflage jacket, carrying an American-made M16 rifle. His men wore red bandannas around their foreheads with Islamic text written on them. These were the so-called red units, the Taliban's own version of special forces, the most elite fighters. One of them pulled a small pink handheld mirror and matching comb out of his pocket and began running it through his hair, which was falling down in thick curls under his red headband, getting himself ready for the camera.

"America will be defeated," the commander said, standing several feet in front of his men. He had cold eyes and looked past me as he spoke, in keeping with strict Islamic practices. "And they will be humiliated when they leave." The rattle of gunfire continued in the distance.

I had come to talk to the Taliban to gauge their morale as their leadership negotiated with the Trump administration. It was the first time representatives of the U.S. government were holding official face-to-face talks with them. U.S. envoy Zalmay Khalilzad was leading a team that was negotiating in Doha. Few were aware of what that deal would look like. The United States didn't need the Taliban's permission to leave the country. They wanted to negotiate a neat retreat, not one where American soldiers were attacked on the way out.

The war in Afghanistan by 2019 had become so restrictively opaque that it was easier to access it through the Taliban than through the Pentagon. The fighting was increasingly done by special forces, both American and Afghan, as the local regular forces struggled to keep up. Special forces were not allowing any media embeds, and even the Afghan special forces had to ask the Americans for permission, which was always a hard no, a senior government official admitted in his office, embarrassed.

Air strikes were also, alarmingly, at their highest levels since the surge a decade ago, when over 100,000 American troops were in the country and I was a cub reporter for Gulf News. The Trump administration had eased the rules of engagement when it came to air strikes just as it had in Iraq and Syria during the bombing campaign against ISIS. According to an in-depth study carried out by Brown University's Costs of War Project, during the period from 2017 to 2019, the number of Afghan civilians killed in U.S.-led air strikes in Afghanistan increased 330 percent. Absolutely none of this was covered by America's TV networks. News from Afghanistan seemed to bring with it overwhelming fatigue. Even at PBS I had to argue hard to get out on this assignment.

As we wandered through the villages damaged by air strikes, it was clear how vulnerable families were to U.S. air strikes. Two-story mud homes, made of wooden frames and dried earth, collapsed completely under missiles. Here there was no rubble, just clumps of earth and broken wood. Village elders, a small lineup of old men in traditional shawls and turbans, were keen to show me the damage. They were as surprised to see a foreigner like me as I was when they took my hand and cupped it between theirs. Nearby the Taliban fighters watched disapprovingly, leaning on their parked motorcycles, huge radio antennas sticking out of their bags.

The civilians were trapped between two warring sides. While we toured the nearby villages, Taliban fighters implored us to move on at the sound of chopper blades overhead. Occasionally, groups of villagers would come out to talk to us or simply to watch, sometimes growing to several dozen at once. I pleaded with them to go back in their houses, aware that we were a rich target for any drone pilot looking for gatherings of men in Taliban territory.

In the years since the United States had pulled back, Afghan security forces had struggled to hold off the Taliban. As the war grew more intense, so, too, did the number of civilian casualties. The year 2018 had been the deadliest for ordinary Afghans since the war began, the loosening of the rules of engagement for air strikes leading to a massive increase in the deaths of innocent people. These air strikes were meant to pressure the Taliban in the ongoing negotiations with U.S. officials.

Meanwhile, the Kabul government increasingly relied on raids by the Afghan special forces, especially those tied to the CIA— shadowy, secretive units of fighters answerable only to intelligence officials. They flew into Afghan villages at night looking for Taliban leaders, rarely took prisoners, and often killed with impunity. No one was keeping count. As the war had slipped away from the world's gaze, it had become dirtier, more indiscriminate, fought in the shadows by the most cynical men still standing after nearly two decades of bloodshed.

According to a Human Rights Watch report issued weeks before I arrived in Afghanistan, these fighters had been on the rampage, executing suspects and kidnapping and disappearing people without trial. They were out of control and far beyond the reach of the law, in large part because they operated under the command of the Afghan military's intelligence unit. They were recruited, trained, and equipped by the CIA. U.S. forces had Afghan civilian blood on their hands.

But the media was not publicizing these records. Numbers and statistics couldn't do the job, and I bristled with anger at the American military's success at keeping reporters away from this war. "You work for the American people," I told a U.S. military press officer over the phone from my room at the Serena Hotel in Kabul. He had just hung up the phone when I'd asked to put through a request for a formal interview with the force commander General Austin Miller, and I called back, enraged.

Years of obfuscation and blocking reporters had hampered the West's understanding of this war. The fact that they had been successful—the American public had very little information about the war—made that all the harder to swallow. This press officer's snarky arrogance pushed me over the edge. This was bullshit.

"You work for our viewers, they deserve to know something about the war!" The person on the other end of the phone, speaking from a U.S. military base in the same city, remained unmoved. General Miller, America's commander in Afghanistan at the time, refused to give interviews to international reporters based in Afghanistan, effectively blocking everyone from *The New York Times* to *The Washington Post* and PBS. Afghanistan was a war few wanted to answer difficult questions about. And not many Americans seemed to miss the updates.

Regular Afghan soldiers and police were also being slaughtered in the fighting. In January 2019, President Ashraf Ghani said 45,000 members of the Afghan security forces had been killed since he took power in late 2014. This number was virtually impossible to grasp and didn't account for the hundreds of thousands who had been badly injured, all leaving extended families without incomes. I had sat down with former deputy defense minister Tamim Asey in the gardens of the Serena in September 2019, and he told me it was true. The deaths were so atrociously regular he began measuring his time in casualties.

"I would go home and sleep well for four or three hours on a

day that I could count in every hour I didn't lose two or three people," he said, his haunted eyes looking into mine. "That would be my
best day. Because in every hour, on average, we used to lose one or
two ANDSF [Afghan National Defense and Security Forces], and in
twenty-four hours we are talking twenty-four people, or forty people,
or forty-eight people."

At the final village I visited on that trip to Taliban territory, a local
elderly man called Shir Hasan had come out of his home and sat in
a plastic chair in front of the main mud wall perimeter wall of the
compound. He was old, with a long, thick white beard, and he wore
the traditional small white hat. The Taliban fighters told us he had
recently lost family members in night raids before wandering off, not
particularly interested. We had just finished fitting a radio microphone
to his shirt when I asked him to tell me what had happened.

His face crumpled in despair, he attempted a few words but burst into
tears. Around a dozen small children, boys and girls, had come out of
the home and stood behind him. They looked on silently, scared. Special
forces had come in the night to their home, he eventually said, trembling.
There were Americans among the Afghan soldiers, he said. They pulled
his two nephews from the house, one of them a teenager.

"I told them, 'We are not Taliban, don't do this to us,'" he said, stopping
to compose himself as his emotions rose again and his voice trembled.

Soon after, they heard bullets fired.

"One American was standing here at the door, I saw him myself," said
Hasan. "I don't know if the Americans shot them or the others did. There
were a lot of them." He stopped and wept for a moment. "When the
shooting happened, my brother shouted, 'They killed my little children!'"

He pointed behind him. Another elderly man stood behind the
children, leaning against the wall, staring straight ahead. He was silent,
and a single tear rolled down his cheek.

I had kneeled in the dirt next to Shir Hasan as he told us his story and
felt like my heart was on fire. I had never seen a Pashtun Afghan man
break down so publicly, an elder, from tough rural stock, so undone.

Despite the fact we'd heard helicopters overhead and it was getting late, we knew custom demanded we stay for a meal. I was sent off to eat with the women in a large house, while the rest of the team, all Afghan men, ate with the Taliban commander and his red brigade soldiers. The women of this Taliban-controlled village delighted in having temporary custody of me. A blond Western woman, I was a remarkable curiosity in their care. An elder, smiling lady produced an ornate handmade wedding dress. She handed it to me and insisted I try it on. The collection of around a dozen women of several generations roared with laughter as I put it on. I looked at myself in a mirror on the wall and thought of my own wedding, just months before, and how out of place I had looked in my wedding pictures.

The women had left potatoes and eggs frying untended in the yard outside while they crept into the room to see me, and the smells of the food wafted in. The Taliban commanders and fighters waited in the next building to be fed. *Maybe the Talibs hear the cackle of intergenerational female laughter?* I thought. That afternoon I really wished that I could speak Pashto because all I wanted to do was talk to these women. I didn't want to grin and nod and hug, I wanted to ask them dozens of questions and answer all of theirs. Instead, I had to accept simply making them chuckle, holding their babies while they all laughed adoringly at their offspring flailing around in my arms.

I could hear the fighting outside getting closer, the rat-a-tat of gunfire from beyond the apple orchards, and knew I should be ready to move. It wouldn't be safe to drive the roads back to Kabul after dark. I headed outside and pulled my boots on at the doorway. Clomping through an old wood door, I looked back and waved at the ladies. The older ones leaned out, smiling and waving back. A woman in the yard was hand-slicing crinkle-cut French fries with a metal slicer. I had to get back to work, but everything was so interesting, touching, and scary. I wished for more moments like this one; I wished for less violence.

In January 2021, I was back in insurgent areas of Wardak. The Trump administration had arranged for American troops to leave, and the

Taliban were confident President Biden would see the deal through. This time I brought a Western camerawoman/producer with me.

On this second trip, just before we had to leave, I wanted to try to speak with a civilian in private, beyond the watch of Talibs. By now they had followed us into a health clinic, peering beady-eyed at the doctor as we chatted to him about access to drugs. They had followed us into a busy marketplace and listened as we talked to people in the street.

In the village we visited, a man had come out of his house to see us. He spoke some broken English and decent Arabic. I grabbed the camerawoman, told the Taliban we were going to talk to him inside his home, and disappeared into the inner sanctum of his compound. I knew the Talibs could not follow us, as nonrelatives were not allowed in a home with women inside. Being two women, we were permitted this rare privilege.

Free of our escorts, I relaxed and turned to the man. He gave his name simply as Salim. Tall and bearded and likely in his fifties, wearing a black turban, he had exhausted, pleading eyes. He stood next to me in the open yard outside the main home. It had modern plastic window frames and doors and was built with brick, not mud. He had worked for years in Abu Dhabi to pay for it.

He looked incredibly stressed—a combination of fear of the Taliban, desperation for the war to end, and an urgent wish not to let this opportunity to speak with us pass. I let him catch his breath, grateful for the moment inside this man's calm home without any gunmen, just the sun on our faces and the soft cluck of chickens around. It was so rare I could chat with people in Pashtun-speaking areas, and between English and Arabic, I was delighted to find we could manage. A few little girls skipped around the yard, shuffling closer to listen in.

"Mr. Joe Biden," he began, looking at me with strained, heartfelt intensity. "We want the war to be over and the Americans to leave from here. America is good, but they need to go back to America." He was being so gracious, so respectful and polite to us, journalists from the country he wanted to be rid of. I had seen this same courtesy in Yemen, Gaza, and Iraq, and always felt a little embarrassed and astonished that civilians so rarely blamed us reporters from the very countries that were bombing them.

I asked him what he hoped for in the future, for himself and his family. He didn't hesitate, not for one second.

"Schools," he said. "This is my daughter," he added, pointing to one of the girls. "This is my daughter," he repeated, pointing to another. "I want them to go to school."

Salim would get one of his wishes. It wouldn't be the second one.

25

"There Is Not a Future for You Here"

THAT TRIP TO AFGHANISTAN HAD come just at the right time. As 2020 came to a close, I had just finished a semester of teaching at Princeton, which, owing to COVID-19 lockdowns, I did from my kitchen counter in Manhattan. Ben and I had stopped arguing, and not in a good way. We shuffled past each other in our new apartment, a space vastly smaller than the sprawling home we had enjoyed in Beirut. We swung between cheerful friendship and a kind of deafening silence, neither of us acknowledging that we had become no more than roommates.

The reality of it all was still too painful to look straight at. I knew I wanted to leave, but I couldn't entertain the thought of being alone, without him. I didn't know what to do. So I did what I always had done. I went on assignment.

My camerawoman and I had landed in Kabul two weeks before Biden's inauguration for an extended assignment for PBS. U.S. forces were due to leave in three months. The entire country seemed to be asking if they would. After our visit to the Taliban, it was time to talk to those they menaced most.

When Anisa Shaheed's phone rang, I didn't have to understand the Dari she spoke to know she was trying to calm the nerves of someone on the other end, checking up on her. It was her office back at the TOLO TV headquarters in Kabul, from which the most-watched TV news in the country was produced and broadcast. Anisa was one of the network's lead reporters, a household name in Afghanistan.

Now that trusted recognition, however hard-earned it was through years of good, brave work, was a dangerous liability. The Taliban had circulated a list of a hundred names of female journalists, peace and rights activists, and those working in high-profile jobs in civic leadership—all with a stark threat: quit your jobs or be the next to be assassinated. Anisa's name was on that list.

"Yes, yes, don't worry, she is not suspicious," she said into the phone, looking out the back window of the car. "No, no, I investigated, don't worry."

Anisa was heading to the outskirts of the city, where she had a lead on a local crime story. A woman had been murdered by her husband, and the dead woman's mother called her because the police refused to act. By January 2021, as the Afghan state continued its slow-motion collapse, desperate people called Anisa asking for her to find the truth or pressure officials to do their job. She reported on destitute injured soldiers being denied their tiny compensation payments by their commanders, murders of women that were going entirely uninvestigated, and corruption of officials. Insurgents were also aware that Anisa would respond to a news tip. She had been warned by the intelligence services of Afghanistan that the Taliban were planning to lure her into a trap.

Although I hid it well, I was intimidated by Anisa. She coveted none of the attention we provided, following her around and profiling her on national TV in the United States. She shrugged off our presence with a casual smile and ironic laughter and got on with her work. Small in build, she wore a traditional Afghan fox-fur hat and camel-colored coat. She was a mixture of cool-girl toughness and confident elegance.

Clambering through the laneways of a poor Kabul suburb to find the family she would interview, Anisa led the way and I followed, watching her smile and chat with locals. Once inside the simple home, she sat on the floor of a small, carpeted living room and listened to the family at great length. They were grateful she had come, and the mother of the murdered woman held her hand for a long time as

Anisa made her way out afterward. Several little girls of various ages were hanging out windows to steal a glimpse of her as we pulled our boots back on in the small yard of the house. Their expressions were a mixture of smiles and utter wonderment. I looked at them and knew that in that moment something extraordinary was likely happening in their lives, a quiet little revelation, proof of What Can Be. To inspire people, little girls in particular, is to leave a kind of magic behind in this world, a wonderous, immeasurable bundle of possibilities.

But this was dangerous work. I was nervous; spending over an hour in a house in an area with a well-known Taliban presence, where the entire neighborhood saw you arrive, was not wise. I was aware throughout the hour that the one muddy narrow path we came in on was our only way out.

"I can't not come here just because I'm scared or because I'm under threat," Anisa said to me as we left. "If I don't, who will make this family's voice heard? Who will make sure their words reach officials?"

As we drove back to her office, I was for once quietly pleased we were stuck in Kabul traffic, grateful for the time to sit and listen to Anisa talk. The Afghan government offered so little support to citizens that those in need often approached the media instead, she told me. A woman from Kunduz Province had come to Anisa the week prior. Her three sons had been badly disabled in the war, yet the Afghan officials had offered no help.

"She came to TOLO and she was screaming at our front gate," Anisa said. "On the one hand, there is a fear in the office that these women are coming to kill us women, so they wouldn't let her in. I said, 'Search her, and then let her in so I can talk to her.'"

After Anisa's interview with the woman about her sons had been aired, the Ministry of Defense finally promised to treat them. Anisa didn't have to do this work to be on the air. She could have taken safer, studio-based work. Being in the field talking face-to-face with people was what she loved, chasing stories and seeing things for herself. I understood.

I returned to TOLO TV to interview her in a more formal context. We spoke in a quiet office upstairs from the newsroom. Our team had come through steel doors and blast walls to enter the building, past shelves filled with well-worn flak jackets and neatly arranged helmets. It reminded me of the entrance to the Gandamack, which had been forced to shut several years prior after Taliban attacks on guesthouses became constant.

"In all the years I've been working at TOLO we have lost ten colleagues," she told us. We all knew the number of deaths had increased in recent months. A well-known TOLO TV anchor was killed in a targeted bombing of his car just weeks before this interview. He was Anisa's best friend. She described the killing, as tears began to fall.

My camerawoman/producer and I sat in silence and listened to Anisa describe what it was like to wonder each day who it would be next. Which face or name would appear on her phone in a news report or a shared text.

"I don't fear death, I've never feared death," she said, and no one doubted her. "The fear that I could lose somebody, that's a much more difficult fear. If you die, it's done, life ends. But to see a friend covered in blood, unable to get up, that's very difficult."

My producer asked Anisa if she missed her friends. "Yes," she said. Something in her face changed. She stared blankly in the space in front of her. In a whisper, she said, "I miss you." It was unclear if this was patchy English, or she was speaking to a person in her mind.

"Do you have dreams? When you dream, what comes up for you?" the producer prodded as she wept.

"That's enough," I snapped.

The producer and I argued in the parking lot outside afterward. People who find their homes turned into war zones, who have spent years here watching war devastate their communities, who live in constant fear, may appear well put together. But they are not, I argued. They're merely surviving. We cannot tear that down just to get more emotion on-camera. My producer was angry and defensive; she felt patronized.

She hadn't been to war before, and she didn't understand the emotional toll of ripping away those defenses. These people have no therapists, no escape, no hope. We don't have a right to dig up their deepest anguish for our assignment, I said in the car ride back to the hotel.

"Jane's right," said Aleem, the fixer, looking out the window as we drove back to the hotel. "Everyone here looks normal, but we are all so affected deep down. It's very bad."

We drove to meet Shaharzad Akbar, the young and brilliant head of Afghanistan's Human Rights Commission. I interviewed her in 2019 shortly after her appointment, and she struck me as the embodiment of women's advancement in Afghanistan. I knew few others as optimistic about the future of her country.

"It changes a lot for the younger girls who are watching us," she had said back then. "Every day I am conscious of being watched."

Shaharzad was totally self-made as a professional woman. Since first arriving in Kabul, first in 2009 and then living there in 2013 and 2014, I had seen a generation of young Afghan women from middle-class families complete their educations there and go on to build careers. These were not the elites who had flown back from the States or the children of powerful politicians and warlords. No other group was as dedicated to building the country than these young women.

Shaharzad was one of them. She was just thirty-one years old when she was selected by President Ghani as the new head of the Human Rights Commission, an independent body charged with investigating abuses across the country and pressuring the government to act. She had won a prestigious scholarship to Smith College in the United States and had returned to Afghanistan to pursue her dreams of helping build stronger institutions in her home country. If she was blessed by luck early in life, it was by having a father who insisted his daughter receive the best education possible.

Back in 2019, as we chatted with her in her office, a huge cold space that dwarfed her tiny frame, the Trump administration was negotiating with the Taliban. The prospect of a deal that would bring the Taliban into a power-sharing agreement was growing.

"Women were stoned by the Taliban, flogged by them, and this is continuously happening in areas under their control," she said, her smile fading. "Now imagine the possibility of them not only coming back to power, but also determining what the laws of Afghanistan look like. That's really scary."

By the time I walked back into her office in 2021, Shaharzad looked thinner, exhausted. Her smile remained, but her broken heart was plain to see. The Taliban's assassinations campaign was her worst nightmare. Those who were being killed—journalists, judges, politicians, and others in the public sphere—were the result of twenty years of education and audacious hope.

"They are the backbone of running a system of governance. They are in civil society. They are in media. They are religious scholars, teachers, prosecutors. They are judges, and the message to them is 'there is not a future for you here,'" she said, her voice weak.

Everyone from her family to her friends and colleagues had begged her to leave the country, but she refused. She would raise her child in Afghanistan, she had said. No one predicted what would happen in just over six months. Because right now, it was hard to imagine anything getting worse.

"There is still hope," she said, her wide eyes pleading. "Afghanistan is not a lost cause. It's not a lost cause for me. And Afghanistan needs us, all of us. More than anything I believe all Afghans deserve basic human rights like everybody else on the planet. I think staying here for me is staying true to that belief."

Shaharzad had lost two members of her team six months before, she told us, including a close friend. The moment our conversation turned to that time, her face shifted. The resolve it showed before faded. No amount of professionalism could block the pain. All of us were silent, listening.

"I don't know if I have the strength in me for any more loss of that kind. Not knowing, that's scary for me. I know I need to have that strength, but . . ."—she paused, swallowing back tears—"I think losing my colleagues really tested my strength, really tested my faith, and really tested my hope. But it didn't stop me."

Our interview had ceased to be an interview. We were just people, listening. I sat in the chair, fighting every impulse to reach forward and take her hand, breathing deeper and feeling a slow-moving wave of grief grow inside me. And I stayed silent.

My heart burned for Shaharzad when she voiced doubts about her own abilities, even her emotional strength.

The team packed up our mics and filming gear in sober silence while Shaharzad wiped her face and returned to her brave public smiling face. I worried about the intense pressure she was under, in every possible way. For months after our interview with her, I held my breath in panic every time I read a headline from Kabul about another killing.

The Taliban had denied these killings to us, but few believed them. I certainly didn't. "The Taliban's leadership claims responsibility for every operation we carry out," the commander in Wardak had said a couple of weeks earlier when we first arrived. I had asked if they were responsible for the killings. His answer was rote, and he was unable to suppress his smirk. It was a lie so stark it insulted my intelligence, which I supposed was part of the dance.

The country's vice president, Amrullah Saleh, the former head of the intelligence services, admitted us into the main intelligence services' prison to interview one of the Taliban assassins. Finally we could ask the right questions of the right people. After my days of witnessing the pain inflicted on these women, I was more than ready to get in there, roiling with disgust and rage.

After much security searching and checking and stalling, I sat down in front of a teenage boy, handcuffed, slumped over, terrified. The security forces had set up a small windowless room for us to light and film in. Men in old brown suits walked in and out, their faces serious, unclear how a journalist had been granted such permissions. Everything led me to believe we were about to speak with a killer. Instead, this teenage boy cut a pitiable, tragic figure.

I listened as he explained how he'd arrived in the prison. His older cousin had instructed him to watch an election official. He had been told to wait outside the person's house and report on his daily routine of coming and going.

Large in build but baby-faced and completely lost, the boy sat on a chair in front of me wearing a simple shalwar kameez and a pair of black plastic sandals. We would not give away his identity in our story because he had not yet been tried. He had given his cousin the house address and the time the person left for work. Then one morning he was gunned down. Not by this boy—his job was done. He didn't pull a trigger, probably had never even held a gun in his life. But he was all the authorities had, so he would pay the price. Vice President Saleh was pushing for the death penalty.

"I want to study, to go to school," he mumbled, studying his feet. "I had ambitions growing up, but my cousin destroyed everything."

He began to cry silent tears, raising his two hands, tethered together, to wipe them away. I felt my rage melt. I didn't want it to, though. I wanted the clarity of blame, the cathartic pain of my anger and someone to direct it at. It was simpler that way. This boy had done a terrible thing. But he was also a victim of the war. Of his Talib cousin.

"Where is your cousin now?" I asked. "What Taliban area is he in?"

"Wardak," he whimpered.

26

Taliban on the March

I SAT AT MY KITCHEN counter in New York, trembling and filled with dread, and waited for Ben to walk in the door from work. I needed to say aloud the word that had been inside my head for months: divorce. He was in love with twenty-four-year-old me, a ghost of the past. A young girl sitting on the steps of the Gandamack Lodge in Kabul, trying to find a driver. The woman I had become was different, more surefooted, less needy. She was confident, had turned her dreams into reality and was building new ones.

After the shouting stopped and the door slammed shut, my PBS foreign editor, Morgan, called. "What can I do? What do you need?" he asked when my tears began to ease and I could breathe again. "I need to go on assignment," I said. I would rush between Yemen, Dubai, New York, and Afghanistan in the coming months, filled with a mixture of fear and relief and liberation from the weight of the guilt I had carried around as our love had faded. These had been my first-ever assignments without Ben in my life, without him to call at the end of the day. I was racked with guilt, if not regret.

A part of me had died, and it was the part Ben was still in love with, that young, lost, needy woman. She simply wasn't there anymore, and I didn't want her to come back. Ben was in love with a ghost, patently dissatisfied with the thirty-six-year-old me.

"I'm sorry," I told him in my head again and again for months in those quiet moments. I knew I owed him loyalty. But I owed myself loyalty first.

Between preparations to return to Afghanistan in the summer of 2021, I stood in line at City Hall in lower Manhattan, shuffling forward down a dusty corridor in a long line of masked people, all clutching their paperwork and avoiding eye contact like good New Yorkers. I suffered this indignity as the agreed dues on my way toward what society at the time was calling the COVID Divorce.

Ben and I met for a peacekeeping chat over coffee under a tree on the Upper West Side to discuss arrangements for the divorce. He asked what story I was reporting next. "Afghanistan," I said, sparing him the details.

"No one cares about Afghanistan," Ben snapped.

"I care" was my response.

The worst thing you can do at a front line is drive around not knowing where you are. That's exactly what we were doing.

An hour north from Kabul in a car with a driver from the area, cameraman Zach Fannin, ace producer Ali Latifi, and I headed west off the highway and up toward the Ghorband Valley. The Taliban had taken vast territory in the north and were now descending through this area toward Kabul. The main highway out of the city was peaceful, flanked by flat farmland and rows of poplar trees. The Hindu Kush appeared ahead in the distance as the morning mist faded and colors sharpened in the sun. A few tractors and cars moved in each direction. As we entered the valley itself, the road was suddenly quiet. We traveled along the road, passing some cars and open-topped trucks, all loaded high with belongings, headed in the opposite direction. People were fleeing with whatever they could.

"Are we sure this is right, Ali?" I asked, leaning in from the back seat and struggling with my iPhone map. We had lost all phone reception and had not expected to drive this far without coming upon our hosts. I was getting nervous.

"This is dangerous," the driver mumbled toward Ali, in Dari. "There is Taliban up ahead." He was stoic, leaning far forward over the steering wheel of his little yellow taxi, peering through the windscreen.

The valley rose on either side of us now as we chugged along the road. *We are in an incredibly vulnerable position,* I thought. Talibs in the hills could open fire on us from up above. We passed several spots where government army Humvees and emerald-green Toyota Hilux trucks were parked by the side of the road, stunned-looking soldiers gathered around them, seemingly avoiding the fight. The army were now to the rear of the local militias, whom we were going to find. I worried we had passed them and crossed over into no-man's-land, or worse, Taliban territory.

"Let's turn around," I told the driver as the rat-a-tat of gunfire in the hills became as impossible to ignore as the knot growing in my gut. This carload of people was my responsibility. I had brought us here, and we had gone too far.

As we did what felt like a painfully slow three-point turn in the middle of the abandoned road, I was grateful we had decided to put our flak jackets on for the drive. This beat-up old taxi might have helped us blend in, but it gave us no protection against bullets. We passed a tiny defunct gas station with a couple of local men sitting outside, old hunting rifles slung over their soldiers, a part of their brave but futile resistance effort. The driver stopped and asked for directions to the front. "Jesus fucking Christ," I grumbled. After all these years I knew this was not how it is supposed to be done.

It was early July 2021 and the war in Afghanistan was unraveling. The American soldiers had left their last base, Bagram Airfield, abandoning it in the night and telling no local staff, and the Taliban were advancing at a rapid pace. There were no more embeds, and there was no real central command. The presidential palace was in disarray and denial.

The government had, in an act of utter desperation, told local people to arm themselves and fight alongside the government soldiers. *Join or form a local militia* was the message, *and God be with you.* A local member of Parliament called Abdul Zahir Salangi had formed a militia in the Ghorband Valley, distributed guns, and was leading the men from the front. Ali secured us incredible permission to visit Salangi.

When we finally found his men, they had taken up a position inside a cluster of houses on one side of the valley.

We walked into a small abandoned cinder-block home and found Salangi surrounded by fighters, commanding others in the valley on the radio. He sat, slumped over on the floor, in khaki-green military fatigues and a traditional woolen Afghan hat. There were dark circles around his eyes, and he spoke with a slow, labored effort. He hadn't slept in four days. There could not have been a starker image of how much Afghanistan had slipped backward from the hopes of a democratic peaceful future than this MP, surrounded by irregular fighters, at war. We could have been with the mujahideen from the 1980s struggle against the Soviets. In fact we were. The MP had fought the Russians, and a fair few of his men as well.

"We thought the partnership with the United States would be long-term," he said, looking at me with exhausted eyes. Outgoing fire from just outside ripped through the room as we all scattered and lay flat. The Taliban were creeping closer.

I wanted to see where Taliban positions were. I grabbed a small handheld camera and left the team downstairs to film with the fighters. I stayed low behind a short wall while a militiaman guided me across the flat roof of the house. Similar to the others, he wore a traditional shalwar kameez, a flat cap, and a camouflage overcoat. Radio in hand, he ran ahead, crouched behind a collection of cinder blocks, then turned and waved me over. I ran to him, keeping him in the camera's frame. He pointed up the hill in front of us, just across the valley. The Taliban were close. They had the higher ground.

In a break from the fighting, they politely asked us to leave. Just as I felt responsible for the team, they worried about our safety. Before we jumped back in the car, I jogged back to ask one more question. The tallest, biggest fighter had been hanging around me all morning, looking as though he wanted to speak to me. He towered over me, binoculars in one hand and a huge green ammunition belt around his broad chest. The scarf wrapped around his head had small tassels that dangled over his forehead. What did he think about the U.S.

drawdown? I asked, a question so obvious and crude, I bristled a little as it came out. But I needed to know.

"We feel left behind by the Americans," he said, flanked by the other men, listening and nodding with serious faces. "They abandoned us in the middle of the road."

As we drove away from the valley and the tension began to ease from my body, I worried we hadn't stayed long enough. Did we get what we needed? I fretted over the footage we had. Did we have enough? "Let's come back soon, Ali," I said. "Sure, of course," he said. But we would never come back. Several weeks later the Taliban took the entire valley.

Ali insisted we stop on the road home for an unlikely ice cream at a little wooden shop in Charikar town. Made by hand, the ice cream was a fusion of cream and sugar and ice, scented with cardamom, cold and soft on my tongue. Back in the car I looked out the window as I had done a thousand times before, heading home from a day of filming somewhere so real and urgent, and at the center of things. The countryside raced by, and I felt myself relax. I barely slept now and felt tired in my bones. I was covered in dried sweat and dust and was sunburned. Yet, with the rusty smell of red earth in the warm breeze and this ice cream cooling my belly, I felt gratitude that I was there. It even, odd as it might sound, felt like joy.

There's a common misperception that war zones are solely places of misery. But misery is unsustainable to the human spirit. Every day societies continue to function in their own way: on the front lines, fighters tell jokes; in refugee camps, couples make love; children play tag in bomb shelters. The misery, when it comes, provides a contrast so sharp the good times feel more meaningful, however cruelly they are parsed out. Witnessing the horrors of war, we find it hard not to appreciate even more the simple pleasures—an ice cream on a tough day, a favorite song on the radio, a good sunset.

Days later we were driving to another valley of Afghan resistance. We were going to see Ahmad Massoud. As our SUV moved alongside the rushing Panjshir River, the sheer rock face of the narrow valley entrance cold and gray next to us, I thought of the last time I had been there to meet with Massoud. The son of famed Tajik mujahideen commander Ahmad Shah Massoud was holding meetings with his commanders and inspecting new recruits. His father had led the fight against the Soviets and then went on to fight the Taliban. Throughout the group's rule from 1996 to 2000, the Panjshir Valley was the only small strip of land the Taliban were never able to conquer. Massoud senior had long warned his American allies that Al Qaeda were a growing threat, and two days before the 9/11 attacks they sent an assassin to kill him. They knew he would be a skilled foe in the war that was coming after the attacks in the United States. His son, named after him, was twelve years old then.

Massoud's people had told us he had reopened twenty-four of his father's old bases to new recruits. The Taliban had been fighting successful military campaigns in the north of the country, above the Panjshir. Now they were attacking the valley from various sides, spreading Massoud's forces thin. He was addressing his followers in the shadow of his father's huge mausoleum, rallying support and attempting to keep morale high. Several generations of fighters sat before him in rows of plastic chairs; others stood around, craning to hear.

I suspect this son had none of his father's warring appetite. No sons of fathers like that can ever be quite as exceptional as their fathers, I jotted in my notebook. They'll never have had such formative years. The men who bled on these hillsides to keep the Soviets—and then the Talibs—at bay grew fat from America's presence. They sent their kids to private schools in Europe, bought themselves suits and gold watches, surrounded themselves with entourages, drove around in armored SUVs, benefited from cushy jobs such as cabinet ministers and provincial governors, while they were hustling opium and security racket deals on the side. Their sons came back from Europe with neat haircuts and soft hands. The generational divide was never fully concealed by the khakis and bodyguards and traditional Afghan hats.

Ahmad seemed to have gained confidence. Perhaps it was experience. He engaged the commanders, who sat cross-legged and stony-faced, stroking thick graying beards. An intimidating crowd, these older men who knew his father and all his battlefield prowess. The pressure must have been unbearable. For all the yells of "Allahu Akbar" in support of the young leader's comments, these old hands did not appear convinced.

Roya Heydari, a young and well-known Afghan photographer, moved around the crowd taking photographs. Impossibly glamorous, Roya had a huge following on social media. I had cherished the photos of Afghan children she had taken for the UN for years. The night before we had met for dinner in a restaurant in Kabul and she had asked if she could tag along to the Panjshir, keen to meet and photograph Massoud in person for the first time. I agreed, making her promise to take a picture of me with him also. I was, deep down, glad of some female company.

The new recruits sat under a tree nearby, cross-legged and slouched in the grass, with old hunting rifles and AK-47s at their feet, not yet entitled to seats in the plastic chairs. A single modest ammunition belt wrapped each rifle, brass-colored bullets shining in the sun. These farmers' sons were about to go to war. They were being drilled earlier by an old mujahideen fighter, hollow-cheeked and wrinkled, shouting at them as they marched around out of sync, their guns slipping off their skinny shoulders.

As Massoud finished his address, a hot wind blew around us. Thunder rumbled in the hills and a dark cloud floated over the mausoleum, threatening heavy rain. We waited for the skies to clear before sitting down nearby with Massoud for our interview. Behind him old Soviet tanks sat rusting in the sun, now museum pieces hauled up for visitors. This war, he said, would have to be fought by militias once more. With the Americans gone, the Afghan army would collapse. His men would be the ones the government should send to war.

"The Americans in the last twenty years, the model that they based Afghanistan's army on, it's an American-based model," he said. "An army that is dependent always on technology and aerial support."

Before we left, Roya took a picture of Ahmad and me together, with the valley behind us. As we drove back to the city and waved goodbye to each other, she and I made plans to work together again. I hoped to come back to Afghanistan in late August, perhaps September. The next time I saw her, she was fleeing for her life.

27

The Fall

I PACKED UP THE NEW YORK apartment I had initially rented with Ben before our divorce. A war reporter friend who was traveling for a while offered me her loft downtown while I figured out my life.

I arrived at the new place during a massive summer storm. The rain soaked through and softened the brown cardboard box in my hands, causing it to crumple around the edges, rather like my hair, wet clothes, and personal resolve.

Once I was inside, the smell of books calmed me. Rows and rows of shelves framed antique wooden furniture, leather seats, and a grand piano. The old books gave the room the smell of a library. Stormy nighttime New York City faded into rain on a windowpane.

I placed my soggy box down on the dining table and sighed in deep, honest relief. In the box were an old HP printer and a ream of printing paper. I had two suitcases, one filled with clothes for yacht club parties at the beach and dinner dates in Manhattan with my new boyfriend. The other held combat clothing and a flak jacket and helmet, as well as a burka I would need shortly in Afghanistan. The printer was to make copies of my divorce paperwork. I couldn't afford a lawyer.

I walked softly through the apartment, my eyes adjusting to the dim lighting and my fingertips drifting over the covers of the books belonging to the collection of a decades-long activist. A cat meowed and brushed against my leg. Janine had mentioned she had rented an apartment once belonging to a famous feminist writer. As I gazed, astonished, at the bookcase, I realized I was in Kate Millett's Bowery apartment. Everything from Millett's own books—*Sexual Politics, The Politics of Cruelty, Sita,* and *The Basement*—to anthologies of lesbian and feminist history and culture and politics and argument and thought all sat quietly in the soft light in front of me. Her belongings were everywhere, from the clothes in the wardrobe to paintings and pottery. Millett had died in 2017 and her widow had rented out the apartment as is before handling her estate. Her presence felt palpable.

I opened a bottle of wine and sat alone under the lamplight, in this other woman's life, feeling like I was under her gaze. The overwhelm of that summer began to drain away. Life's messaging is sometimes so brash you have to laugh out loud, even if you are alone in a loft under a lamp, wet with rain, and surrounded by generations of women's radical, independent thought on yellowing pages.

Two weeks later, I stood at midnight on the tarmac of Dubai airport, trying to make the toughest decision of my career. My cameraman Eric, a tall, gentle Coloradan in a khaki shirt with a camera slung over his shoulder, looked at me for an assessment. We had checked in for our flight to Kabul, canceled, and checked in once again. Now we were standing on the tarmac by a small bus while Fly Dubai Airline staff waited. There were about a dozen Afghans on the bus to take us to the plane. "Okay, we'll go," I said. I'd never been so indecisive in my life.

The Taliban had just taken Kandahar and were marching north to Kabul. There was talk of flights being canceled and people getting trapped inside the capital as it was surrounded by the Taliban. All the newspapers, from *The Wall Street Journal* to *The New York Times,* were evacuating. A few hours prior *The New Yorker* had canceled my commission, saying it was too dangerous. "It's up to you, whatever you decide," said Morgan Till at PBS.

I looked at Eric and then across at the bus. Eric had never been to an active war zone before. I would be responsible if we got there and were stuck. If we didn't go, we could miss the most important moment in Afghan history for decades. This was a story I had to get to; the last twelve years of my life had led me there. We climbed on the bus.

Walking up the stairs to the plane I shouted back to Eric, over the roar of the engine, "Don't worry, if there is fighting in Kabul when we get there, the plane will never land." We both knew it wasn't that simple.

In the quiet hum of the dark airplane, at 30,000 feet, I journaled. The simple act always helped calm me down. But as I scribbled on the page, I felt regret wash over me. My life in New York was settling into an exciting version of almost normal. In reality, it was a balancing act between assignments to Afghanistan and Yemen, and then weekends at the beach and dinner and cocktails out with friends, jogging in Central Park. I was living two lives that seemed at great odds. I didn't want to do this anymore, this war life. In that moment, when I couldn't turn back, I picked the New York life. I had left behind a wonderful new relationship with a man who admired my work.

"Why am I doing this?" I wrote under the soft airplane light. I was afraid. My life of contentment in New York called to me. I craved different things now: security, children, a normal life. *I'll find those things if I get out of this assignment in one piece,* I thought. I was trying to change my life, but by this stage it felt like I was halfway across a rickety rope bridge, staggering away from a life I once loved but no longer wanted, and toward one I never felt was a real possibility for a woman like me.

When we arrived in Kabul, the city felt strangely normal. The same market stalls sold neat piles of oranges from the airport road, bicycles wove through the cars, and small children begging for money pushed their tiny grubby fingers against the car window.

The Taliban had taken Jalalabad while we were in the air. It was the last provincial capital that remained under the control of the Afghan government. Now only Kabul remained.

Eric and I had planned to make our trip weeks later, but the Taliban's advance far outpaced the gravest predictions. Much of the Afghan military abandoned their posts after the provincial governors fled.

We pulled into the Serena shortly after eight a.m. on August 15. We checked in and headed to our rooms for some sleep. We had been up for days. My phone pinged at around 11:15 a.m. with Twitter updates. The Taliban had entered Kabul. There were pictures.

I hammered on Eric's door. "Get your camera," I said, hoping he didn't see the trembling in my hands. "It's happening."

We ran up onto the roof of the hotel with several other news crews. Helicopters were racing back and forth across the sky from embassies to the airport. We spent some time filming the scene and doing stand-ups. I didn't want to lose the other reporters. There felt like a kind of safety in numbers. I looked down over the edge of the building at the street. It was completely empty. The emerald-green Hilux trucks of the special police forces that had been parked outside at checkpoints along this intersection of the city center were empty, abandoned, their doors swung open.

My phone beeped again with an update. Rumors were circulating on twitter that President Ghani had fled the country. Security staff at the palace had told local reporters he was gone. We were witnessing the collapse of a state.

Suddenly, we heard chanting in the distance. Stuart Ramsay, the Sky News correspondent, was doing a live shot about thirty feet away from us on the roof as it happened. Coming down the empty road were a group of about a hundred men with beards and turbans, waving Taliban flags and shouting slogans in Pashtu. They walked past the hotel and down the road toward the presidential palace. I steeled myself for what was to come. Surely, I told myself, the Taliban will not harm foreign journalists, even Americans. But the likelihood of rioting or looting was high. I knew all too well that the Serena Hotel was vulnerable. We needed to move.

Eric and I stumbled into the Baron hotel complex by the airport, a series of cement housing blocks around a main grassy garden in the center. It was in the process of being turned into part evacuation center, part British military base. Every space was packed with British paratroopers, walking around frantically, sitting on the ground, some sleeping wherever they could, others clutching guns and moving back and forth from the entrance points of the complex. Helicopters roared overhead, ferrying the last of staff from foreign embassies in the city to the tarmac of the airport, just beyond our walls.

In the next couple of days most of the journalists who packed the Baron's lobby flew out on evacuation flights, leaving a final group of eight there: four from Sky News, the defense editor of the British newspaper *The Independent,* a Pakistani Dutch correspondent for Dutch TV 2, and Eric and me.

Eric and I had both agreed we would stay as long as we could. We both knew this was one of most consequential stories we would ever cover, history that needed to be documented. Morgan, an ace to the last, an editor who had consistently had my back, supported our decision and helped calm nerves in the head office in Washington.

Simi Jan was the Dutch reporter, and she had flown in by herself in a hurry, just like us, but her cameraman hadn't made a flight to Kabul in time. Eric filmed for her on occasion, and we often teamed up, sharing everything from makeup to laundry soap to phone chargers. Simi was a lively, ever-smiling, passionate reporter with the kind of positive attitude a moment like this desperately needed. We dubbed ourselves the "Baron Eight," which sounded intrepid enough. We leaned on each other for help and support for the next two weeks.

On the first morning, we all marched off to the main gate of the Baron complex, a huge, twelve-foot-tall steel door at the end of a long gravel driveway, flanked by high walls and razor wire. On the other side of the metal gate were thousands of Afghans, pounding their fists on the metal and begging to be let in. It was a terrible sound.

Half a dozen British paratroopers, fully armed with rifles and wide ammunition belts, stood behind the gate. One officer shouted, "Hold the line! Hold the line!" He sounded afraid. The gate could give way. On the other side gathered in the road were thousands of people, many women with small children. Across the street was the main perimeter wall to the airport runway, where huge C-17 military planes carrying evacuees were taking off.

Around fifty yards down the street to the right was the main entrance there, called the Abbey Gate, guarded by American Marines. To the left it was Taliban fighters. The group had sent them to secure the perimeter of the airport, throwing up checkpoints all along the way. They beat Afghans on their way to the airport, their gunmen using sticks and firing in the air, sending terrified crowds of women and children in all directions. They were unable to stop the sea of humanity rushing past them, so they lashed out in anger, flailing around like madmen as clouds of dust gathered around them. Foreigners were not allowed back into the city, we were told. If they caught us at the checkpoints trying to get in, they would not be firing in the air.

At the Baron gate, the British troops guarded a smaller doorway in the large gate, their guns cocked. As they yelled, "British passports only!" and the fear and tension among the jumpy soldiers peaked, a mass of human arms and hands would reach in, and somehow someone would push beyond the crush of clothes and flesh and make it through with a small bag of belongings in one hand and a passport in the other. "British passports only!" screamed the soldiers, but there was no real way of checking. Simi, Eric, and I asked if we could go out and film and the British officer in charge said no fucking way. "If this crowd attacks you, I have to send my guys to rescue you," he shouted. "Not happening!"

We heard intermittent sounds of automatic gunfire. Sometimes it was Afghan special forces, on the tarmac still trying to help coordinate crowds and secure the airport for evacuations, and other times it was the Taliban down the street. We needed to get pictures.

With no help from the British, we wandered back to the main hotel office to push management to let us leave. "Follow me," said the American contractor in charge that day, a tall, bald man with a thick beard and no patience for a reporter. He walked Eric and me into the main security surveillance room, where a wall of flat-screen TVs showed us exactly what was happening not only on the street outside but at the airport itself. "You want to go out there? You won't come back," he said. We watched the screens in awe.

Tens of thousands of people were rushing across the tarmac toward planes. Special forces Humvees careened through the crowds, firing their huge guns in the air, trying to keep them back just long enough for planes to take off and land. Black Hawk helicopters swooped in and strafed the crowds. The cameras fixed on the walls of the airport showed people climbing over the top at various points. The entire scene was out of control. The contrast between such chaotic horror and the quiet, cool room we stood in was difficult to reconcile.

We were finally able to step outside onto the street the next day. The soldiers had placed abandoned SUVs and rolls of razor wire to the left, between the main crowds and the entrance, trying to slow the crowds headed for the airport's gates.

At the front of the crowd, I could see Taliban gunmen pacing up and down, and occasionally a British soldier would wander up with an interpreter and a tense conversation would ensue. The Taliban were, for now, cooperating, and allowing the NATO troops to pack up and leave. Watching the British officers and the Talib gunmen together, standing around talking, was so surreal, even the Talibs looked amazed. The reality of the fall of Kabul seemed a surprise to them, and their new role of violent, crude crowd control was likely not how they had pictured victory.

Farther down the street outside the Abbey Gate, groups of U.S. Marines were milling about, trying to keep crowds of desperate Afghans back. I had never, in all my years of covering war in Afghanistan, seen American troops simply mingling with the crowds of civilians in the street. They had always been behind blast walls, on bases, or encased inside armored vehicles. Now they were completely exposed. All norms had fallen away. Small groups of uniformed troops from NATO countries were also wandering about, a few Canadians here, a half-dozen Germans there, all looking for their people—embassy staff, interpreters, the families of diplomats.

I looked at the scene around me in astonishment. It felt like a movie set, where actors were in costume but not playing the role they had been cast for. Then someone grabbed my arm.

"Please help me," a woman said in English. "I need help." She was a surgeon from Herat, she told me. The Taliban had taken Herat weeks before. She was living with her mother, a widow, and her sister, a divorced woman. She was single. The Taliban had gone door to door she said, informing communities that single women would not be allowed to live independently without a male guardian. She was to be married off. Her sister stood nearby. They had finally bolted to Kabul but arrived just as the Taliban had taken the city. They had rushed straight to the airport. They had no contingency plan.

She had not wanted to leave Herat, she explained. She had no choice. "I had a good life," she said, as though to herself, and started to cry. She wore a black abaya and a blue headscarf and was clutching only a purse and an iPhone. I was overcome with grief, watching her life implode around her and hearing those words I now more than ever dreaded to hear: "Please help me." I gasped back tears between my questions, promising I would talk to some of the British soldiers, and squeezed the top of her arm. I never saw her again.

That night I lay in bed for a couple of restless hours, listening to the sound of gunfire and helicopters flying low overhead, and wept. I knew that just a few dozen feet away, thousands of desperate people were sleeping in the street, clutching their babies and their precious documents and photographs, whatever small items they could carry. Inside the hotel complex, the British sorted through the paperwork of those who had been allowed in. The chosen few had been told to wait for an escort to the flight line.

Something inside me flipped. I didn't want to be a spectator anymore. *I refuse,* I told myself. *I refuse to just watch this happen.* Tomorrow I was going to figure out how to help get people the hell out of here.

All the existing systems for sorting through people—whether they needed to have a green card or an American passport or a valid visa—collapsed within the first few days. American soldiers were often trying to simply hold back the crowds outside the Abbey Gate while desperate Afghans begged them for help, or even for just some idea about what they should do. The exhausted soldiers were coming face-to-face with desperate civilians in need, but they had little in the way of assistance to offer. The main chaplain at the airport base told us in an interview that she was sleeping three hours a night because soldiers needed her spiritual council so often.

Near where she sat, a group of around two dozen children were waiting under a shaded area just outside the airport military hospital. They ranged in ages from four to seventeen and looked around with wide, frightened eyes. These children had been separated from their parents in the crush and were being looked after by American soldiers inside the airport complex. One little boy wore a sunhat and carried a teddy bear backpack. Someone had prepared him for the journey. Some of the children's parents had been killed in the crush outside the airport gates. The soldiers had yet to tell them. Others had USA written on the back of their little hands, where they were bound for. One twelve-year-old was trying to tell us how he got lost in the crowd when he started to cry.

My phone had already been buzzing with callers trying to get Afghans out they knew or had worked with. Journalists trying to get their fixers out, or the families of former interpreters, young academics, soldiers. I had to film a piece every day, write a script, and then go live with it from the hotel garden between one a.m. and three a.m. But if I got up early in the morning, I could also work on finding people, contacting them, and then begging the soldiers to let them into the complex. I didn't have a plan other than to go out and search for the people desperate friends and colleagues in the United States were trying to get out. The Al Jazeera office continued to work, unimpeded, in the city. Qais had long since left Afghanistan for asylum in Canada with his family. Mahmoud and the others continued to work at the bureau. I thought of them often amid the chaos, remembering all the happier times we had spent together.

A certain cycle took hold. A friend or colleague would send me a message on WhatsApp saying their former interpreter or fixer was near the gate and asked if I could help them get in. I would get in touch with that person directly and coordinate with them on the phone, asking them to send me their live location so I could guide them through the crowds. I knew that once they were inside the compound, they could get their names on flight lists for the evacuation flights going to the United States and elsewhere. They just needed to get inside. The soldiers had no real idea who was allowed in, so they kept almost everyone back unless I could persuade them otherwise. If they were close, I would ask the soldiers at the front to let them in. At first they told me no. During one such negotiation, a British officer saw what I was trying to do and said, "You need Canadian Dave."

Canadian Dave was a tall, ginger-haired former Canadian special forces soldier who was running a private security company from Kabul when it fell. His business had disappeared in minutes, and now he devoted every moment of the day to getting people out. He ran up and down the street outside Abbey Gate and the Baron with lists of people, their names, and their IDs. Then he found them in the crowd, persuading the soldiers to let them through. The British soldiers especially were allowing him through with people.

"What you need to do is get them to wear something identifiable," he explained. "Like a red hat or a yellow headscarf." He also told me about the secret back gate at the Baron. A smaller gate through which staff brought in food and water supplies, it was opened only once or twice a day. A small crowd of people had gathered outside there.

One former journalist with *The New York Times* who had been trying for years to get visas for his wife and children coordinated with me as they tried to make it to the front gate. A mixture of American Marines and British paratroopers had now pulled shipping containers across the road to keep the crowds back. I climbed onto the containers using a small ladder the soldiers had and stared down at a sea of humanity, all desperate, exhausted, dangerously hot. One little girl held up a sign that said AUS, WE HAVE VISA, hoping any Australian would notice. Several dozen people had been killed in the crush. Terrified parents had handed babies up to soldiers on top of the walls to save them. Soldiers occasionally dropped water hoses over the wall, trying to keep people from succumbing to the worst midday heat.

The Taliban fighters circulated through the crowds, their role unclear. They saw me standing there, looking for the journalist's wife and children, a brazen Western woman in jeans and a shirt, staring down at them, and waved their guns and shouted at the American Marines, who eventually asked me to get down.

I rushed to the back gate and told the journalist's family to meet me there. Then began the constant requests to the soldiers to let them in. The paratroopers were by now completely exhausted. They got little to no sleep and were unsure of what exactly the protocols were as to who was allowed in at all. "Fuck off!" one officer yelled at me. Moments later, he pulled his helmet on, grabbed his gun, opened the gate, dove into the crowd of panicked Afghans and belligerent Taliban, found the family, and pulled them inside. "I'm sorry about that," he told me later, placing a hand on my shoulder.

Later that night, as I was walking back to my room, I saw an Afghan man walk up to a British soldier on the base and ask him where he could get some food. The young infantryman pulled a hard-boiled egg and a banana out of his pocket and handed them to him. "It's not much," the soldier said, with sadness. The hours became a series of constant favors to ask, as I recognized the outsize and entirely unjustified power that fate had placed with me.

When I asked to get people into the Baron hotel complex, provided they had some sort of visa or paperwork with them, they were usually admitted. If we weren't pulling them out of the crowds, imploring the soldiers for "just one more," currying favor with cups of coffee from the canteen and boxes of pizza ferried to the gates, then they were left outside. The system was completely unfair because in truth there was no system. Once inside the Baron, people were placed on lists according to which nation they were headed for and were escorted to the various flights by that nation's soldiers.

My phone pinged with a message. It was Roya. She had been hiding for five days in an apartment with another renowned female Afghan photographer, Fatimah Hossaini, while the Taliban lurked in the streets outside. Finally they decided to make a run for it. They filled their backpacks with their laptops and cameras, rushed out into the street, waved down a car, dove in the back seat, and called me. Roya was terrified, gasping for air as they raced past Taliban checkpoints. Eric and I waited for her, afraid she would be stopped. Canadian Dave came and helped, taking us to a watchtower over the top of the wall. We looked down and saw them. Dave rushed out the gate, grabbed Roya and Fatimah, and pulled them inside. As they fell inside, they were overcome, exhausted, filled with relief. We embraced, and they wept.

I brought Roya and Fatimah to my room for a moment of rest. Sitting cross-legged on my bed, they told me about the last week. "I cannot believe it, I just cannot believe it," Roya kept repeating. Their lives were completely suspended. They discussed where to go, what to do. Would they fly to the United States? What would they do there? "On my God, my photographs," Fatimah lamented. She'd had to leave much of her life's work behind in her apartment, a collection of photographs of Afghan people and places, a love letter to her beloved nation.

"I'm going to go for a little while and then come back," declared Roya. I looked at her and worked hard to hide my sadness. She had just uttered the same words spoken by millions of war refugees, those who never wanted to leave, and who would spend years coming to terms with the fact that it was permanent. All was lost to memory.

Word had spread that I was getting people out, and the constant calls and messages and voices begging for help weighed on me terribly. There was so much need.

We ourselves were under pressure to leave now. PBS managers kept asking when we were going to get on a flight out, and the British officers running the evacuations also asked us politely each day if we were leaving. "One more day," we all implored. The story was still happening, and as soon as Eric and I left, there would be no more U.S. broadcasters at the airport. The Sky News team felt exactly the same exhaustion, emotionally and physically. The cameraman had a serious conversation with his wife about adopting an Afghan child. Kim Sengupta from *The Independent* wept in the hotel garden after witnessing women crushed to death by the crowds. Simi used her language skills to help many of those struggling to know where to go, by translating for them in Dari and Pashtu. We discussed what to do every day.

Finally the British officer in charge came to us one night as a group. "You need to get on a flight out tomorrow," he said plainly. "The day after, we are handing this place over to the Taliban and flying ourselves and our equipment out." The Taliban would not let us back into the city, so this was our only chance to leave. PBS management told Eric and me we must take this plane.

That night, I waited for the bursts of gunfire to stop long enough to make the call. I needed to hear a voice from New York, the other world in my life, from someone who knew me as more than a war reporter. I needed to speak with someone who would tell me everything was going to be okay, that I was doing the right thing. I was torn with guilt at the thought of leaving.

American security officials kept warning of a possible suicide attack at the airport. Although I played down the dangers to my producers back in Washington, D.C., it seemed like only a matter of time before it would come, that horrifying thump and shake of a murderous explosion I had come to know.

I spoke to my boyfriend in a whisper, sitting on the cement step of the building. It was dark, save for some lamplight and a bright moon. "I'm trying my best here," I said into the phone, a tear rolling down my cheek. "But I just have a feeling something really bad is about to happen."

I climbed the ramp into the C-17 with several hundred other Afghans, its engines roaring as we were swallowed into the bare metal interior of the windowless aircraft. The lights inside were green, and we were all instructed to sit on the floor. All the seats had been removed to fit more people inside. Men, women, and children all sat down, crammed together. Each was allowed to bring only a small purse. They would begin their new lives with absolutely nothing. One little girl, around four years old, wore a sparkly dress for the occasion.

At the front of the plane an American flag hung from the wall. It felt like we were on a spacecraft about to fly to another planet.

As the plane roared down the runway and took off, the initial relief and even excitement from the families as they had boarded, knowing they had made it to freedom, fell away. A somber sense of what was being left behind filled the cavernous space. We all clung to one another, a huddled mass of people holding arms and hands, meeting each other's eyes with a knowing nod. Eventually everyone lay down and slept. I had lost 10 percent of my bodyweight during the previous ten days in Kabul, and the metal bolts of the aircraft floor poked into my bony sides. I was so exhausted not even a jet engine could keep me from sleep.

When we landed in Doha at the military air base, government officials escorted us to a hotel in the city. Walking ghosts, we blinked in the morning light, clutching our bags and body armor. I had barely changed my clothes in ten days, having packed only an overnight bag from the Serena, believing I would return the day after Kabul fell. The hotel staff gasped at the sight of us.

My phone pinged again with news. A suicide bomber detonated an explosive vest among the crowd outside the Abbey Gate. Over a hundred and fifty Afghans, the people waiting desperately trying to get on flights out, had died. Thirteen American soldiers were also killed. Once again, I was spared, narrowly, while others had lost their lives.

My whole career I had been blessed with such grace. I didn't understand it, but I was grateful. Despite the horror and pain of much of the war I had seen, I felt it had all been a privileged journey, a remarkable responsibility to see it and know it and tell stories about it all. And to know that, however little I could change the outcome of the war, I had done my best to document the lives of those who lived through it. I had, I hoped, done my part.

Epilogue

ONE CHILLY SPRING MORNING IN 2022, I woke up in a hotel room, stepped over to the window, and gazed out at the antique tiled rooftops and church spires of central Kiev. An air raid siren wailed softly in the distance. Still jet-lagged, I made my way downstairs to breakfast. The room was buzzing with energy and chatter as dozens of journalists, all of whom I knew—the best in the business, friends and colleagues—munched on big breakfasts ahead of another day spent out reporting. I looked around the room and I knew this part of my life was over. Something inside me had shifted. For the first time in my career reporting from the road, I knew I wanted to go home.

I felt a hint of this when I returned to Afghanistan a few months after Kabul fell to the Taliban. As if I was in the wrong place, a spark gone. *I'm just exhausted,* I told myself. *I need some time off.* But it was a permanent shift. I cared enormously about the war in Ukraine. But I'd learned in my fifteen years of reporting that there would always be another front, always people whose suffering in the face of war and whose joys despite it would be worth capturing. War wasn't going to end, no matter how badly I wanted it to. I knew my time living from assignment to assignment, doing this work independently, spending most of each year on the road, was over. That scene in *Forrest Gump* when he has been running all over America and suddenly stops in the middle of nowhere, turns, and says to his followers, "I'm pretty tired. I think I'll go home now," came to mind. I felt as if I'd grown the same scraggly beard as Forrest Gump. *This work is for a new generation of reporters to learn from and channel their outrage and curiosity into,* I thought. The streets of Kiev were already teeming with them. This story does not need me.

I'll always be a journalist. These days I report from New York as a *PBS NewsHour* foreign correspondent—"the same assignments, just with jet lag," I say in jest to my friends and colleagues. I'm learning to dive in headfirst less, to curate the assignments I take, to find a balance between my work and private life. Working on stories about climate change, writing articles for the print media, and teaching university students are new passions. I don't have a clear plan, but when have I ever had, really? For me, a plan has only ever been a desire for something that seems unattainable, something you can ache for just enough to follow it into the distance. That ache now tugs me back to this new life, in New York, the city where there are no outsiders.

When I got home after the fall of Kabul, once the initial intensity of studio interviews and the constant questions and answers about Afghanistan calmed down, I felt as if my life was beginning again. As I sat in the huge window of an old crumbling downtown loft, surrounded by books and rugs and the muffled sound of Manhattan traffic, I marveled at the wonder of my life until this point. My days had taken on a certain tentative routine. I attend a regular yoga class, take care of my plants, meet friends in places other than hotel bars in war zones. Make plans with my boyfriend. Learn how to accept another person's love.

As I jog through Central Park, the leaves turn the color of the mountains surrounding Sana'a. Then snow falls like it does in the Hindu Kush, and the spring follows, bringing buds and blossoms like those on the balconies of Beirut. I'm reminded constantly of all that has been given to me and what is now past.

My phone still pings with messages and images from Yemen, Afghanistan, Lebanon, and beyond, places I have been lucky to call home, from friends who are now farther away. I feel emotion well up when I hear their voices on the phone and think of these places I loved like a chosen family. When assignments take me to these places that welcomed me as a younger reporter, I feel a tenderness toward my younger self. Whether I'm in Beirut or Sana'a or Baghdad, I remember how hard on herself she was, and I finally offer her some grace.

At times the transition is harder to ease into. I wake in the darkness sometimes from dreams of crowds of desperate Afghan people begging me to help them get into Kabul airport, or of dead bodies in the streets of Mosul. As I wake from the nightmare, Manhattan's skyline glows beyond my window, and the fear drains away. *New life,* I remember as I drop back to sleep. *I'm safe.*

I still struggle to feel worthy of my life in New York and the people in it, as though I don't deserve to belong, but I'm learning to get past that. "If you hadn't lived that life before you would never have been ready for this one. You had to be there to get here," a wise friend reminded me. I can sit with the discomfort of my safety now. When I am at dinner in a nice restaurant with friends, browsing in bookstores on a rainy afternoon, or giving a speech at an industry event, and I feel that familiar uncertainty, I remember with greater ease now that I deserve to be happy. I can allow myself to be happy without needing to be moving, in constant motion. I can stand still in my apartment, look out over the city, and be at peace.

Sometimes I feel guilt at having been able to move forward like this. Afghanistan continues to flounder under a deeply repressive Taliban rule and hunger crisis. At the time of this writing, Afghan girls over fourteen are still not allowed to attend public school. Yemen stumbles between cease-fires but remains one of the world's worst humanitarian disasters. Lebanon's economy has largely collapsed, its young bright people once again fleeing abroad to make a living, some of which they can send back home. Mohammed Saif and Fuad are still in Sana'a, surviving under repressive Houthi rule and Saudi air strikes. Sami has long since moved to Sweden with his wife and son. Qais owns several Afghan restaurants in Canada. His daughters excel at school. Adiba moved to Geneva, where she works for the United Nations. Anisa Shaheed made it out of Kabul on an evacuation flight to the United States and lives in Virginia. Eric continues to film in conflict zones around the world, especially Ukraine. Pete Reed, the former Marine and volunteer medic in Mosul, also shifted his focus there following Putin's invasion. In February of 2023, he was killed by a Russian missile in Bakhmut while helping move an injured civilian into an ambulance.

As I waited for Eric to arrive at breakfast that morning in Kiev, I thought of all the young reporters ready and willing and driven to get here and do this work. The truth is, however much people lionize war reporters, we are not heroes. We are privileged to do this work. If it's not something you leap out of your hotel bed or military cot or camping spot each morning to do, then it's time to stop. Posing the question "If not me, then who?" is a vanity. Behind us, back at the head offices of news organizations around the world, are armies of talented, brave, and brilliant young journalists waiting for their chance to tell these stories, too.

I look across at other tables and see a younger reporter hunched over his phone, his overcoat already on, scrolling for news updates online. I see him looking around the room nervously at the rest of us and smile to myself, recognizing that feeling of inadequacy yet optimism. I hope he and all the others waiting back in the newsrooms are given a shot to tell these stories well, to enable others to see the humanity all around us, especially in the darkest of times, and to reach their potential as communicators to a wider world. From the deepest parts of me, I wish them all the wonder, joy, and fortitude in the world. I hope they cross paths with incredible people and their lives are filled with a sense of purpose and service. I do not wish them spared the tough times, because I know these will make them stronger, humbler, and more empathic. The experiences ahead of the next generation of international reporters will mold them, shape them into the storytellers their subjects deserve and viewers need.

We in the news media have found ourselves in a time of sensational news, loud opinions, and celebrity reporters. As the industry stumbles and leaves paper and television behind, heading online for good, the nature of news and reporting from around the world is changing, too. As reporters become famous for the first time since the early days of the Iraq war, I hope our focus remains on our subjects and on the stories we tell, instead of on who is narrating them.

I am a rare optimist when it comes to journalism today. I know storytelling will endure because it's so deeply entrenched in our DNA as humans. Since our ancestors spent their time etching tales on cave walls, we've needed to record our stories. The truth needs no defense, and those who pursue it doggedly, with humility and grace, may not have the most glamorous careers in the business, but they will do the most good. To those who do, I wish you a brilliant, defiant, and most unordinary life.

Acknowledgments

IF YOU HAVE READ THIS BOOK, you will know I have been blessed throughout my life by the kindness of strangers. The process of writing the book itself was no less fortunate, with kind and clever people helping me throughout. I owe my agent, George Lucas, a massive debt of gratitude for spotting what he believed to be a unique story and guiding me through the process of making ideas and chapter scribblings into a less unruly outline of a book. My editor at Mariner, Ivy Givens, has been the major driving force behind this book, working tirelessly on edits and supporting me through every step of the process. From the very beginning, Ivy saw its uniqueness and championed and campaigned for *No Ordinary Assignment* throughout all its stages.

I cannot thank my fiancé, Charley Cooper, enough. His council, patience, love, and support at every step has meant the world to me. Charley's sister, Meade, and mother, Regina, have encouraged me along the way and celebrated every little milestone throughout the process. I'm so grateful to have them by my side. Thanks also to good friends who have talked me off emotional ledges in moments of doubt and cheered me on throughout: Ruth Maclean, Catherine Philp, Gillian Tett, Janine di Giovanni, Kati Marton, Pat Mitchell, Kate O'Brian, and many more remarkable women I'm thankful to call friends. Thanks must also go to Steve Capus for being such an encouraging friend and reader through the process. David Holbrook has, as always, guided and supported my work, encouraging me to take risks and make bold, brave choices. Ali Latifi has been always on the end of the phone when I needed him, a true friend and trusted guide. Thanks also goes to Tom Freston for his encouragement and guidance. I owe Cindi Berger much thanks for her belief in this project and support.

I'm grateful to my foreign editor at *PBS NewsHour,* Morgan Till, without whom much of my most significant reporting mentioned in these pages would not have happened. Judy Woodruff has been a tremendous supporter and inspiration throughout my years at the *NewsHour* and I am very grateful to her. Special thanks also goes to David Rohde, my editor at *The New Yorker,* for his patience, kindness, and generosity when it came to the entire process of writing the book. I am also immensely grateful to Jon Sawyer and everyone at The Pulitzer Center for Crisis Reporting for funding and supporting some of the most important journalism in the U.S. today.